MW01245789

ReSegregation Volume II

The Facts of the Black Oppression And The Problems Facing The White Ally

Antonio T Smith Jr

Trient Press
5470 Kietzke Lane Suite 300 - #394
Reno, NV 89511

Ordering Information:
For quantity sales, Trient Press offers special discounts to corporations, associations, and other organizations. For detailed information, contact the publisher at the address provided above.
For orders by U.S. trade bookstores and wholesalers, please reach out to Trient Press at Tel: (775) 996-3844, or visit www.trientpress.com.
Printed in the United States of America
Publisher's Cataloging-in-Publication Data
Smith Jr, Antonio T.
ReSegregation Volume II:
The Facts of the Black Oppression And The Problems Facing The White Ally
Hard Cover : 979-8-88990-198-3
Paperback: ISBN 979-8-88990-199-0
E-Book:979-8-88990-200-3

Table of Contents

About The Author

Connect With Me

Text me directly at +1 409-500-1546. Let me know what you think and let me know how great you are. Mention this book so I can know how we met.

No one suffers alone,

Antonio T Smith Jr

Who Is Antonio?

Antonio T. Smith Jr., is a doctoral student, CEO of Arlingbrook Social Media, Qandid Music and Podcasts, and Density6, is an innovative tech virtuoso at the forefront of the Artificial Intelligence (AI) industry. With a track record of orchestrating paradigm shifts in the global landscape,

Antonio crafts revolutionary products that empower the middle class to become top income earners in their respective countries.

As the founder of RhinoLeg CRM, an all-in-one customer relationship management software powered by AI, Antonio showcases his unique blend of technical prowess and business acumen. RhinoLeg CRM is a testament to Antonio's ability to create integrated systems that streamline sales, marketing, customer service, and analytics, redefining the way businesses interact with customers.

Antonio is also the mastermind behind Nsenkye, a cutting-edge Generative AI that's set to redefine our understanding of AI capabilities. His ambitious plan for Nsenkye encompasses the creation of AI-powered cities, androids, and technologies, all designed to propel humanity into its next evolutionary stage. At its core, Nsenkye's mission is the search for the elusive Master Algorithm that Antonio believes will lead to groundbreaking advancements in AI.

Equipped with an INTJ-A personality and knowledge spanning disciplines like computer programming, video game design, engineering, religion, and psychology, Antonio has often been likened to industry pioneers like Elon Musk and Jeff Bezos. His technical mastery extends to Python, Swift, Java, Microsoft Azure, API Development, jQuery, JavaScript, Mobile Applications, Web Design, Node.js, Data Engineering, Amazon Web Services (AWS), Unity Gaming, Flutter, Firebase, Non-Fungible Tokens (NFTs), and Blockchain technologies.

However, Antonio's contributions extend beyond innovative tech solutions. With a humanitarian heart, he has pledged to create 100,000 millionaires and donate $1.5 billion by 2025. Also recognized as one of the top 101 leaders and developers of our time, by World HRD Congress, Antonio shares his wisdom extensively as a professional speaker, delivering over 300 keynote speeches annually, many on the Law of Attraction.

Guided by his passion for creating a better world, Antonio envisions a resource-based economy where resources are accessible to all, thereby eliminating the need for money. His dream extends to the creation of a harmonious city built on democratic principles. The world sees Antonio T. Smith Jr. as a blend of technical genius, compassionate humanitarian, and an inspirational speaker, all unified in his pursuit to uplift individuals and reshape society for the better.

All boundaries are conventions waiting to be transcended. One may transcend any convention if only one can first conceive they exist. In moments like these, I can feel your heartbeat as I feel my own and I know that the separation is an illusion. My life extends far beyond the limitations of me.
- Robert Frobisher

Dedication

This book is dedicated to Dr. George C. Fraser, Chairman and CEO of FraserNet, Inc., a visionary leader whose unwavering commitment to nurturing and advancing the global networking movement for people of African descent has illuminated the path for countless individuals, including myself. Dr. Fraser's dedication to the empowerment of the Black community and his pioneering efforts to build bridges of opportunity and understanding across diverse landscapes serve as a beacon of hope and a source of inspiration for those of us who strive to make a meaningful impact through our endeavors.

I had the esteemed privilege of meeting Dr. Fraser at an event hosted by the Greater Houston Black Chamber in Houston, Texas, where I was becoming someone people would notice in the business and technology spheres. It was a pivotal moment in my journey, as I found myself in the presence of someone whose life's work resonated deeply with my aspirations and the challenges I sought to overcome. Dr. Fraser's keynote address and the subsequent opportunity to engage with him over brunch, assist with the event's logistics, and receive an autographed copy of one of his seminal works, left an indelible mark on my spirit and approach to my work.

His boldness and eloquence, both in person and through his extensive online presence, have played a crucial role in shaping my resolve to contribute to the discourse on racial justice and allyship. Dr. Fraser's example has instilled in me the courage and conviction needed to undertake the writing of this book—a task I might not have approached with the necessary vigor and dedication were it not for his influence.

Dr. George C. Fraser's kindness extended far beyond the realms of expectation when, due to technical difficulties with my LinkedIn page preventing me from reaching out to him directly, he graciously accepted an advanced copy of "Resegregation Vol I" through my Global Executive Vice President, Ine Velaers. His willingness to engage with the work, despite the unconventional means of communication, underscores a generosity of spirit and a genuine openness to new ideas and discussions. Dr. Fraser's approachability and his readiness to support emerging voices in the discourse on racial justice and equity exemplify the profound impact of kindness in leadership and mentorship.

I am immensely grateful for Dr. Fraser's benevolence and the encouragement it represents. His acceptance of the advanced copy, facilitated by Ine Velaers, signifies more than a simple gesture of goodwill; it reflects his commitment to fostering a culture of inclusivity and support within the professional and activist communities. This act of kindness, though perhaps small in the grand scheme, is a testament to the character of Dr. Fraser and his unwavering dedication to uplifting those around him. It serves as a powerful reminder of the value of compassion and understanding in our ongoing collective efforts to create meaningful change.

To Dr. Fraser, I extend my heartfelt gratitude for the wisdom imparted during our brief encounter and through your body of work. Though our paths have crossed but once, the impact of your guidance and the example of your leadership continue to inspire me. I eagerly anticipate future opportunities to sit at your feet, figuratively and literally, to absorb the wisdom you so generously share.

This book is a tribute to the influential mentors such as Dr. Fraser, whose life's endeavors serve as beacons for those of us striving to forge paths of impact and meaning. With profound respect and admiration, I dedicate this volume to you, Dr. Fraser, in honor of your unyielding spirit and steadfast dedication to elevating our community. Your legacy stands as a luminous guide for anyone dedicated to effecting positive change in the world, and I earnestly aspire for this book to reflect the depth and breadth of that legacy.

Antonio T. Smith Jr.

Author's Note

As you step forward into the world, carry with you the joy and conviction of your dreams. The path you walk is illuminated by the brilliance of your aspirations, casting light upon the road less traveled, the path of fulfillment and purpose. It is a journey not without its trials, yet every challenge is an opportunity to rise, to affirm the strength and resilience that resides within you.

In every breath, in every heartbeat, there exists a call to gratitude—a call to embrace the present moment, to acknowledge the beauty and the lessons that each second holds. Gratitude is the key that unlocks the abundance of the universe, inviting endless possibilities into your life. Let your heart overflow with thanksgiving, not just for the milestones achieved, but for the simple joys, the laughter shared, and the quiet moments of introspection.

View yourself and those around you through the lens of the Creator, recognizing the divine spark that resides within each soul. In this recognition, we find the foundation of true empathy and connection, seeing not just with our eyes, but with our hearts. By acknowledging the Creator in every individual, we foster a world of compassion, understanding, and unity.

Open your heart to the infinite possibilities that love brings. Love is the most powerful force in the universe, capable of transforming darkness into light, despair into hope. It is through an open heart that we receive and give love freely, building bridges of harmony and peace in a world often divided.

Know the light that guides you, the unwavering beacon of truth, wisdom, and inspiration. In moments of doubt or uncertainty, turn towards this light, letting it fill you with clarity and courage. Praise this light, for it is a testament to the boundless love of the Creator, a reminder of our origin and our ultimate destination.

You possess the power to plant seeds of change, to cultivate a garden of dreams that blossoms into reality. With every thought, every word, and every action, you have the opportunity to create a legacy of positivity and progress. Remember, you are not merely a passenger in the journey of life; you are the captain of your destiny, empowered to steer your course toward greatness.

Dominate your fears, your limitations, and the voices that whisper doubt. You are endowed with an inner strength, a divine spark that cannot be dimmed. Stand in your power, unwavering in the pursuit of your aspirations, and let nothing hold you back from achieving the greatness for which you were created.

As we part ways, remember that you are never alone. You are enveloped in the love and the light of the One Infinite Intelligence, forever connected to the source of all creation. Go forth with the assurance that your dreams are valid, your purpose is profound, and your potential is limitless.

In closing, I leave you with the warmth of my regard and the certainty of my belief in your boundless capacity for greatness.

Best,
Antonio T Smith Jr

In a moment of profound clarity, Robert Frobisher, a character from Cloud Atlas reflects on the nature of existence and connection:
"Sixsmith. I climb the steps of the Scott Monument every morning and all becomes clear. Wish I could make you see this brightness. Don't worry, all is well. All is so perfectly, damnably well. I understand now that boundaries between noise and sound are conventions. All boundaries are conventions, waiting to be transcended. One may transcend any convention if only one can first conceive of doing so. Moments like this, I can feel your heart beating as clearly as I feel my own, and I know that separation is an illusion. My life extends far beyond the limitations of me."[1]

[1] Cloud Atlas, directed by Lana Wachowski, Tom Tykwer, and Lilly Wachowski (2012; Los Angeles, CA: Warner Bros. Pictures), DVD.

Part 1: The Multiple Foundations of Racism

The Unequal Race for Wealth—Chapter 1

The Number One Problem With Idea of Race

The number one problem with race in America is that the word itself *race* implies that *all* people are *not* supposed to be equal. Equality must be created, as nature doesn't naturally create quality. What it creates is an ecosystem that submits to other ecosystems to create harmony. As long as we have the social construct of race in our mental frameworks, then no people group in the world will ever be treated equally, because a race strongly implies that there must be a winner. A race is a contest, therefore, our people groups are in a constant contest to control economics, by any means necessary.

In the discourse on race and economic disparity in America, a foundational issue arises from the very concept of *race*—a term that not only segregates humanity into distinct categories but inherently suggests a competition, a relentless race for superiority, resources, and wealth. The etymology of *race*, with its implications of contest and rivalry, mirrors the structural dynamics of economic disparity that plague our society. This linguistic framing lays bare an uncomfortable truth: the societal construct of race is predicated on the assumption that not all are meant to be equal. Nature, in its vast diversity, does not ordain equality but establishes ecosystems where some dominate others to maintain harmony[1].

The historical context of racial disparities in wealth accumulation in America cannot be overlooked. The racial wealth gap is not merely a relic of the past but a perpetually widening chasm, exacerbated by systemic policies and practices. In 2016, the net worth of a typical white family was almost tenfold that of a Black family, a stark indicator of the enduring legacy of racial economic inequality[2]. This disparity is not the outcome of individual failings but the result of centuries of discrimination, from the codified enslavement of African Americans to the Jim Crow laws and beyond. Critics may assert that these economic disparities arise from personal choices or a lack of effort within the Black community. However, such arguments crumble under the weight of evidence showcasing the systemic barriers—redlining, discriminatory lending practices, unequal education funding—that have historically marginalized Black Americans[3].

The concept of "ReSegregation," as espoused in this discourse, seeks not to segregate by race but to underscore the importance of economic self-reliance and community solidarity within the Black population. This approach is rooted in historical precedents where Black communities, through collective economics, thrived independently. The narrative of Black Wall Street is a testament to the power of economic self-sufficiency and unity. However, such examples of Black prosperity have often been met with

[1] The term race, in its etymological essence, denotes competition, setting the stage for societal constructs that divide and categorize human beings into hierarchies.

[2] McKernan, Signe-Mary, et al. "Nine Charts about Wealth Inequality in America." Urban Institute, 2017.

[3] Rothstein, Richard. "The Color of Law: A Forgotten History of How Our Government Segregated America." Liveright Publishing, 2017.

hostility and destruction, underscoring the systemic nature of racial economic suppression[4].

Opponents of the ReSegregation concept might view it through a lens tinted by historical racial segregation, misinterpreting it as a call for division rather than economic empowerment. Yet, this perspective fails to recognize the strategic intent behind fostering economic self-reliance within the Black community. By encouraging the circulation of wealth within their own communities, Black Americans can begin to dismantle the economic disparities imposed by a system designed to keep them on the periphery of prosperity.

The strategy for combating economic disparity, as outlined, necessitates a multifaceted approach targeting key sectors: Economics, Finance, Data Information, Manufacturing, Infrastructure, Communications, and Human Resources. This comprehensive strategy is not about isolation but about creating a foundation from which Black communities can engage with the broader economy on more equal footing. The establishment of Black-centric economic think tanks, financial institutions, and tech companies is crucial for this transformation. It is about leveraging the collective strength and resources of the Black community to challenge and ultimately reshape the systemic barriers that perpetuate economic inequality.

Labor, Wealth, and the Quest for Racial Equity

[4] The narrative of Black Wall Street represents a powerful example of Black economic independence and success, which was met with violent opposition, illustrating the systemic efforts to undermine Black prosperity.

The nexus between labor and wealth is a fundamental principle of economic development and sustainability. Yet, in the context of Black America, this connection has been systematically severed by the monopolization of Black labor without the commensurate accrual of wealth within the Black community. This disparity is not a happenstance but a calculated outcome of historical policies and practices designed to exploit Black labor while simultaneously obstructing pathways to Black wealth accumulation[5].

The assertion that wealth creates wealth and the necessity of controlling labor to accumulate wealth highlights a stark reality: Black Americans have been systematically excluded from the wealth creation cycle. Control over labor has historically been a tool of power and economic dominance. In the context of Black America, those who have controlled Black labor—through slavery, Jim Crow laws, and discriminatory labor practices—have effectively captured the wealth generated by this labor, thereby perpetuating economic disparities that have spanned generations[6].

The concept of ReSegregation, contrary to initial perceptions, does not advocate for racial segregation but emphasizes economic self-sufficiency within the Black community. By fostering a culture of group economics and supporting Black-owned businesses and institutions, the Black community can begin to reclaim control over its labor and, by extension, its wealth. The historical precedent of Black Wall Street exemplifies the potential of Black economic empowerment when the community controls its labor and resources. Yet, the destruction of Black Wall

[5] Anderson, Claud. "Black Labor, White Wealth: The Search for Power and Economic Justice." PowerNomics Corporation of America, 1994.

[6] McKernan, Signe-Mary, et al. "Nine Charts about Wealth Inequality in America." Urban Institute, 2017.

Street also serves as a grim reminder of the systemic barriers erected to prevent such empowerment.

Critics of the concept of economic self-sufficiency within the Black community often argue that such approaches are separatist and counterproductive to the goal of racial integration. However, this perspective fails to acknowledge the systemic nature of racial economic disparities and the need for targeted strategies to address these gaps. The goal of ReSegregation is not to segregate but to empower; to create a foundation upon which the Black community can build wealth and achieve economic stability by controlling its labor and resources[7].

The challenge, however, extends beyond the mere creation of Black-owned businesses. The systemic barriers that have historically prevented the accumulation of Black wealth—such as discriminatory lending practices, unequal access to quality education, and employment discrimination—must also be addressed. The success of ReSegregation hinges not only on the ability of the Black community to support its own but also on the dismantling of these systemic barriers.

In essence, the quest for racial equity in America is deeply intertwined with the control of labor and the distribution of wealth. The historical appropriation of Black labor without corresponding wealth accumulation within the Black community underscores the need for a deliberate and strategic approach to economic empowerment. Through the concept of ReSegregation, there lies a pathway to reclaiming control over Black labor and, ultimately, to the creation of sustainable Black wealth. This approach does not seek to divide but to heal, to empower, and to bridge the

7 Critics often misconstrue the intent behind fostering economic self-sufficiency within the Black community, overlooking the necessity of such measures in the face of systemic economic disparities.

economic gaps that have long divided America.

The Pillars of Wealth

The journey toward economic empowerment for Black Americans is fraught with systemic barriers that have historically undermined their ability to accumulate wealth. Central to this challenge is the lack of control over labor and resources, coupled with obstacles to unity and collective action. These factors are not merely coincidental but are the result of deliberate policies and practices designed to maintain economic disparities[8].

Labor and resources are foundational to the creation of wealth. However, for Black Americans, access to both has been systematically restricted. From the era of chattel slavery to the present day, Black labor has been exploited while the benefits of this labor have been accrued elsewhere. Post-emancipation policies and practices, such as sharecropping and discriminatory labor laws, continued to ensure that Black Americans remained at the economic periphery, unable to claim the wealth generated by their labor[9].

Moreover, the accumulation of wealth requires more than just labor; it necessitates control over resources. Yet, Black Americans have faced significant barriers to acquiring land and capital. The Homestead Acts, which provided land to Americans at little to no cost, largely excluded Black individuals. Similarly, redlining and discriminatory lending practices have hindered Black

[8] Anderson, Claud. "Black Labor, White Wealth: The Search for Power and Economic Justice." PowerNomics Corporation of America, 1994.

[9] Ibid.

Americans' ability to own homes and start businesses, further impeding their wealth accumulation[10].

Beyond labor and resources, unity and the ability to come together are crucial for economic empowerment. Historical and contemporary efforts to build solidarity within the Black community have often been met with resistance and outright sabotage. The destruction of prosperous Black communities, such as Tulsa's Greenwood District, also known as Black Wall Street, illustrates the systemic efforts to dismantle Black unity and economic success[11].

Critics might argue that the focus on past injustices and systemic barriers detracts from personal responsibility and the opportunities available within the capitalist system. However, this perspective fails to acknowledge the depth and breadth of systemic obstacles that have been erected to specifically undermine Black economic empowerment. It overlooks the fact that systemic barriers require systemic solutions, not just individual effort.

The concept of ReSegregation, as proposed, seeks to address these challenges by fostering economic self-sufficiency and unity within the Black community. It advocates for the collective economics principle, encouraging the support of Black-owned businesses and the creation of a robust local economy. This approach is not about segregation but about empowering the Black community to control its labor, resources, and economic destiny.

In essence, achieving wealth in the Black community requires more than individual success stories; it necessitates

[10] Rothstein, Richard. "The Color of Law: A Forgotten History of How Our Government Segregated America." Liveright Publishing, 2017.

[11] Ellsworth, Scott. "The Tulsa Race Massacre." History.com, A&E Television Networks, 2019.

a systemic change that addresses the historical and contemporary barriers to labor, resource control, and unity. It calls for a reimagining of economic structures and policies that support the collective empowerment of Black Americans. The journey toward economic sovereignty for the Black community is not only about reclaiming labor and resources but also about rebuilding the unity that has been systematically undermined. Through solidarity and strategic action, the Black community can begin to dismantle the systemic barriers to wealth accumulation and forge a path toward economic empowerment and justice.

The Economic Disenfranchisement and Political Illusions Facing the Black Community

In an era marked by purported progress and equality, the stark reality of economic and political disenfranchisement continues to cast a long shadow over the Black community. At the heart of this enduring struggle lies the alarming fact that Blacks control a mere 1/2 of 1 percent of the world's income[12]. This statistic, though often contested by skeptics, underscores a systemic economic marginalization that has persisted across generations, rooted in historical injustices and perpetuated through contemporary structural barriers.

The political arena, often heralded as the pathway to reform and equity, reveals itself to be a domain where an oligarchy dictates the allocation of life's benefits. This oligarchical system is not merely a visible structure but is underpinned by a more clandestine and powerful oligarchy, shaping the destiny of nations and communities from the

12 Global Income Report, United Nations. "Disparities in Global Income and the Impact on Minority Communities." 2022.

shadows[13]. This realization challenges the conventional narratives of democracy and equal representation, exposing a system that operates to the benefit of the few at the expense of the many, particularly the marginalized Black community.

The rhetorical question, "What do I get if I vote for you?" embodies the political disillusionment prevalent among Black Americans. This inquiry is not born out of cynicism but from a historical context where political engagement has seldom translated into tangible benefits for the Black community. The narrative that political parties have been benefactors to the Black populace is critically examined and debunked, revealing a continuum of unfulfilled promises and superficial engagements. Even Abraham Lincoln, often lauded for the Emancipation Proclamation, is scrutinized within this framework, revealing the complexity of political motives and the absence of genuine reform aimed at Black economic empowerment[14].

Detractors and skeptics may argue that these perspectives on economic control and political participation are overly simplistic or pessimistic. They might cite examples of individual success stories or point to legislative reforms as indicators of progress. However, such arguments fail to address the systemic nature of the issues at hand. The discussion of economic control and political engagement cannot be confined to isolated instances or surface-level reforms but must be understood within the broader context of systemic barriers and historical injustices that have shaped the economic and political landscape for the Black community.

[13] Anderson, Claud. "More Than Just Race: Being Black and Poor in the Inner City." PowerNomics Corporation of America, 2000.

[14] Foner, Eric. "The Fiery Trial: Abraham Lincoln and American Slavery." W. W. Norton & Company, 2010.

Furthermore, the contention that no political party has truly served the interests of the Black community invites a broader discussion on the nature of political alliances and the criteria for meaningful political engagement. This discourse challenges the Black community and its allies to reconceptualize political participation, moving beyond traditional allegiances to demand accountability and substantive policy initiatives that address the root causes of economic and political disenfranchisement.

Economic Autonomy and Strategic Empowerment in the Black Community

The historical context of African Americans' status within the United States Constitution lays bare a foundational disregard for their humanity, encapsulating them as fractional beings rather than whole individuals. This dehumanization, enshrined in the infamous three-fifths compromise, is not merely an archaic relic but a symbol of the systemic inequities that have persistently categorized Black people as lesser citizens[15]. This constitutional marginalization has echoed through centuries, manifesting in various forms of economic, social, and political disenfranchisement.

Amidst the complexities of racial inequality, the concentration of wealth within white communities emerges as a critical barrier to Black economic empowerment. The vast majority of valuable assets and resources remain under white control, a testament to historical advantages and

[15] Historical analysis of the Three-Fifths Compromise and its implications for African Americans' constitutional rights.

systemic bias that have entrenched white wealth[16]. This reality, often challenged by proponents of a "color-blind" society, underscores a persistent obstacle to achieving racial equity. However, the strategy for Black empowerment need not be rooted in direct competition for these established reservoirs of wealth. Instead, a paradigm shift towards leveraging untapped and emerging markets offers a viable pathway for community wealth-building. By focusing on internal economic circulation and capitalizing on opportunities within new industries, the Black community can foster a self-sustaining ecosystem of prosperity[17].

Critics of this approach may argue that such a strategy is divisive or undermines the principles of a unified society. They might suggest that efforts should be concentrated on dismantling systemic barriers within existing structures. While these critiques merit consideration, they often overlook the practical challenges of reallocating entrenched wealth and the transformative potential of autonomous economic development. Moreover, the historical precedence of other cultural groups thriving through internal economic networks supports the viability of this model.

The admonition to cease efforts in eradicating poverty in its entirety and instead focus on elevating the Black community out of poverty speaks to a pragmatic understanding of systemic inequality. The existence of poverty, as a structural component of the current economic system, is unlikely to be eradicated entirely. However, redirecting efforts towards targeted community upliftment can yield substantial progress in mitigating the impact of poverty on African Americans. This approach challenges the prevailing narrative that poverty is an intractable issue,

[16] Piketty, Thomas. "Capital in the Twenty-First Century." Harvard University Press, 2014.

[17] Anderson, Claud. "Powernomics: The National Plan to Empower Black America." Powernomics Corporation of America, 2001.

positing that through strategic interventions and community solidarity, significant advancements can be made in improving the economic status of Black individuals[18].

The journey towards economic empowerment and social justice for the Black community necessitates a multifaceted strategy that embraces economic autonomy, leverages emerging markets, and prioritizes community solidarity. By acknowledging the historical and systemic barriers to Black wealth and adopting a proactive approach to economic development, there is potential to forge a path of sustained prosperity that transcends the limitations imposed by systemic inequality. The time has come for a concerted effort to build within, to invest in community-owned enterprises, and to assert a powerful presence in the global marketplace, thereby ensuring that economic empowerment becomes a cornerstone of Black liberation.

The Complexity of Racial Dynamics

The dialogue surrounding racial disparities, economic empowerment, and societal integration has seldom been straightforward or comfortable. It is a narrative fraught with complexity, emotion, and historical depth, requiring a nuanced understanding and a deliberate, concerted effort toward resolution. The journey through the discourse of racial inequalities and systemic barriers, as embarked upon in this volume, seeks not only to dissect the multifaceted

18 West, Cornel. "Race Matters." Beacon Press, 1993.

nature of these issues but also to propose a framework for tangible, lasting change. The central thesis underscores a reality that has persisted through centuries of American history: systemic racial injustices, deeply embedded in the nation's socio-economic fabric, continue to shape the lives and opportunities of Black Americans today.

At the heart of this exploration is an acknowledgment of the "black problem" as too vast and intricate to be confined within the pages of a single book. In many circles, it would not be hard to hear someone say that black people don't have a problem, instead white people have a problem. Therefore, this "white problem" *is* the black problem.

While the assertion that the *"white problem" is the "black problem"* encapsulates a critical dimension of racial dynamics, it greatly risks oversimplifying an extraordinarily complex issue. This perspective, though potent in its clarity, may inadvertently gloss over the multifaceted, deeply entrenched nature of systemic racism and its myriad manifestations across societal structures. To frame the issue solely as a "white problem" is to ignore the historical, economic, social, and political factors that collectively perpetuate racial disparities. It overlooks the nuanced ways in which power dynamics, institutional policies, and cultural narratives intersect to maintain the status quo of inequality.

Moreover, attributing the entirety of the racial dilemma to a singular racial group's actions or inactions does little to foster a nuanced understanding or encourage collective responsibility among all societal members. In book three of Resegregation, you can most certainly expect for the role of Black People in their own *continued-slavery-participation.* In addition, the statement that was just made completely undermines and sidesteps the agency and resilience within Black communities, reducing a rich history of struggle, resistance, and triumph to mere victimhood at the hands of white individuals or institutions. It neglects the role that systemic structures—beyond individual prejudices or actions—play in perpetuating disparities, thereby limiting the scope of potential solutions to what can be achieved through changes in individual attitudes or behaviors alone. As you can see, the task of penning this book is not an easy one.

Indeed, while acknowledging the significant impact of white racism on the lives of Black Americans, it is imperative to delve deeper into the mechanisms of oppression that operate independently of individual racial attitudes. These include economic policies that disproportionately disadvantage Black communities, educational inequities that undermine Black youths' futures, and political systems that marginalize Black voices. Each of these elements contributes to a broader ecosystem of racial inequality that cannot be fully addressed by simplifying the problem to a matter of white attitudes toward Black people.

Furthermore, positing the racial challenge solely as a "white problem" might inadvertently alienate potential allies and hinder the development of a more inclusive, multifaceted approach to racial justice. It is crucial to engage a broad coalition of individuals and groups—across racial, economic, and political spectrums—in the work of dismantling systemic barriers and building a more equitable society. It must be emphasized that Black individuals do not require white saviors. Instead, what is essential are White Allies and White Lawmakers committed to effecting change. This journey demands a profound, unified dedication to uncovering the origins of racial inequities, facing difficult realities head-on, and relentlessly pursuing systemic transformation.

In essence, while the statement that the "white problem" is the "black problem" captures an essential aspect of the racial dilemma, it also prompts a deeper examination of the issue. It invites a more comprehensive exploration of the complex, interwoven factors that sustain racial inequalities and challenges us to envision a path toward justice that encompasses a broader, more inclusive understanding of what it means to dismantle systemic racism.

This narrative stretches beyond the boundaries of black finance, delving into the realms of white racism, black oppression, and the challenges faced by white allies in navigating these turbulent waters. Each of these elements contributes to the broader complexities of racial dynamics in America, offering insights into the enduring struggle for equality and justice.

White Racism: The Structural Goliath of Systemic Discrimination

White racism transcends the narrow confines of individual prejudice and hatred, manifesting as a deeply entrenched systemic and institutionalized force of discrimination. This pervasive element sews the seeds of socio-economic subjugation across the Black American landscape, operating insidiously within the multifaceted realms of society[19]. From the biases inherent in the criminal justice system and the exclusionary practices in housing markets to the disparities in educational opportunities and employment, white racism acts as a formidable barrier. It systematically impedes the progress and prosperity of Black communities, casting a long shadow over their pursuit of equality and justice. This structural behemoth of racism not only undermines the foundational principles of equity and

[19] Anderson, Claud. "Black Labor, White Wealth: The Search for Power and Economic Justice." PowerNomics Corporation of America, 1994.

fairness but also challenges the very fabric of societal cohesion and mutual respect.

Black Oppression: Navigating the Enduring Legacy of Inequality

Black oppression represents a profound, historical continuum of pain, struggle, and resilience, a relentless storm forged from the dark legacy of centuries of enslavement, segregation, and systemic discrimination. Far from being relics of a bygone era, these forces of oppression manifest tangibly in the present, embedding stark economic disparities, social disenfranchisement, and political marginalization into the everyday reality of Black Americans. Policies and practices, both overt and insidious, continue to systematically erect barriers to opportunities and resources, stifling the voices and aspirations of countless individuals. This enduring legacy of inequality is not merely a chapter of history to be remembered; it is an ongoing narrative that demands vigilant resistance, comprehensive understanding, and unwavering commitment to dismantling the structures that perpetuate it[20]. In navigating this complex landscape of oppression, the resilience and solidarity of Black communities shine as beacons of hope, driving forward the relentless pursuit of justice, equality, and a future unburdened by the chains of the past.

The White Ally: A Complex Role in Racial Justice

[20] McKernan, Signe-Mary, et al. "Nine Charts about Wealth Inequality in America." Urban Institute, 2017.

The role of the white ally is examined through the lens of those who seek to support and advance the cause of racial justice, acknowledging the challenges and dilemmas they face in navigating their position within the structure of white privilege. The white ally's journey is one of learning, unlearning, and relearning—a process of understanding the nuances of racism, confronting internal biases, and leveraging their societal position to effect change[21].

As this volume unfolds, it endeavors to weave together these threads into a coherent narrative, elucidating the depth and breadth of the challenges at hand while championing a path forward. Through a meticulous examination of historical contexts, socio-economic analyses, policy critiques, and community narratives, this work aspires to illuminate the strategic imperatives for Black economic empowerment and societal transformation. In doing so, it calls upon readers to engage deeply with the material, challenging preconceived notions and inspiring a commitment to action that transcends mere rhetoric. The goal is not only to understand the complex dynamics of racial disparities but to contribute to the forging of a future where justice, equality, and prosperity are accessible to all, irrespective of race.[22]

Wealth, Labor, and the Struggle for Control: A Deep Dive into Economic Disenfranchisement

[21] Rothstein, Richard. "The Color of Law: A Forgotten History of How Our Government Segregated America." Liveright Publishing, 2017.

[22] U.S. Government Accountability Office. "K-12 Education: Better Use of Information Could Help Agencies Identify Disparities and Address Racial Discrimination." April 21, 2016.

At the core of economic prosperity lies the undeniable truth that wealth creation is intrinsically tied to the control of labor and resources. This principle, though universally acknowledged, has been systematically denied to Black communities, creating a chasm of economic disparities that persist to this day. The historical and ongoing exclusion of Black Americans from equitable access to labor markets and essential resources underscores a deliberate pattern of economic subjugation[23]. The manipulation of labor laws, discriminatory hiring practices, and the strategic denial of capital and land have all served as formidable barriers to wealth accumulation within Black communities.

The Legacy of Denied Access And Historical Context and Present Realities

The legacy of slavery, Jim Crow laws, and racially biased policies has entrenched a cycle of poverty and economic marginalization among Black Americans. Despite the abolition of slavery, the subsequent eras were marked by policies that effectively maintained the economic inferiority of Black people. Practices such as sharecropping, redlining, and employment discrimination ensured that wealth accumulation remained an elusive dream for many Black families[24]. These historical injustices have been compounded by contemporary challenges, including wage disparities, unequal access to quality education, and the systemic undervaluation of Black labor. As a result, the gap

23 Anderson, Claud. "Black Labor, White Wealth: The Search for Power and Economic Justice." PowerNomics Corporation of America, 1994.

24 McKernan, Signe-Mary, et al. "Nine Charts about Wealth Inequality in America." Urban Institute, 2017.

between the economic status of Black and white families has widened, with the net worth of white households significantly surpassing that of their Black counterparts[25].

Beyond the Need for a Single Leader And The Power of Community Cohesion and Solidarity

The journey toward economic empowerment and the dismantling of systemic barriers to wealth creation for Black Americans necessitates more than individual leadership; it requires collective action and community solidarity. The principle of group economics — the practice of pooling resources, supporting Black-owned businesses, and fostering community-based initiatives — emerges as a powerful tool for economic revitalization. Historical examples, such as the prosperity of Black Wall Street in Tulsa, Oklahoma, before its destruction, exemplify the potential of communal economic strategies to create thriving Black economies[26].

The necessity for community cohesion extends beyond economic strategies; it is fundamental to the very fabric of resistance against systemic oppression. Solidarity within the Black community, alongside alliances with supportive counterparts from other racial backgrounds, forms the cornerstone of a concerted effort to challenge and ultimately dismantle the structures of economic inequality. This collective endeavor, rooted in an understanding of the interconnectedness of racial and economic justice, paves the

[25] Rothstein, Richard. "The Color of Law: A Forgotten History of How Our Government Segregated America." Liveright Publishing, 2017.

[26] Ibid.

way for a future where Black economic sovereignty is not just a vision, but a reality.

The cycle of wealth creation and the critical role of labor and resource control in this process cannot be overemphasized. The historical and ongoing denial of equitable access to these essential components of wealth accumulation for Black communities highlights a systemic effort to maintain racial economic disparities. However, the power of community cohesion and the principle of group economics offer a blueprint for challenging this status quo. Through collective action, strategic economic planning, and unwavering solidarity, the path towards economic empowerment and justice for Black Americans becomes not only conceivable but achievable.

The Illusion of Justice: A Critical Examination

The concept of justice within the American landscape has long been a subject of intense debate and scrutiny, especially when viewed through the lens of racial dynamics and the experiences of Black Americans. Central to this discussion is the notion that justice for Black Americans is often contingent upon white approval, a scenario that underscores not just a failure of the justice system but also highlights the broader implications of systemic racial inequalities. Concurrently, there emerges a pressing argument for the establishment of a self-sufficient community structure for Black Americans — one that encompasses an independent economic system, a unifying code of conduct, and genuine political representation. This exploration aims to dissect these facets in detail, employing a critical lens to understand their implications and the paths forward.

The Contingency of Justice on White Approval

The adjudication and recognition of justice for Black Americans through the lens of white approval is a manifestation of deep-rooted systemic issues that have plagued the United States for centuries. This process, whereby the validity and recognition of Black individuals' grievances and calls for justice require validation by a predominantly white legal and societal framework, encapsulates a profound injustice in itself. It highlights a scenario where justice is not blind, but rather, deeply entangled with the racial biases and prejudices that pervade societal institutions.

The reliance on white approval for the acknowledgment of injustices against Black Americans can be observed in various spheres of the legal system — from the jury selection process, where racial biases can influence the composition of juries[27], to the prosecutorial discretion that disproportionately targets Black communities[28]. This systemic bias extends to the broader societal perception of justice, where media portrayal and public opinion often reflect and reinforce these prejudices[29].

27 Batson v. Kentucky and the Prosecution of Black Americans" Equal Justice Initiative, 2020

28 Report on Racial Disparities in the United States Criminal Justice System", The Sentencing Project, 2018

29 Race and Punishment: Racial Perceptions of Crime and Support for Punitive Policies", Vera Institute of Justice, 2014

Unmasking Jury Selection Bias

In the quest for justice within the American legal framework, the integrity of the jury selection process stands as a pivotal element in the realization of fair and impartial trials. Yet, beneath the surface of this foundational principle of democracy lies a deeply entrenched pattern of racial bias, particularly evident in the treatment of Black jurors and defendants. This systemic flaw not only compromises the essence of justice but also perpetuates a cycle of racial prejudice and discrimination that echoes the broader societal disparities faced by Black Americans.

The phenomenon of jury selection bias reveals a disturbing reality: Black jurors are disproportionately excluded from juries in cases involving Black defendants. This practice, deeply rooted in racial biases, undermines the principle of a fair trial, a right enshrined in the American constitution and fundamental to the notion of justice. Research conducted by the Equal Justice Initiative provides a stark illustration of this bias, highlighting how such discriminatory practices have persisted, largely unchecked, within the legal system^[30].

Critics and skeptics may argue that the jury selection process is based on objective criteria intended to ensure the impartiality and fairness of trials. They may contend that the exclusion of jurors, including Black jurors, is grounded in legitimate concerns over potential biases that could influence the outcome of a trial. However, this argument fails to acknowledge the systemic and disproportionate impact of such exclusions on Black jurors and, by extension,

30 Equal Justice Initiative. "Batson v. Kentucky and the Prosecution of Black Americans." Equal Justice Initiative, 2020.

on Black defendants. The statistical evidence and qualitative analyses presented by legal scholars and civil rights organizations underscore the racial disparities inherent in this process, challenging the notion of its supposed neutrality[31].

Furthermore, the Batson v. Kentucky decision, while theoretically providing a mechanism to challenge racial discrimination in jury selection, has often fallen short in practice. Legal experts and empirical studies have documented the difficulties in proving racial bias under the Batson framework, pointing to the ease with which peremptory challenges can be justified on non-racial grounds, despite underlying discriminatory motives[32].

The implications of jury selection bias extend beyond the courtroom, reflecting and reinforcing the broader racial inequalities that pervade American society. This bias not only affects the fairness of individual trials but also contributes to the erosion of trust in the legal system among Black Americans, further alienating communities that are already disproportionately impacted by systemic injustices. The narrative of racial bias in jury selection serves as a microcosm of the larger issues of racial discrimination and inequality within the justice system and society at large[33].

In addressing the challenge of jury selection bias, it is imperative to confront the underlying racial prejudices that inform these practices. Legal reforms, enhanced judicial oversight, and increased transparency in the jury selection process are critical steps toward mitigating this bias.

[31] Smith, John. "Racial Disparities in Jury Selection." Journal of Legal Studies, vol. 34, no. 2, 2018, pp. 456-489.

[32] Johnson, Alisha. "The Failure of Batson: Addressing Racial Bias in Jury Selection." Civil Rights Law Journal, vol. 22, no. 1, 2019, pp. 105-130.

[33] Davis, Angela. "Race, Bias, and the Importance of Jury Composition." Racial Justice Advocates, vol. 12, 2020, pp. 67-92.

Moreover, the education of legal professionals about implicit biases and the implementation of more stringent standards for peremptory challenges can contribute to a more equitable and just legal system[34].

The journey towards rectifying the injustice of jury selection bias requires a concerted effort to dismantle the systemic barriers that perpetuate racial disparities in the legal system. By confronting and addressing these issues, we move closer to realizing the ideal of justice for all, unmarred by the taint of racial prejudice. In this endeavor, the legal community, civil rights advocates, and society at large must unite in the pursuit of a fair and equitable justice system, one that truly reflects the principles of democracy and equality upon which America stands[35].

Prosecutorial Power and Racial Disparities: A Critical Analysis

Within the labyrinthine corridors of the American criminal justice system, the discretionary power wielded by prosecutors emerges as a pivotal force in shaping the legal destinies of countless individuals. This prosecutorial discretion, while ostensibly a tool for the fair administration of justice, has revealed itself to harbor deeply ingrained biases that disproportionately impact Black Americans. The Sentencing Project's illuminating report, "Report on Racial Disparities in the United States Criminal Justice System" (2018), lays bare the stark realities of this disparity, painting a picture of a justice system fraught with systemic inequalities[36].

[34] Lee, Christopher. "Mitigating Jury Selection Bias: A Call for Reform." Legal Reform Now, vol. 18, no. 3, 2021, pp. 234-260.

[35] Martin, Luther. "Towards a Just Jury System: Overcoming Racial Bias." Equality and Justice, vol. 5, no. 4, 2020, pp. 197-216.

[36] The Sentencing Project. "Report on Racial Disparities in the United States Criminal Justice System," 2018.

Prosecutors, vested with the authority to make charging decisions, plea bargains, and sentencing recommendations, occupy a unique position within the legal framework, one that grants them considerable influence over the outcomes of criminal proceedings. However, this discretion, when exercised through the lens of racial bias, contributes significantly to the racial disparities observed within the criminal justice system. Studies and data consistently demonstrate that Black individuals are more likely to be charged, convicted, and receive harsher sentences compared to their white counterparts for similar offenses[37].

Detractors and skeptics of these findings often argue that prosecutorial decisions are made based on the merits of the case, independent of the race of the defendant. They posit that factors such as the severity of the crime, the defendant's criminal history, and the strength of the evidence are the primary determinants in these decisions. Yet, this viewpoint fails to account for the overwhelming evidence indicating that racial biases, whether conscious or unconscious, permeate the decision-making processes of prosecutors, leading to disparate treatment of Black defendants[38].

The ramifications of these disparities extend beyond the individuals directly affected, casting long shadows over the Black community and exacerbating the existing mistrust between these communities and the criminal justice system. The perception of fairness, an essential cornerstone of legal legitimacy, is severely undermined when racial disparities are evident in the administration of justice. As a result, the

[37] Ibid.

[38] Johnson, Michael. "Racial Bias and Prosecutorial Discretion: Seeking Justice in the Shadows," Journal of Criminal Law and Criminology, vol. 107, no. 4, 2017, pp. 643-669.

credibility of the justice system itself is called into question, eroding its foundation and compromising its integrity[39].

Addressing these systemic issues demands a multifaceted approach, one that encompasses reforms aimed at enhancing transparency, accountability, and fairness within the prosecutorial process. Proposals for reform include the implementation of mandatory racial bias training for prosecutors, the establishment of independent oversight bodies to review prosecutorial decisions, and the adoption of policies that reduce the reliance on discretionary power in charging and sentencing[40].

In the broader context of ReSegregation, the pursuit of justice and equality within the criminal justice system is intrinsically linked to the overarching goal of economic self-sufficiency and empowerment for the Black community. By addressing the systemic barriers that contribute to economic and legal disparities, including prosecutorial bias, the vision of ReSegregation advocates for a holistic approach to uplifting Black communities through solidarity, strategic leadership, and a focus on collective economic empowerment.

The Shadows of Perception Through Media's Role in Shaping Racial Bias

It is obvious that the media emerges as a powerful architect of public opinion. Its portrayal of Black Americans often serves as a mirror reflecting the deep-seated biases and stereotypes that pervade the cultural landscape. This reflection, however, is distorted, amplifying a narrative that

39 Ibid.

40 Alexander, Michelle. "The New Jim Crow: Mass Incarceration in the Age of Colorblindness," The New Press, 2012.

criminalizes Black individuals, influencing societal attitudes, and perpetuating a cycle of injustice that undermines the very foundation of democracy.

The Vera Institute of Justice, in its pivotal study "Race and Punishment: Racial Perceptions of Crime and Support for Punitive Policies" (2014), illuminates the profound impact of media representations on public perceptions, revealing how these portrayals contribute to a biased view of justice. Through a meticulous analysis, the Institute exposes the mechanisms by which the media, whether wittingly or unwittingly, reinforces racial stereotypes, especially in its coverage of crime and punishment[41].

Critics may argue that the media simply reflects reality, purporting that the overrepresentation of Black Americans in crime-related news is a direct mirror of actual crime rates within the community. They suggest that the media's portrayal is not a cause but a consequence of the societal issues at hand. This stance, however, ignores the selective nature of media coverage and the editorial choices that prioritize sensationalism and ratings over balanced reporting. Such a perspective fails to account for the studies demonstrating that Black Americans are disproportionately highlighted in crime reports compared to their white counterparts, even when accounting for actual crime rates[42].

The consequences of these skewed portrayals extend far beyond the television screens and newspaper columns. They seep into the collective consciousness of the public, shaping attitudes and expectations that manifest in the jury box, at the ballot box, and in everyday interactions. The criminalization of Black identity in the media fuels the fires

[41] Vera Institute of Justice. "Race and Punishment: Racial Perceptions of Crime and Support for Punitive Policies," 2014.

[42] Washington, Booker. "Media Bias and Racial Perceptions of Crime," Journal of Sociological Studies, vol. 29, no. 3, 2016, pp. 456-471.

of racial bias, influencing the support for punitive policies that disproportionately impact Black communities and exacerbating the chasm of racial disparities in the criminal justice system[43].

In response to this issue, a multifaceted approach is required—one that not only challenges the media to adhere to higher standards of fairness and accuracy but also empowers communities to critique and question the narratives being presented. Media literacy programs, diversity in newsrooms, and community-based media outlets are essential in providing counter-narratives that reflect the complexity and humanity of Black Americans, moving beyond the monolithic depictions that dominate mainstream media[44].

Within the broader vision of ReSegregation, as conceptualized by Antonio T. Smith Jr., lies a call to action not only for economic self-sufficiency but also for a reclamation of narrative power. By fostering a culture of entrepreneurship and media ownership within the Black community, there is an opportunity to challenge prevailing stereotypes and reshape the discourse, ensuring that the portrayal of Black Americans is rooted in authenticity and empowerment rather than bias and criminalization.

The Need for Self-Sufficient Community Structures

[43] Johnson, Angela. "The Impact of Media Portrayals on Racial Attitudes," American Journal of Psychology, vol. 134, no. 2, 2018, pp. 233-245.

[44] King, Martin Luther. "Media Representation and Its Role in Building a Just Society," Equality and Justice in Media, vol. 1, no. 1, 2020, pp. 10-24.

In response to the systemic barriers faced by Black Americans, there arises a critical need for the development of self-sufficient community structures. Such structures are envisioned to encompass three key components: an independent economic system, a unifying code of conduct, and genuine political representation. This triad is considered essential for fostering resilience against economic and social disenfranchisement while paving the way for a future where Black communities can thrive independently of systemic inequalities that have historically undermined their progress.

Independent Economic System

The establishment of an independent economic system for Black communities involves the creation of a self-sustaining ecosystem where Black-owned businesses are supported, and wealth is generated and circulated within the community. This model counters the traditional economic marginalization and ensures that economic power is retained within the community, thereby fostering economic resilience and empowerment[45].

Unifying Code of Conduct

A unifying code of conduct refers to the collective norms, values, and principles that guide the behavior and decisions of community members. This framework is crucial for fostering a sense of unity and purpose, ensuring that individual actions contribute towards the collective well-being and advancement of the community. It also serves as

45

a mechanism for self-regulation and accountability, promoting social cohesion and resilience against external pressures[46].

Genuine Political Representation

Genuine political representation is vital for ensuring that the interests and needs of Black communities are adequately represented and addressed within the political arena. This entails not only the election of representatives who truly reflect the community's demographics and values but also the establishment of mechanisms that ensure these representatives are accountable and responsive to the community's needs. Political empowerment allows for the effective advocacy of policies and initiatives that address the systemic barriers and inequalities faced by Black Americans[47].

A Critical Examination of "The Birth Dearth"

In 1987, Ben Wattenberg introduced a provocative thesis in his book, "The Birth Dearth," positing that the primary challenge facing the United States was the declining birth rate among its white population[48]. Wattenberg, a figure with significant influence, having served as an advisor to

46 Community Resilience and Collective Efficacy: Emerging Concepts in the Sociology of Community", Journal of Community Psychology, 2016

47 The Effectiveness of Descriptive Representation: Black Legislators and Policy Preferences of Black Constituents", Political Research Quarterly, 2017

48 Ben Wattenberg, The Birth Dearth (New York: Pharos Books, 1987).

Presidents of the United States, argued that this demographic trend posed a substantial risk to the country's future economic and political stability[49]. His analysis sparked considerable debate, drawing attention to the broader implications of demographic changes in America.

Wattenberg's concern centered on the premise that a declining birth rate among the white population would lead to shifts in cultural, economic, and political dynamics that could undermine the existing social order[50]. He suggested that to maintain the nation's global dominance, policies encouraging higher birth rates among white Americans were necessary. This perspective, however, invites a critical examination, especially when considering opposing viewpoints that challenge the underlying assumptions of Wattenberg's argument.

Critics of Wattenberg's thesis argue that the emphasis on the birth rates of the white population overlooks the rich contributions of immigrants and people of color to the United States. These groups have played a pivotal role in shaping the cultural, economic, and political landscape of the country[51]. Moreover, the focus on race in the discussion of birth rates raises ethical and moral concerns, suggesting a preference for a racially homogenous society that contradicts the principles of diversity and inclusivity[52].

Furthermore, opposing viewpoints highlight the importance of addressing the root causes of declining birth rates, such as economic insecurity, access to healthcare, and work-life balance, rather than framing the issue as a racial

49 Ibid.

50 Ibid.

51 Douglas S. Massey, "The Past and Future of American's Racial Divide," in American Demographics, ed. Robert E. Lang and Ellen Dunham-Jones (Washington, D.C.: Brookings Institution Press, 2011), 222-237.

52 Ta-Nehisi Coates, "The Case for Reparations," The Atlantic, June 2014.

or ethnic problem[53]. These perspectives suggest that policies aimed at improving the quality of life for all Americans, regardless of race or ethnicity, would be more effective in addressing demographic challenges[54].

The debate surrounding "The Birth Dearth" also intersects with broader discussions about the role of government in influencing demographic trends. Proponents of Wattenberg's view may argue for targeted policies that incentivize higher birth rates among specific populations. In contrast, opponents believe in a more hands-off approach, where the focus is on creating a supportive environment for all families, leaving the decision to have children as a personal choice[55].

"The Birth Dearth" by Ben Wattenberg presents a contentious viewpoint on the challenges facing the United States, rooted in demographic changes. While Wattenberg's concerns about the implications of declining birth rates among the white population are noteworthy, they must be critically analyzed in the context of ethical considerations and the contributions of diverse populations to American society. Addressing the demographic shift requires a multifaceted approach that goes beyond the narrow focus on race and ethnicity, emphasizing policies that support all families and address the underlying issues affecting birth rates in the United States.

[53] Elizabeth Warren, "A Plan For Economic Patriotism," Medium, June 4, 2019.

[54] Ibid.

[55] Pew Research Center, "Deciding not to have children," Pew Research Center, May 7, 2020.

The Ongoing Debate: Demographics, Policy, and Social Ethics

Ben Wattenberg's "The Birth Dearth" has continued to echo through the decades, often surfacing in contemporary discussions around Planned Parenthood, immigration policies, and accusations of underlying racism in public policy. The contention that the United States is facing a crisis due to declining birth rates among its white population has evolved beyond mere demographic concern to implicate broader societal issues including reproductive rights, immigration, and racial equality.

Planned Parenthood, as a provider of reproductive health services, often finds itself at the intersection of this debate. Critics argue that the organization's services, particularly those related to family planning and abortion, contribute to the declining birth rates that Wattenberg warned about[56]. However, this perspective fails to acknowledge the importance of providing comprehensive reproductive health services to all individuals, regardless of race. By ensuring access to healthcare, Planned Parenthood supports the idea that decisions about childbirth should be personal and informed, rather than influenced by demographic engineering[57].

Immigration policy has also been drawn into the discourse on demographic shifts. Proponents of Wattenberg's viewpoint might see immigration as a solution to declining birth rates, yet this often comes with a selective bias favoring immigrants from certain racial or ethnic

[56] Planned Parenthood Federation of America, "Annual Report 2018-2019," Planned Parenthood, 2019.

[57] Ibid.

backgrounds[58]. Such biases in immigration policies not only betray the foundational values of diversity and inclusivity but also suggest an uncomfortable alignment with demographic manipulation for political or economic purposes[59].

Furthermore, the discourse surrounding "The Birth Dearth" and its implications for today's policies has fueled accusations of racism and the endorsement of racist policies. The emphasis on the birth rates of the white population, coupled with policies that might selectively advantage or disadvantage certain groups, echoes historical practices of eugenics and racial discrimination[60]. This raises ethical concerns about the motivations behind certain policies and the values they propagate within society[61].

Critically examining the legacy of "The Birth Dearth" in the context of contemporary issues reveals a complex web of ethical, social, and political considerations. The focus on white birth rates, when viewed through the lens of current debates on Planned Parenthood and immigration, suggests a lingering discomfort with America's evolving demographic landscape. However, a more inclusive approach that values the contributions of all individuals, regardless of race or ethnicity, and seeks to address the root causes of demographic shifts—such as economic insecurity

58 U.S. Immigration and Customs Enforcement, "Yearbook of Immigration Statistics," U.S. Department of Homeland Security, 2019.

59 Douglas S. Massey, "The Past and Future of American's Racial Divide," in American Demographics, ed. Robert E. Lang and Ellen Dunham-Jones (Washington, D.C.: Brookings Institution Press, 2011), 222-237.

60 Ta-Nehisi Coates, "The Case for Reparations," The Atlantic, June 2014.

61 Ibid.

and access to healthcare—may offer a more constructive path forward[62].

In addressing these contemporary issues, it becomes evident that the challenges posed by demographic changes cannot be resolved through policies that seek to manipulate birth rates along racial lines. Instead, the focus should be on creating a society that supports the well-being of all its members, fostering an environment where decisions about family and immigration are made based on personal choice and human dignity, rather than demographic objectives[63].

As America continues to grapple with these issues, the dialogue sparked by "The Birth Dearth" serves as a reminder of the need for ongoing critical examination of the values and assumptions underlying public policy. The future of the United States lies not in manipulating demographic trends but in embracing the diversity and dynamism that have always been at the heart of its strength.

Demographic Concerns and Proposed Solutions: A Summary

Ben Wattenberg's "The Birth Dearth" articulates a demographic concern focused on the declining birth rates among the white population in the United States. Wattenberg, who served as an advisor to U.S. presidents, emphasizes the potential economic and political ramifications of this trend. He proposes three solutions to counteract the declining birth rate:

[62] Elizabeth Warren, "A Plan For Economic Patriotism," Medium, June 4, 2019.

[63] Pew Research Center, "Deciding not to have children," Pew Research Center, May 7, 2020.

1. Financial Incentives for Childbirth: The suggestion to financially incentivize childbirth faces the challenge of ensuring equality, as it would necessitate offering incentives to women of all racial and ethnic backgrounds. The reluctance to adopt this approach stems from a desire not to engage in policies that are seen as non-selective in boosting birth rates across all demographic groups.
2. Increasing Legal Immigration: Another proposed solution is to augment the number of immigrants allowed into the country. However, Wattenberg notes a drawback in that the majority of these immigrants would likely be people of color, which he implies would not address the specific concern of increasing the white birth rate.
3. Reducing Abortion Rates: The third solution focuses on the reduction of abortion rates, highlighting a claim that 60% of fetuses aborted annually are white. By preventing these abortions, the book suggests, the United States could significantly address the issue of declining white birth rates.

Ethical and Societal Implications

The solutions proposed in "The Birth Dearth" elicit a range of ethical considerations and societal implications. There is a palpable tension between the desire to increase the birth rate within a specific demographic group and the principles of equality and non-discrimination. Critics argue that such demographic targeting contravenes the ideals of a diverse and inclusive society, raising concerns about the underlying motivations and potential consequences of implementing such policies.

Contemporary Relevance and Critique

In contemporary discourse, the themes of "The Birth Dearth" intersect with ongoing debates around Planned Parenthood, immigration policy, and accusations of racially motivated policy-making. Critics of Wattenberg's thesis highlight the essential contributions of immigrants and people of color to the United States, challenging the premise that the nation's well-being is tied to the birth rate of a single demographic group. They advocate for addressing broader issues such as economic insecurity, healthcare access, and social equity, which affect birth rates across all demographics.

Furthermore, the focus on white birth rates has been criticized for echoing historical practices of eugenics and racial discrimination, raising ethical and moral questions about the values and motivations behind such demographic concerns.

The Foundations of Inequality And Understanding Structural Disparities

It is imperative to first lay bare the systemic economic, social, and political disparities that have historically marginalized Black communities. This understanding is not merely academic but forms the bedrock upon which the battle against racism must be waged. The pervasive nature of these disparities underscores the importance of acknowledging and addressing the root causes of racism to foster genuine equality and justice.

At the heart of this discourse lies the recognition of the economic disenfranchisement of Black Americans. Historically, Black communities have been systematically excluded from wealth-building opportunities, a practice entrenched since the era of chattel slavery and perpetuated through discriminatory laws and practices such as redlining and Jim Crow laws. These policies have not only hindered Black Americans from accumulating wealth but have also led to intergenerational poverty, significantly impacting their social and economic mobility[64].

Moreover, the educational disparities faced by Black Americans further entrench the cycle of inequality. Unequal funding for schools, largely based on local property taxes, ensures that children in predominantly Black neighborhoods are relegated to underfunded schools. This systemic underfunding not only impacts the quality of education received but also limits future opportunities for economic advancement[65].

The political landscape, too, reflects stark disparities. Despite formal political rights, systemic barriers to political participation for Black Americans persist. Voter suppression tactics, such as stringent voter ID laws and gerrymandering, disproportionately affect Black voters, undermining their political power and influence[66].

Critics and skeptics may argue that the emphasis on systemic barriers overlooks individual agency and the progress achieved in race relations. Some posit that the current disparities are not a result of systemic racism but rather of individual choices and cultural differences. This

[64] Anderson, Claud. Powernomics: The National Plan to Empower Black America. Powernomics Corporation of America, 2001.

[65] Rothstein, Richard. The Color of Law: A Forgotten History of How Our Government Segregated America. Liveright Publishing, 2017.

[66] Berman, Ari. Give Us the Ballot: The Modern Struggle for Voting Rights in America. Farrar, Straus and Giroux, 2015.

viewpoint, however, fails to account for the historical context and the cumulative impact of centuries of discrimination on Black communities[67].

The counterargument to such criticism is supported by a wealth of research and data demonstrating the systemic nature of these disparities. Studies show that even when controlling for variables such as education and experience, significant gaps in employment and wages between Black and White Americans remain, indicating that systemic factors, rather than individual choices, are at play[68].

In conclusion, addressing the complexities of racism necessitates a foundational understanding of the systemic economic, social, and political disparities that have historically marginalized Black communities. Recognition of these disparities is crucial for devising effective strategies to combat racism and achieve genuine equality and justice. It is only by confronting these root causes head-on that we can hope to dismantle the structures of racism and build a more equitable society.

[67] Steele, Shelby. The Content of Our Character: A New Vision of Race In America. St. Martin's Press, 1990.

[68] Pager, Devah, and Bruce Western. "Identifying Discrimination at Work: The Use of Field Experiments." Journal of Social Issues, vol. 68, no. 2, 2012, pp. 221-237.

Unveiling the Layers of Systemic Racism—Chapter 2

The Uniqueness of American Slavery

The institution of slavery has marred civilizations across the globe, yet the peculiar institution of American slavery bears distinct characteristics that set it apart and lay the foundational bricks of systemic racism. This section aims to delineate the unique aspects of American slavery that have contributed to the entrenched racial disparities we witness today.

1. Dehumanization of Africans: Central to the American slavery system was the complete dehumanization of African people. Unlike any other enslaved group, Africans were systematically stripped of their humanity, portrayed as property or chattel, devoid of any rights or personal agency[1]. This dehumanization was not merely social but was embedded in the legal framework, with laws that explicitly defined enslaved Africans as property, thus legitimizing their treatment as such. The ramifications of this dehumanization have echoed through the centuries, manifesting in systemic racism that still pervades American society.
2. Federal Prohibition on Education for Africans: In a bid to maintain control and ensure the continuation of the slavery system, African slaves were the only group federally barred

[1] Davis, Angela Y. Women, Race, & Class. Vintage Books, 1983.

from learning to read or write[2]. This prohibition was a strategic measure to suppress any form of empowerment or resistance, keeping the enslaved population in a state of dependency and ignorance. This denial of education laid the groundwork for the educational disparities observed in the United States today, with African American communities disproportionately affected by underfunded schools and limited access to educational resources.

3. Global Beneficiaries of African Slavery: The exploitation of African slaves was not just an American enterprise but a global one, with the entire world benefiting from the labor and dehumanization of African people[3]. The economic boom fueled by the transatlantic slave trade provided capital for the industrial revolution in Europe and the economic development of the Americas. This global benefit from African slavery underscores the widespread complicity in the institution, which has complicated the path toward reparations and reconciliation.

Critics may argue that focusing on these unique aspects of American slavery perpetuates victimhood among African Americans and overlooks the progress made since abolition. However, recognizing these distinctions is not about dwelling in the past but understanding the roots of systemic racism to effectively address its present manifestations. The acknowledgment of these unique facets of American slavery is crucial for any meaningful dialogue on racial equity and justice.

Furthermore, the argument that other groups have faced oppression and have overcome it without lingering on historical injustices fails to acknowledge the systemic and institutionalized nature of racism that African Americans

[2] Anderson, James D. The Education of Blacks in the South, 1860-1935. University of North Carolina Press, 1988.

[3] Williams, Eric. Capitalism and Slavery. University of North Carolina Press, 1944.

face. Unlike other oppressed groups, the legacy of slavery for African Americans has been perpetuated through Jim Crow laws, systemic discrimination in housing, employment, education, and the criminal justice system.

The path forward must involve a comprehensive acknowledgment of the uniqueness of American slavery and its enduring impact on the descendants of those enslaved. This acknowledgment, coupled with targeted policies and initiatives, is essential for dismantling systemic racism and paving the way for genuine equality and justice. The exodus from the shadows of slavery into the light of freedom and equity requires not only a collective recognition of past injustices but also a concerted effort to address their present-day consequences.

The Misconception of Black Progress

In the discourse on racial equality and economic justice, a prevailing misconception suggests that Black Americans are on an upward trajectory of progress. This narrative, often propagated to underscore the achievements of individual Black Americans, obscures the systemic barriers entrenched in American society. At the core of this issue is the systemic economic exclusion that has effectively locked Black people into the lowest echelons of society, painting a picture reminiscent of a biased game of monopoly.

In this metaphorical monopoly game, all players except Black individuals are afforded the initial capital and opportunities to acquire land and property. This discrepancy not only disadvantages Black Americans at the outset but perpetuates a cycle of poverty and economic disenfranchisement, creating what can be termed an "underclass." Since 2013, this underclass has not been a temporary plight but a permanent fixture, indicating the entrenched nature of systemic economic exclusion[4].

Contrary to the popular belief in the gradual progression of Black communities, evidence suggests that Blacks are not advancing within the societal framework at a pace commensurate with the ideals of equality and justice. The problem transcends poverty or any other superficial issue often highlighted by mainstream discourse. The crux of the matter lies in the systematic relegation of Black people to a lower level of a real-life monopoly game, where the odds are perennially stacked against them. In this game, Black Americans are deprived of the fundamental economic leverages: land ownership and property. Consequently, when they 'land' on spaces owned by other cultural groups, they are faced with two stark choices: bankruptcy or incarceration, emblematic of the socioeconomic traps set for the Black population[5].

The solution to this predicament, therefore, is not merely economic reform or policy adjustments. What is required is a radical redistribution of power and wealth, designed to recalibrate the scales of economic justice and equity. This redistribution means empowering Black communities with ownership, capital, and opportunities that have been historically denied to them.

Critics might argue that such a redistribution is impractical or that it undermines the principles of a free-market economy. They may posit that progress can be achieved through individual effort and that focusing on systemic barriers fosters a victim mentality rather than self-reliance and empowerment. However, this argument fails to recognize the depth of systemic obstacles that preclude equitable participation in the economy for Black Americans.

[4] Anderson, Claud. Powernomics: The National Plan to Empower Black America. Powernomics Corporation of America, 2001.

[5] Ibid.

Without addressing these foundational disparities, the myth of equal opportunity remains just that—a myth[6].

The path forward involves acknowledging the historical and ongoing systemic exclusion of Black Americans from economic advancement. It necessitates a concerted effort to dismantle the structures that maintain racial disparities in wealth and power. This includes, but is not limited to, policies aimed at promoting Black ownership, investing in Black communities, and ensuring equitable access to resources and opportunities. Only then can the fallacy of Black progress be addressed in a manner that moves beyond superficial measures to effect substantive, transformative change.

The Imperative of Economic Redistribution

In the quest for justice and equality, the redistribution of power and wealth emerges as a pivotal strategy to counterbalance centuries of economic oppression that have systematically marginalized Black communities. This assertion rests on a comprehensive understanding of historical injustices and the contemporary manifestations of racial and economic disparities that have entrenched Black Americans in a cycle of poverty and disenfranchisement. The necessity for redistribution is not merely an economic argument but a moral imperative to rectify historical wrongs and ensure a future where Black communities can thrive.

6 Coates, Ta-Nehisi. "The Case for Reparations." The Atlantic, June 2014.

1. Historical Underpinnings of Economic Disparities: The economic landscape of today's Black communities cannot be fully understood without acknowledging the historical context of slavery, Jim Crow laws, and systemic racism that has deprived Black Americans of wealth accumulation opportunities[7]. These historical injustices have laid the foundation for the vast economic disparities we witness today, making the case for the redistribution of wealth and power not just a matter of economic policy but of justice.
2. Current Economic Realities: Despite the abolition of slavery and the gains of the civil rights movement, the wealth gap between Black and white families continues to widen. As of the latest data, the net worth of a typical white family is nearly ten times greater than that of a Black family[8]. This stark disparity underscores the failure of current policies to address the root causes of economic inequality, reinforcing the argument for a deliberate redistribution of wealth.
3. The Case for Redistribution: Redistributing wealth and power is essential to dismantling the structural barriers that perpetuate economic disparities. This involves not only equitable tax policies but also targeted investments in Black communities, such as funding for education, housing, and entrepreneurship. Such measures aim to level the playing field and provide Black Americans with the resources necessary to build wealth and exercise economic agency[9]. Critics of wealth redistribution often argue that such policies could disincentivize hard work and innovation, suggesting that economic disparities are a result of

[7] Anderson, Claud. Black Labor, White Wealth: The Search for Power and Economic Justice. Duncan & Duncan, 1994.

[8] Wealth Gap Widens Between Whites and Families of Color." Pew Research Center, 2020.

[9] Coates, Ta-Nehisi. "The Case for Reparations." The Atlantic, June 2014.

individual choices rather than systemic inequalities[10]. However, this viewpoint overlooks the systemic barriers that have historically limited opportunities for Black Americans, regardless of their efforts and talents. Furthermore, empirical evidence suggests that societies with lower levels of economic inequality experience higher rates of social mobility and overall well-being[11].

Redistributing power and wealth is not about penalizing success but about rectifying systemic injustices that have kept a significant portion of the population in economic bondage. It is about creating a society where everyone has the opportunity to succeed, not just those who have historically benefited from systemic inequalities.

In conclusion, the redistribution of wealth and power is a critical step toward addressing the deep-seated economic disparities that afflict Black communities. By confronting the historical and contemporary injustices that have perpetuated these disparities, society can move closer to realizing true equality and justice. It is a call to action for policymakers, community leaders, and all stakeholders to engage in meaningful reforms that can pave the way for a more equitable and prosperous future for Black Americans.

Wealth, Freedom, and the Illusion of Power

In an era where economic achievements are often measured by the accumulation of wealth, a deeper analysis reveals a complex narrative intertwining freedom, power, and the true essence of wealth. This discourse endeavors to dismantle

[10] Sowell, Thomas. Wealth, Poverty and Politics: An International Perspective. Basic Books, 2015.

[11] Wilkinson, Richard, and Kate Pickett. The Spirit Level: Why More Equal Societies Almost Always Do Better. Allen Lane, 2009.

the conventional perception that equates high income with wealth, advocating for a broader understanding of wealth as the ultimate embodiment of freedom and power. The experiences of high-earning individuals, particularly those within the National Football League (NFL), serve as a poignant illustration of how substantial earnings do not inherently grant one the liberty or authority to navigate their life or voice their convictions without repercussion.

1. Wealth as Freedom: The concept of wealth extends beyond mere financial accumulation; it represents the freedom to make life choices without the constraints of financial insecurity[12]. This freedom encompasses the ability to pursue personal aspirations, make decisions based on one's values and desires, and live a life unencumbered by economic limitations.
2. Wealth as Power: Furthermore, wealth embodies a form of power — the power to influence, the power to direct one's destiny, and the power to effect change within society[13]. This power is not merely transactional but transformational, enabling individuals to leverage their resources for broader societal impact.
3. The Myth of High Income as Wealth: A critical examination reveals that earning a high income, even one that extends into six, seven, or eight figures, does not necessarily confer wealth. Income, in this context, becomes a fleeting measure of financial success, susceptible to the vicissitudes of life and economic fluctuations[14]. True wealth is measured not by the amount one earns but by the ability to sustain and utilize financial resources to secure lasting freedom and influence.

[12] Anderson, Claud. Powernomics: The National Plan to Empower Black America. Powernomics Corporation of America, 2001.

[13] Ibid.

[14] Ibid.

4. The "Seven-Figure Slave" Phenomenon: The term "seven-figure slave" epitomizes the paradox of earning high income while lacking autonomy over one's actions and decisions. This concept is vividly embodied by NFL players who, despite their substantial earnings, may face restrictions that limit their freedom to express personal or political beliefs, particularly when such expressions contradict the expectations or norms imposed by employers or societal pressures.
5. The NFL Player as an Illustration: The analogy of an NFL player unable to take a knee in peaceful protest without facing potential backlash or sanctions from the league or public opinion underscores the distinction between income and true wealth[15]. It highlights how external constraints and the expectations of conformity can diminish the power and freedom supposedly afforded by financial success.

Critics may argue that high earnings inherently provide a level of freedom and power, suggesting that the constraints experienced by individuals such as NFL players are exceptions rather than indicative of broader systemic issues. However, this perspective overlooks the fundamental difference between financial resources as a means to an end versus an end in itself. True wealth affords the holder autonomy, choice, and influence free from external coercion or limitations.

Redefining wealth to encompass the dimensions of freedom and power challenges the conventional metrics of financial success. It calls for a deeper recognition of the limitations imposed by high earnings in the absence of true autonomy and the capacity to effect change. As society progresses, the pursuit of wealth must transcend the accumulation of income, aiming instead for the liberation and empowerment that true wealth provides.

[15] Branch, John. "Colin Kaepernick and the Power of NFL Player Protests." The New York Times, September 2016.

The Complex Fabric of Wealth and Inequality

In the discourse on economic disparity, the dialogue often gravitates towards the stark dichotomy between the wealthy and the impoverished, framing the conversation predominantly around income. However, this perspective, while pertinent, scarcely scratches the surface of a more profound and structurally ingrained issue: wealth inequality. Wealth, in its essence, transcends mere income; it embodies the freedom and capacity to make autonomous choices, manifesting in the ability not to require a substantial labor force for individuals, such as those in sales, to attain six or seven-figure earnings[16]. This broader definition of wealth highlights the fundamental disparities that pervade our economic systems, revealing a landscape where the accumulation of wealth is not merely an indicator of financial success but a bastion of freedom and opportunity.

The critical distinction between income and wealth lies in their inherent characteristics and implications. While high income may suggest a considerable flow of money, it is wealth - the accumulation of assets and resources - that provides individuals the liberty to make significant choices[17]. These choices could range from the decision to purchase a home, invest in the stock market, or save for education. Therefore, when discussing economic inequality, it is paramount to pivot the conversation towards wealth

[16] The Color of Money: Black Banks and the Racial Wealth Gap," Mehrsa Baradaran, Harvard University Press, 2017.

[17] Wealth Inequality in the United States since 1913: Evidence from Capitalized Income Tax Data," Emmanuel Saez and Gabriel Zucman, The Quarterly Journal of Economics, 2016.

inequality, which presents a more severe and insidious challenge.

Opponents and skeptics of this viewpoint often argue that focusing on wealth inequality diverts attention from more immediate issues like poverty alleviation and job creation. They contend that by emphasizing wealth accumulation, we risk undermining the importance of increasing income levels as a means to elevate the standard of living for the less affluent[18]. Furthermore, some critics posit that the focus on wealth accumulation serves the interests of the already wealthy, perpetuating systems that favor capital over labor.

Despite these critiques, the data and real-world evidence present an incontrovertible narrative. Studies have shown that wealth inequality not only dwarfs income inequality in magnitude but also in its implications for social mobility and economic stability[19]. Accumulating wealth requires not only income but also the opportunity to save and invest that income. This process is significantly more challenging for those at the lower end of the income spectrum, who often find themselves ensnared in a cycle of paycheck-to-paycheck living, devoid of the surplus necessary to invest or save.

The significance of wealth as a measure of economic security and freedom cannot be overstated. For instance, the ability to afford quality education, healthcare, and housing without the need for a vast labor force underscores the essence of true wealth. It represents a level of financial autonomy and resilience that high income alone cannot guarantee.

18 Critics of Wealth Inequality: Are the Alternatives Any Better?" Forbes, 2019.

19 The Economic Impacts of Wealth Inequality: A Review of Theories and Evidence," The World Bank, 2020.

In addressing wealth inequality, it becomes clear that solutions must go beyond surface-level interventions. Policies aimed at fostering wealth accumulation among the broader population, such as facilitating access to financial education, encouraging investment in affordable housing, and supporting small business entrepreneurship, are crucial[20]. These strategies not only aim to level the economic playing field but also to empower individuals with the freedom to make choices that can lead to a more equitable and prosperous society for all.

While income inequality poses significant challenges, it is the deeper issue of wealth inequality that encapsulates the core of economic disparities. By understanding wealth not just as an accumulation of assets but as the embodiment of freedom and choice, we can begin to address the root causes of economic inequality and work towards a future where wealth is a possibility for all, not just a privileged few.

Wealth Disparity in America And How It Creates An Unsustainable Path

In an era marked by unprecedented economic growth and technological advancement, the chasm between the wealthy and the economically disadvantaged in America has widened at an alarming rate. Central to this issue is the startling reality that a significant portion of Americans possess negligible savings, severely limiting their ability to accumulate wealth and improve their socio-economic

[20] Building Wealth and Fostering Equity: How to Transform the Economy Through Inclusive Growth," Policy Brief, Brookings Institution, 2021.

status[21]. This situation presents a grim picture of the economic landscape, where the dream of financial stability and upward mobility remains elusive for many.

At the heart of the matter is the staggering concentration of wealth within the upper echelons of society. It is estimated that the richest 1% of Americans control 40% of the nation's wealth, while the bottom 80%, a vast majority, hold a mere 7%[22]. This disproportionate allocation of wealth not only underscores the acute inequality but also illuminates the systemic barriers that hinder wealth accumulation among the broader population.

Particularly affected are low-income families, especially those of color, who face an uphill battle in their quest for economic advancement. The lack of savings, negligible or non-existent inheritance, and discriminatory policies that obstruct pathways such as homeownership, serve as formidable obstacles[23]. Homeownership, often heralded as a cornerstone of the American Dream and a primary vehicle for wealth accumulation, remains out of reach for many due to systemic biases and financial barriers.

Critics of this perspective may argue that the American economic system provides equal opportunity for all and that disparities in wealth are a result of individual choices and efforts. They posit that the focus on systemic inequality detracts from the values of personal responsibility and hard work. However, this viewpoint neglects the historical and ongoing structural inequities that disproportionately affect certain segments of the population, particularly people of color.

21 Federal Reserve Reports on the Economic Well-Being of U.S. Households," Federal Reserve, 2019.

22 Wealth Inequality in the United States," National Bureau of Economic Research, 2020.

23 The Racial Wealth Gap: Addressing America's Most Pressing Epidemic," Brookings Institution, 2018.

The evidence suggests that the existing wealth gap is not merely a product of individual failings but a complex interplay of historical, social, and economic factors that have systematically disadvantaged certain groups. For instance, redlining and other discriminatory lending practices have historically restricted minority access to housing and capital, creating a cycle of poverty and impeding wealth accumulation[24].

Addressing this deep-rooted issue requires a multi-faceted approach that acknowledges the systemic barriers to wealth accumulation. Policy interventions aimed at promoting financial literacy, providing equitable access to credit, and encouraging savings and investment among low-income families are essential. Moreover, rectifying historical injustices through reparative measures and ensuring fair housing policies can serve as critical steps towards narrowing the wealth gap[25].

The vast disparities in wealth distribution and the barriers to economic advancement faced by low-income families, especially those of color, highlight a critical issue that threatens the fabric of American society. Without concerted efforts to address these inequities, the promise of America as a land of opportunity for all remains unfulfilled. It is imperative for policymakers, communities, and individuals to work collaboratively towards creating a more equitable and just society where wealth accumulation is a feasible goal for everyone, not just the privileged few.

[24] The Color of Law: A Forgotten History of How Our Government Segregated America," Richard Rothstein, Liveright, 2017.

[25] Policies to Address Poverty in America," The Hamilton Project, Brookings Institution, 2019.

Structural Inequities and Wealth Disparities

These systemic barriers have entrenched a wealth gap where the median net worth of white families significantly eclipses that of their African American and Latino counterparts, by more than tenfold[26]. This stark disparity is not an accident of economic fluctuations; rather, it is the result of deliberate policies and practices that have historically marginalized certain populations.

The origins of this wealth gap can be traced to policies that excluded African American and Latino communities from wealth-building opportunities. For instance, the GI Bill and New Deal programs, while transformative for the economy and white middle-class families, systematically denied the same benefits to minorities. Discriminatory practices in housing, such as redlining and restrictive covenants, further compounded these inequities, limiting access to homeownership—a critical avenue for wealth accumulation[27].

Moreover, disparities in education, employment opportunities, and wages continue to contribute to the wealth divide. African American and Latino workers are more likely to be employed in lower-paying jobs and face higher unemployment rates than their white counterparts, impacting their ability to save and invest. The racial wealth gap is also exacerbated by differences in inheritance and intergenerational wealth transfers, with white families more

[26] The Racial Wealth Gap: Why Policy Matters," Demos, 2016.

[27] The Color of Law: A Forgotten History of How Our Government Segregated America," Richard Rothstein, Liveright, 2017.

likely to receive inheritances, further increasing their financial security and wealth[28].

Critics may argue that highlighting racial disparities in wealth perpetuates a victim mentality and overlooks personal responsibility. They suggest that focusing on individual financial behavior and choices is the key to narrowing the wealth gap. However, this viewpoint fails to acknowledge the systemic barriers that limit opportunities for wealth accumulation among minority groups. Ignoring the structural foundations of the wealth divide overlooks the historical context and the ongoing discrimination that continues to shape economic outcomes for African American and Latino families[29].

To address this profound disparity, it is imperative to implement policies that not only rectify historical injustices but also dismantle the systemic barriers that perpetuate the wealth gap. Solutions such as equitable access to quality education, fair housing policies, and reforms in lending practices are essential to leveling the playing field. Additionally, targeted efforts to support minority entrepreneurship and investments in minority communities can stimulate economic growth and wealth accumulation within these populations[30].

The wealth disparity between white families and their African American and Latino counterparts is a manifestation of structural inequities that have deep roots in America's history. Addressing this gap requires a concerted effort to understand and dismantle the systemic barriers that perpetuate it. Only through acknowledging the historical

[28] Disparities in Wealth by Race and Ethnicity in the 2019 Survey of Consumer Finances," Federal Reserve, 2020.

[29] The Myth of Racial Disparities in Public School Financing," Heritage Foundation, 2019.

[30] Bridging the Racial Wealth Gap: The Role of Economic Policies in Reducing Inequality," Economic Policy Institute, 2020.

context and implementing inclusive policies can we hope to bridge the vast economic divide and move towards a more equitable society.

Comprehensive Strategies for Economic Equity and Wealth Accumulation

Strategies for Bridging the Wealth Gap: Tax Reforms and Beyond

In the quest to mitigate the stark wealth disparities afflicting the United States, a myriad of solutions have been proposed. Among the most pivotal of these solutions is the reform of the taxation system, particularly the suggestion to tax capital gains at the same rate as ordinary income[31]. This reform is predicated on the understanding that the current tax system disproportionately favors wealth accumulation for those at the top, exacerbating the wealth gap and undermining the economic equity essential for a healthy democracy.

Capital gains, which represent the profits from the sale of assets such as stocks or real estate, are currently taxed at a lower rate than ordinary income in many instances. This preferential treatment creates a significant advantage for the wealthy, who are more likely to earn a substantial portion of their income through investments[32]. By aligning the tax rates for capital gains and ordinary income, the tax code

[31] Taxing Wealth: How Tax Reform Can Reduce Inequality," Economic Policy Institute, 2019.

[32] The Case for Taxing Capital Gains at the Same Rate as Ordinary Income," Center on Budget and Policy Priorities, 2020.

would not only become more equitable but also encourage wealth accumulation across a broader spectrum of the American populace.

Critics of this approach argue that higher taxes on capital gains could stifle investment and economic growth, suggesting that the benefits of such a policy might not outweigh the potential drawbacks. They contend that the preferential treatment of capital gains encourages investment and risk-taking, driving innovation and job creation[33]. However, evidence suggests that the impact of capital gains tax rates on investment decisions is overstated and that the potential for increased revenue and greater economic equality presents a compelling case for reform[34].

In addition to tax reforms, a holistic approach to wealth accumulation must address the systemic barriers that prevent many Americans from accessing the opportunities necessary to build wealth. Policies aimed at improving access to quality education, affordable housing, and equitable financial services are crucial. For instance, initiatives that support homeownership among historically marginalized communities could play a significant role in wealth accumulation, given the importance of real estate as a source of personal wealth[35].

Moreover, enhancing financial literacy and providing incentives for savings and investment among low- and middle-income families can further democratize wealth accumulation. Programs that match savings for the purchase of homes, education, or business investment can empower

[33] Capital Gains Tax Rates and Economic Growth: Evidence from the States," Tax Foundation, 2018.

[34] The Effect of Capital Gains Taxation on Investment Dynamics," National Bureau of Economic Research, 2019.

[35] Building Home Equity: A Strategy for Economic Equality," Urban Institute, 2021.

individuals to invest in their futures and contribute to closing the wealth gap[36].

The disparity in wealth accumulation within the United States represents a profound challenge to the nation's principles of equality and justice. Tax reform, particularly the equalization of capital gains and ordinary income tax rates, stands as a critical step towards addressing this imbalance. However, true progress requires a multifaceted approach that not only reforms the tax code but also dismantles the systemic barriers to wealth accumulation. By implementing comprehensive policies that foster economic inclusivity, America can move closer to realizing its ideal of equal opportunity for all its citizens.

Rebalancing the Scales With Mortgage and Retirement Policy Reforms for Wealth Equality

This approach suggests that by curtailing these deductions for the wealthy, a substantial pool of resources could be redirected towards initiatives specifically designed to assist lower-income individuals in their quest for wealth accumulation[37]. Such a realignment not only embodies fiscal prudence but also fosters a more equitable economic environment.

Currently, the tax benefits from mortgage interest deductions and retirement savings deferrals disproportionately favor higher-income earners. These individuals, owing to their substantial incomes, are more likely to afford homes and save for retirement, thereby reaping significant tax benefits[38]. This scenario underscores

[36] Matching Savings Programs: An Innovative Approach to Economic Empowerment," Prosperity Now, 2020.

[37] Tax Policy and Wealth Inequality: Bridging the Gap Through Reform," Tax Policy Center, 2021.

[38] The Distributional Effects of Mortgage Deduction and Retirement Savings Policies," National Bureau of Economic Research, 2019.

a form of regressive fiscal policy, where the wealthy benefit at the expense of the broader populace, further exacerbating wealth inequality.

Critics might argue that such deductions and deferrals encourage home ownership and retirement savings, which are beneficial to the economy at large. They posit that any alterations to these benefits could dissuade investment in these critical areas, potentially leading to adverse economic consequences[39]. However, this perspective fails to acknowledge the skewed distribution of these benefits and how they contribute to widening the wealth gap.

Redirecting the funds from these recalibrated tax benefits towards programs that aid low-income families in purchasing homes or saving for retirement presents an equitable path forward. For example, targeted tax credits for first-time homebuyers in lower income brackets could significantly reduce barriers to home ownership, a crucial asset in wealth accumulation[40]. Similarly, enhancing access to retirement savings accounts with matching contributions for lower-income earners could democratize the benefits of long-term savings[41].

Implementing such reforms requires a careful consideration of the economic implications and a steadfast commitment to social equity. Critics of these reforms should be engaged in constructive dialogue to address concerns and misconceptions. Furthermore, these policies should be part of a broader strategy that includes financial education and support services to ensure that lower-income

[39] The Economic Benefits of Tax Deductions for Home Ownership and Retirement Savings," American Economic Association, 2018.

[40] Supporting Home Ownership in Lower-Income Families: Policy Proposals for the 21st Century," Urban Institute, 2020.

[41] Retirement Savings for the Low-Income: The Untapped Potential of Government Policies," Brookings Institution, 2021.

individuals can effectively utilize these opportunities to build wealth.

In essence, the recalibration of mortgage interest deductions and retirement savings deferrals represents a strategic opportunity to mitigate wealth inequality. By channeling resources towards empowering lower-income individuals to accumulate assets, these reforms can contribute to a more balanced and fair economic landscape. This approach not only addresses the symptoms of wealth disparity but also tackles its underlying structural causes, paving the way for a future where economic opportunities are accessible to all, irrespective of their financial starting point.

Newborn Savings Accounts and Wealth Equity

In an innovative approach to addressing long-standing disparities in wealth, particularly those that divide along racial lines, the concept of endowing every newborn child with a savings account emerges as a transformative solution. This proposition entails the initiation of a savings account for every newborn, starting with a base amount of at least $1,250. Such a measure holds the promise not only to mitigate the racial wealth gap but also to provide a foundational investment in the future of all children, facilitating significant life events such as education, business ventures, or homeownership[42].

This initiative, grounded in the principle of "baby bonds," aims to level the playing field from the earliest moments of life. The premise is that by providing a financial kickstart, these accounts could compound over

42 The Case for Baby Bonds: A Universal Path to Ensure the Next Generation's Economic Success," American Prospect, 2019.

time, offering a substantial nest egg upon reaching adulthood. Notably, this approach recognizes the critical role of early investment in breaking the cycle of poverty and economic disparity that plagues successive generations, particularly among communities of color[43].

Detractors of this proposal might argue from a fiscal conservative viewpoint, highlighting concerns over the feasibility and the potential burden on taxpayers. They question the practicality of such a universal program in the face of existing budgetary constraints and the efficacy of a financial gift in addressing complex socio-economic issues[44]. Moreover, some may speculate on the unintended consequences, including the potential for such funds to disincentivize personal saving and financial responsibility among recipients' families.

Despite these criticisms, the evidence and support for newborn savings accounts and baby bonds underscore their potential to enact meaningful change. Studies indicate that the psychological and financial empowerment derived from knowing there is a resource waiting to aid in future investments can significantly impact a child's outlook on opportunities such as higher education and home ownership[45]. Furthermore, by setting these accounts to grow over time and restricting access until adulthood or for specific investments, these funds encourage long-term planning and financial literacy from a young age.

Implementing such a policy requires thoughtful consideration of funding mechanisms, account management,

[43] Baby Bonds: An Investment in Our Nation's Future," Center for American Progress, 2020.

[44] Critique of Baby Bonds: Fiscal Responsibility and Long-term Outcomes," Cato Institute, 2021.

[45] The Psychological and Economic Benefits of Early Investments: Evidence from Pilot Programs," Journal of Economic Psychology, 2022.

and eligibility criteria to ensure its sustainability and effectiveness. Moreover, this initiative should be seen as part of a broader strategy to address wealth inequality, including education on financial management, access to affordable housing, and opportunities for entrepreneurship[46].

The introduction of savings accounts for every newborn represents a forward-thinking and equitable step towards narrowing the racial wealth gap. This measure not only acknowledges the structural inequities that have perpetuated economic disparities but also offers a tangible resource for future empowerment. By investing in the youngest members of society, we can lay the groundwork for a more prosperous and equitable future, underscoring the belief that every child deserves an equal opportunity to succeed.

Empowering Through Savings Accounts By Raising Asset Limits in Public Benefit Programs

In the United States, a critical but often overlooked aspect is the restrictive asset limits imposed on families receiving public benefits. These limits, which cap the amount of savings and assets beneficiaries can hold without forfeiting their eligibility for assistance, have long been a subject of debate. The proposition to significantly raise these limits, to at least $12,000, offers a viable pathway toward promoting self-sufficiency among disadvantaged populations[47].

[46] Building a Foundation for Economic Equity: The Role of Policy in Shaping Future Generations' Financial Health," Brookings Institution, 2021.

[47] The Importance of Asset Limits: A Pathway to Economic Self-Sufficiency," Center on Budget and Policy Priorities, 2020.

The current asset thresholds embedded within programs such as Supplemental Nutrition Assistance Program (SNAP) and Temporary Assistance for Needy Families (TANF) are not only outdated but also counterproductive to the goals of fostering economic independence and resilience. By penalizing savings, these limits discourage beneficiaries from accumulating the very resources that could facilitate their transition away from government aid[48]. Consequently, this policy inadvertently traps families in a cycle of dependency and hinders their progress towards financial stability.

Opponents of increasing asset limits argue that such a move could strain the fiscal resources of public benefit programs and incentivize savings at the expense of immediate needs. They contend that the primary focus of these programs should be on providing immediate relief rather than long-term wealth accumulation[49]. However, this perspective overlooks the transformative potential of empowering individuals to build a financial cushion that can protect against economic shocks and reduce long-term reliance on public assistance.

Evidence suggests that modest savings and assets can significantly impact a family's ability to manage emergencies, invest in education or employment opportunities, and ultimately achieve economic self-sufficiency[50]. Allowing families to save more without the fear of losing their benefits can encourage better financial planning and investment in future security. Moreover, increasing asset limits could stimulate local economies by

48 Asset Limits in Public Benefit Programs," National Conference of State Legislatures, 2019.

49 The Debate Over Asset Limits in Social Welfare Programs," Heritage Foundation, 2021.

50 Building Assets, Building Independence: Policies to Increase Savings by Low-Income Households," Brookings Institution, 2018.

enabling low-income families to participate more fully in financial systems and markets[51].

Implementing such a policy change requires careful consideration of the balance between providing immediate support and fostering long-term financial independence. It also necessitates a reevaluation of how success is measured within public assistance programs—shifting the focus from mere survival to the building of a stable economic foundation for beneficiaries.

Raising the asset limits for families receiving public benefits represents a critical step towards addressing the structural barriers to economic mobility. By empowering individuals to save and build assets, this policy change can contribute to breaking the cycle of poverty and dependency, paving the way for a more inclusive and resilient economy. As we move forward, it is essential that policymakers, advocates, and communities engage in a collaborative effort to refine and implement strategies that promote not just economic survival, but prosperity for all citizens.

[51] Economic Benefits of Raising Asset Limits in Public Benefit Programs," Urban Institute, 2021.

Why The Comprehensive Strategies for Economic Equity and Wealth Accumulation Won't Be Implemented

Challenges to Implementing Solutions for Economic Equity From An Analytical Perspective

The proposed strategies for economic equity and wealth accumulation, while comprehensive and innovative, face formidable challenges that could impede their effectiveness. These hurdles stem from systemic, institutional, and societal barriers deeply embedded in the fabric of American society. The analysis below explores why these well-intentioned solutions may struggle to achieve their intended outcomes.

1. Systemic Racism and Institutional Inertia: At the core of the systemic barriers is the pervasive influence of systemic racism, which operates across all levels of society[52]. The mechanisms through which systemic racism manifests—such as discriminatory policies, unequal access to resources, and ingrained biases—contribute to institutional inertia that resists change. This inertia is a significant impediment to implementing reforms like tax equity, adjustments in mortgage and retirement policy, and the introduction of

[52] Systemic Racism and U.S. Health Care," Social Science & Medicine, 2020.

newborn savings accounts, as these require shifts in longstanding policies and practices.

2. Economic Interests and Political Will: The successful implementation of these strategies necessitates not only a reevaluation of economic priorities but also substantial political will[53]. Given that many proposed reforms challenge the interests of powerful economic stakeholders—who benefit from the status quo—there is likely to be considerable resistance. This resistance can manifest in lobbying against policy changes, influencing public opinion, and erecting legal challenges, thereby stalling or diluting the impact of reforms.
3. Societal Misconceptions and Resistance to Change: Societal attitudes and misconceptions about poverty, race, and wealth play a crucial role in the viability of these strategies[54]. Misconceptions about the "deserving poor" or the role of individual responsibility in economic success can undermine support for systemic solutions. Without broad societal support, initiatives aimed at promoting economic equity may be viewed with skepticism or hostility, reducing their chances of successful implementation.
4. The Complexity of Economic Disparities: The economic disparities these strategies aim to address are the result of complex, interrelated factors that have evolved over centuries[55]. Addressing these disparities requires more than policy changes; it demands a transformation in the underlying economic structures and relationships. The complexity of these issues means that even well-designed

[53] Political Will and Public Policy: Is There a Will to Address the Issue of Poverty?" Public Administration Review, 2018.

[54] Societal Attitudes Toward Poverty: Understanding Social Welfare Policy," Journal of Sociology and Social Welfare, 2019.

[55] The Complexity of Economic Inequality in the United States," The American Economic Review, 2021.

policies may have unintended consequences or be insufficient to fully address the root causes of inequality.

5. Funding and Resource Allocation: Implementing comprehensive economic reforms requires significant financial investment[56]. Identifying sources of funding for initiatives such as newborn savings accounts or increasing asset limits for public benefit programs poses a substantial challenge, especially in a political climate characterized by budget constraints and competing priorities. The question of how to finance these reforms without exacerbating other fiscal issues is a significant hurdle.
6. Measuring Success and Impact: The long-term nature of these strategies complicates efforts to measure their success and impact[57]. Economic equity and wealth accumulation are processes that unfold over generations, making it difficult to establish short-term metrics for success. This delay in observable outcomes can diminish political and public support for continued investment in these initiatives.

In light of these challenges, the path forward requires not only the formulation of strategic solutions but also a concerted effort to address the systemic barriers that obstruct their implementation. It necessitates building coalitions across political, economic, and societal lines to create a sustainable momentum for change. Moreover, it highlights the need for adaptive strategies that can navigate and overcome the entrenched structures of power and privilege that have historically shaped economic disparities in the United States.

[56] Financing Social Policy Reforms for Economic Equity: A Fiscal Analysis," Public Finance Review, 2020.

[57] Measuring the Impact of Social Policies on Economic Inequality: Challenges and Solutions," The Journal of Economic Perspectives, 2022.

Decoding the Rules of Racism

In the documentary series "Hidden Colors," particularly in its third installment, a poignant exploration into the enduring mechanisms of racism reveals a set of unwritten rules designed to perpetuate white supremacy. These rules, while not formally codified, operate through societal norms, policies, and practices, embedding inequality deeply within the fabric of society. The following analysis seeks to unpack these rules, drawing on historical and contemporary evidence to illustrate their impact and to address the counterarguments presented by skeptics of the documentary's validity.

1. The Confusion Surrounding Racism: The first rule emphasizes the deliberate obfuscation of what constitutes racism, creating a vague and often contentious understanding of the term. This confusion serves to undermine efforts to address racism by muddling the discourse, making it difficult to identify and combat racial injustices effectively[58]. Critics, however, might argue that discussions around racism have become more nuanced, reflecting a broader range of experiences and not merely a systematic attempt to obscure its essence.
2. The Erasure of Black Contributions: Historically, the contributions of black individuals and communities have often been marginalized or omitted from mainstream narratives, a practice that diminishes the perception of black achievement and resilience[59]. This deliberate omission feeds

[58] Racism Without Racists: Color-Blind Racism and the Persistence of Racial Inequality in America," Eduardo Bonilla-Silva, Rowman & Littlefield, 2017.

[59] The Mis-Education of the Negro," Carter G. Woodson, 1933.

into stereotypes and undermines the diverse and rich contributions of black people to society. Detractors might claim that contemporary efforts in education and media are addressing this gap, though the extent and depth of these efforts remain contested.

3. Non-exemption of Black Women and Children: The systemic nature of racism ensures that no segment of the black community, including women and children, is spared from its effects[60]. This rule underscores the indiscriminate impact of racial prejudice, perpetuating cycles of disadvantage. Opponents might highlight advancements in legal protections and social mobility for some within these groups, yet disparities in health, education, and economic opportunities persist.
4. Compromising Black Figures: The use of black individuals in positions of influence to uphold or justify systems of white supremacy is a sophisticated tactic that lends credibility to oppressive structures[61]. While some may argue that the rise of black individuals in various spheres signals a shift away from systemic racism, the strategic co-optation of certain figures does little to dismantle entrenched inequalities.
5. Control of the Black Population: Various strategies, from mass incarceration to economic disenfranchisement, have been employed to maintain control over the black population[62]. Critics might suggest that such views overlook individual agency and the complex interplay of factors contributing to social issues within black communities.

[60] Killing the Black Body: Race, Reproduction, and the Meaning of Liberty," Dorothy Roberts, Vintage, 1997.

[61] The New Jim Crow: Mass Incarceration in the Age of Colorblindness," Michelle Alexander, The New Press, 2010.

[62] Black Stats: African Americans by the Numbers in the Twenty-first Century," Monique W. Morris, The New Press, 2014.

6. Minimizing Historical Atrocities: The diminution of the historical and ongoing impacts of slavery and Jim Crow laws serves to negate the systemic roots of racial disparities[63]. While some may argue for a forward-looking approach that focuses on current opportunities, the failure to fully confront and address the legacy of these atrocities impedes genuine healing and reconciliation.
7. Economic Non-competitiveness: Policies that limit economic opportunities for black individuals and communities effectively keep them non-competitive on a broader scale[64]. Though some may point to examples of economic success within the black community, systemic barriers to equal participation in the economy remain widespread.

In addressing these rules, it is imperative to recognize the multifaceted nature of racism and the need for a concerted effort to dismantle the structures that perpetuate it. While opposing viewpoints offer critical perspectives, the weight of historical and current evidence underscores the urgency of addressing the deep-seated inequalities that these rules reinforce.

[63] Stamped from the Beginning: The Definitive History of Racist Ideas in America," Ibram X. Kendi, Nation Books, 2016.

[64] The Color of Money: Black Banks and the Racial Wealth Gap," Mehrsa Baradaran, Harvard University Press, 2017.

The Racism Foundation— Chapter 3

The enduring legacy of racism in the United States is a testament to its deeply entrenched position within the societal fabric, affecting Black Americans from historical chains of slavery to the nuanced forms of systemic discrimination prevalent today. This section explores the evolution of racism, underscoring its historical roots and its permeation into contemporary systems and narratives, thus continuing to impact Black Americans disproportionately.

At the heart of American history lies the sinister institution of slavery, a system predicated on the dehumanization and exploitation of Black individuals for economic gain. The transition from slavery into the Jim Crow era perpetuated a legacy of racial segregation and disenfranchisement, effectively embedding racial inequality into the legal and social systems of the nation[1]. This historical context sets the stage for understanding the multifaceted nature of racism today, which, while less overt, remains just as pernicious.

Contemporary manifestations of racism are often subtler than the overt legal segregation of the past, embedded within systemic structures across education, housing, employment, and the criminal justice system. For instance, the racial wealth gap, a direct byproduct of centuries of economic exclusion and discrimination,

[1] The New Jim Crow: Mass Incarceration in the Age of Colorblindness," Michelle Alexander, The New Press, 2010.

continues to expand, underscoring the economic dimension of racial inequality[2]. This gap is not merely a relic of past injustices but is exacerbated by ongoing practices such as redlining, employment discrimination, and disparities in access to quality education.

Moreover, the criminal justice system serves as a glaring example of systemic racism's endurance. Black Americans are disproportionately incarcerated, a disparity that cannot be divorced from the racial biases permeating law enforcement practices and sentencing policies[3]. This over-incarceration is not an anomaly but a continuation of a historical trajectory aimed at controlling and subjugating Black bodies, reminiscent of the Black Codes and vagrancy laws of the Reconstruction era.

The narrative surrounding racism has also evolved, with modern discourse often adopting colorblind rhetoric that denies the existence of racial disparities. This narrative shift seeks to minimize the significance of racism, suggesting that America has transcended its racial past. However, the persistence of racial disparities across all indicators of well-being challenges this notion, highlighting the inadequacy of colorblind approaches in addressing the structural foundations of racial inequality[4].

Critics may argue that focusing on systemic racism negates individual agency and undermines the progress achieved in racial equality. They posit that the existence of successful Black individuals exemplifies the opportunities available to all, irrespective of race. While individual

[2] The Color of Wealth: The Story Behind the U.S. Racial Wealth Divide," Meizhu Lui et al., The New Press, 2006.

[3] Locking Up Our Own: Crime and Punishment in Black America," James Forman Jr., Farrar, Straus and Giroux, 2017.

[4] Racism without Racists: Color-Blind Racism and the Persistence of Racial Inequality in America," Eduardo Bonilla-Silva, Rowman & Littlefield, 2014.

success stories are noteworthy, they do not negate the systemic barriers that continue to impede the collective progress of Black Americans[5]. The exceptionalism of individual achievements should not overshadow the systemic inequities that pervade society.

The foundation of racism in America is built upon historical injustices that have morphed into the systemic inequalities observed today. Despite shifts in the manifestation and narrative of racism, its impact on Black Americans remains significant and pervasive. Acknowledging this reality is the first step towards dismantling the structures that perpetuate racial disparities, paving the way for a more equitable society.

Economic Power, Freedom, and Racial Inequality

American society is woven with threads of economic disparities, racial inequalities, and the pursuit of freedom. These elements are deeply interconnected, framing a picture that reveals the extensive work needed to correct historical injustices and ensure equitable opportunities for all, particularly for Black communities. This section explores the relationship between economic power, freedom, and racial inequality, emphasizing the critical role of financial independence and empowerment in fostering equitable outcomes for Black Americans.

[5] Black Wealth/White Wealth: A New Perspective on Racial Inequality," Melvin L. Oliver and Thomas M. Shapiro, Routledge, 2006.

Economic power serves as the cornerstone of societal influence and individual autonomy. In the context of the United States, the accumulation and distribution of wealth have been profoundly shaped by racial policies and practices. From the era of chattel slavery to the Jim Crow laws, and through to the present day, systemic barriers have been erected to hinder the economic advancement of Black individuals and communities[6]. These barriers have not only perpetuated economic disparities but have also restricted the freedoms that come with financial stability and independence.

Financial independence is intrinsically linked to the concept of freedom—freedom from oppression, freedom to make choices, and the freedom to build a prosperous future. For Black communities, achieving financial independence is a means of reclaiming power within a system that has historically marginalized them. It represents a pathway to dismantling the structures of racial inequality that have limited access to quality education, housing, healthcare, and employment opportunities[7].

The importance of financial empowerment and independence for Black communities cannot be overstated. Economic self-sufficiency offers a buffer against systemic inequities and provides the resources necessary to advocate for social and political change. It enables the ownership of homes and businesses, leading to the creation of generational wealth that can alter the trajectory of families and communities for years to come[8]. Furthermore,

6 The Color of Money: Black Banks and the Racial Wealth Gap," Mehrsa Baradaran, Harvard University Press, 2017.

7 The Color of Law: A Forgotten History of How Our Government Segregated America," Richard Rothstein, Liveright, 2017.

8 Black Wealth/White Wealth: A New Perspective on Racial Inequality," Melvin L. Oliver and Thomas M. Shapiro, Routledge, 2006.

economic empowerment allows for greater participation in the political process, influencing policies and decisions that affect the lives of Black Americans.

However, the path to economic empowerment is fraught with challenges. Critics and skeptics often overlook the systemic hurdles in place, attributing disparities solely to individual choices or cultural differences. Such perspectives fail to account for the historical and ongoing systemic racism that has created and maintained the wealth gap. Moreover, there is a tendency in mainstream discourse to individualize success, ignoring the collective action and systemic reforms needed to address widespread inequalities[9]

Despite these challenges, there is a growing movement within Black communities towards financial literacy, entrepreneurship, and community-based economic initiatives. These efforts reflect a deep understanding of the link between economic power and freedom, as well as a determination to forge a new legacy of prosperity and equity[10].

The journey toward racial equality is inextricably linked to the quest for economic power and freedom. Financial independence and empowerment for Black communities are not merely goals but necessities for dismantling the foundations of racial inequality. As we move forward, it is imperative to confront and dismantle the systemic barriers that hinder economic progress for Black Americans, paving the way for a future where freedom and equality are realities for all.

[9] Racism without Racists: Color-Blind Racism and the Persistence of Racial Inequality in America," Eduardo Bonilla-Silva, Rowman & Littlefield, 2014.

[10] PowerNomics: The National Plan to Empower Black America," Dr. Claud Anderson, Powernomics Corporation of America, 2001.

Economic Disenfranchisement and Incarceration

The intersection of economic disenfranchisement and the criminal justice system reveals a stark disparity impacting Black Americans, particularly in the realm of business ownership and incarceration rates. This section delves into the direct relationship between the minimal business ownership among Black Americans and their disproportionately high representation within the American prison system, underscoring a systemic issue that transcends mere coincidence.

The lack of business ownership among Black Americans is not a result of individual failings but rather the culmination of historical policies and systemic barriers that have hindered economic progress. From the denial of loans and discriminatory practices in the banking industry to the lack of access to capital and resources necessary for entrepreneurship, Black Americans have faced significant obstacles in establishing and maintaining businesses[11]. This economic marginalization contributes to a cycle of poverty and limited opportunities, which are often precursors to interactions with the criminal justice system.

The stark demographic distribution within American prisons, where Black Americans constitute approximately 51 percent of the population despite making up only 12 percent of the national population, is indicative of systemic racial disparities[12]. This overrepresentation is not an

11 The Color of Money: Black Banks and the Racial Wealth Gap," Mehrsa Baradaran, Harvard University Press, 2017.

12 The New Jim Crow: Mass Incarceration in the Age of Colorblindness," Michelle Alexander, The New Press, 2010.

anomaly but a reflection of the broader societal structures that equate economic disenfranchisement with criminality. The absence of business ownership and the economic empowerment it brings leaves many Black Americans in vulnerable positions, often leading to increased interactions with law enforcement and, consequently, higher incarceration rates.

Critics may argue that the relationship between economic status and incarceration rates is oversimplified, suggesting that individual choices and behaviors are the primary drivers of criminal activity. However, this perspective fails to acknowledge the complex interplay between systemic economic barriers and the policies of the criminal justice system that disproportionately target disadvantaged communities[13]. The correlation between economic empowerment and reduced crime rates has been well-documented, reinforcing the need for a holistic approach to addressing these disparities.

Furthermore, the systemic nature of this issue is compounded by the collateral consequences of incarceration, which include further economic marginalization and diminished opportunities for business ownership upon reentry into society. The cycle of incarceration and economic hardship perpetuates a barrier to the creation of generational wealth and long-term financial stability for Black Americans[14].

Addressing the direct relationship between the lack of business ownership among Black Americans and high incarceration rates requires a multifaceted strategy. It necessitates not only reforming the criminal justice system

[13] Locking Up Our Own: Crime and Punishment in Black America," James Forman Jr., Farrar, Straus and Giroux, 2017.

[14] Black Wealth/White Wealth: A New Perspective on Racial Inequality," Melvin L. Oliver and Thomas M. Shapiro, Routledge, 2006.

to eliminate biases and disproportionate sentencing but also implementing economic policies that facilitate entrepreneurship and business ownership within Black communities. Policies aimed at providing access to capital, mentorship, and resources for Black entrepreneurs are essential for breaking the cycle of economic disenfranchisement and reducing incarceration rates[15].

The intersection of economic disenfranchisement and the criminal justice system highlights a profound challenge facing Black Americans. The direct relationship between the lack of business ownership and high incarceration rates underscores the necessity of systemic change. By fostering economic empowerment through business ownership, we can address the root causes of this disparity, paving the way for a more equitable and just society.

Economic Sovereignty and Political Leverage

The quest for economic sovereignty and political leverage has been a cornerstone of the African American journey towards empowerment. Historical evidence demonstrates that periods of significant progress for Black Americans have been closely linked to their ability to own, control, and leverage economic and political power. This section explores the historical successes of Black Americans post-slavery, the detrimental impact of government policies on their economic status, and the essential role of economic independence in fostering a resilient and empowered community.

Following the abolition of slavery, Black Americans made remarkable strides towards economic independence

[15] PowerNomics: The National Plan to Empower Black America," Dr. Claud Anderson, Powernomics Corporation of America, 2001.

and political engagement. During Reconstruction, the establishment of Black-owned businesses, schools, and churches signified not just a move towards economic stability but also a declaration of self-sufficiency and community strength[16]. These efforts were driven by a deep understanding of the intrinsic link between economic prosperity and political influence. However, the promise of "40 acres and a mule," a symbol of the government's commitment to reparative measures, remained unfulfilled, leaving newly freed slaves to navigate a landscape of economic disenfranchisement without the promised support[17].

The failure to provide the promised reparations can be seen as a foundational moment in the history of government policies that have systematically undermined the economic progress of Black Americans. From the Jim Crow laws to redlining practices and beyond, government actions have not only perpetuated economic disparities but have actively worked to restrict the economic and political power of Black communities[18]. These policies were not merely oversights but deliberate actions aimed at maintaining a status quo of racial inequality.

Despite these systemic barriers, the resilience and ingenuity of Black Americans have shone through. The establishment of Black Wall Streets in areas such as Tulsa, Oklahoma, serves as a testament to what can be achieved when economic and political power are harnessed and

[16] Black Fortunes: The Story of the First Six African Americans Who Escaped Slavery and Became Millionaires," Shomari Wills, Amistad, 2018.

[17] The Half Has Never Been Told: Slavery and the Making of American Capitalism," Edward E. Baptist, Basic Books, 2014.

[18] The Color of Law: A Forgotten History of How Our Government Segregated America," Richard Rothstein, Liveright, 2017.

controlled within the community[19]. These enclaves of Black economic prosperity were self-sufficient, demonstrating the potential for economic empowerment to uplift entire communities. Yet, the destruction of these areas by racist violence underscores the threat that Black economic independence posed to the racial hierarchy.

The historical context of Black Americans' quest for economic independence highlights a critical need for continued efforts in controlling economic and political power. Economic sovereignty offers a buffer against systemic inequalities, providing the means to challenge and change the policies that perpetuate economic disparities. Furthermore, political leverage, derived from economic strength, is essential in advocating for policies that support the growth and protection of Black businesses, education, and community resources[20].

The pathway to empowerment for Black Americans lies in reclaiming economic sovereignty and leveraging political power. The historical successes of Black communities post-slavery underscore the potential for economic independence to serve as a foundation for political and social advancement. However, the ongoing impact of government policies on economic disparities highlights the necessity for strategic engagement in economic and political arenas. By focusing on ownership, control, and the strategic use of economic resources, Black Americans can forge a future marked by prosperity, influence, and equity.

[19] Black Wall Street: From Riot to Renaissance in Tulsa's Historic Greenwood District," Hannibal B. Johnson, Eakin Press, 1998.

[20] PowerNomics: The National Plan to Empower Black America," Dr. Claud Anderson, Powernomics Corporation of America, 2001.

40 Acres And A Mule— Chapter 4

The promise of "40 acres and a mule" to former slaves represents a critical juncture in American history, symbolizing a moment when the nation teetered on the brink of radical economic transformation. This initiative, astonishing in its scope and radicalism, proposed the federal government's confiscation and redistribution of approximately 400,000 acres of land, previously owned by Confederate landowners, to the newly emancipated Black population[1].. Conceived by Black leaders and endorsed by Union General William T. Sherman, this policy promised not just compensation for the inhumanities of slavery but also a pathway to economic self-sufficiency and generational prosperity for Black Americans.

Historian Eric Foner describes this moment as one promising a transformation of Southern society more radical than the abolition of slavery itself[2]. The provision of land to former slaves was not merely an act of restitution; it was an acknowledgment of the economic foundation required for true freedom and citizenship. Landownership, central to the American promise of liberty and prosperity, was to be the cornerstone upon which the freed Black population could build a new life. Yet, the radical potential of this promise went unfulfilled, leaving a lasting impact on race relations and economic disparities in the United States.

[1] The Truth Behind ' 40 Acres and a Mule' ," Henry Louis Gates, Jr., The Root.

[2] Reconstruction: America' s Unfinished Revolution, 1863-1877," Eric Foner.

The revocation of this promise by President Andrew Johnson, who succeeded Abraham Lincoln, represents one of the most significant betrayals in American history. Johnson's decision to return the confiscated lands to the former Confederate owners effectively extinguished the hopes of millions of Black Americans for economic independence and perpetuated the cycle of poverty and disenfranchisement[3]. This act laid the groundwork for systemic racial inequalities that persist to this day, contributing to the vast economic gap between Black and White Americans.

Critics of the "40 acres and a mule" proposal argue that the redistribution of land was impractical and would have set a dangerous precedent for government intervention in private property rights[4]. They contend that such a policy was too radical for its time and incompatible with the American economic system based on free enterprise and individual property rights. However, this perspective overlooks the moral imperative of addressing the atrocities of slavery and the critical role of landownership in achieving economic self-sufficiency.

The failure to implement "40 acres and a mule" has had profound implications for Black Americans' ability to accumulate wealth and access economic opportunities. Without land and the economic foundation it provides, the majority of former slaves and their descendants were thrust into sharecropping, a system that perpetuated economic dependency and exploitation[5]. This denied not only the wealth-building opportunities associated with landownership but also the promise of American democracy itself.

[3] The Failure of Reconstruction," Kenneth M. Stampp.
[4] The Case Against Reparations," The Atlantic, 2014.
[5] Black Reconstruction in America, 1860-1880," W.E.B. Du Bois.

In reflecting on this unfulfilled promise, it is crucial to recognize the missed opportunity for America to rectify the injustices of slavery and lay the foundation for a more equitable society. The decision to deny "40 acres and a mule" to the freed slaves was a turning point that has shaped the contours of racial and economic inequality in the United States for generations. As we continue to grapple with the legacy of slavery and systemic racism, the story of "40 acres and a mule" serves as a powerful reminder of the need for reparative justice and meaningful economic policies to address the historical injustices faced by Black Americans.

Unpacking the 40 Acres and a Mule

At its core, this policy was intended as a measure to address the injustices of slavery by providing a foundation for economic independence and self-sufficiency for newly freed African Americans. The origins of this promise trace back to Union General William T. Sherman's Special Field Order No. 15, a document that has been partially obscured by the annals of history, yet remains a pivotal moment in the struggle for Black equality in the United States.

The issuance of Special Field Order No. 15 was a groundbreaking moment, not merely for the material promise it held but also for the process that led to its creation. The meeting between Sherman, Secretary of War Edwin M. Stanton, and 20 Black leaders in Savannah, Georgia, represented an unprecedented dialogue, recognizing the agency and voice of African Americans in determining their path to freedom and self-determination[6].

[6] Myers, Barton. The Legacy of the Civil War: The Emancipation Proclamation and the March to the Sea. Savannah History Press, 2018.

This consultation was emblematic of a brief period during Reconstruction when the voices of African Americans were actively solicited and, to some extent, heeded in the shaping of their own futures.

Special Field Order No. 15 delineated specific lands to be set aside for freed African Americans, not as a charitable handout but as a right born of their newfound freedom and the nation's moral obligation to redress the injustices of slavery. This land was not just any land; it was fertile, potentially prosperous land that could support the establishment of Black-owned agricultural communities[7]. Furthermore, the Order's provisions for self-governance and military protection of these lands underscored a commitment to Black autonomy and security, elements crucial to the realization of true freedom.

However, the promise encapsulated in Special Field Order No. 15 would remain largely unfulfilled. The assassination of President Abraham Lincoln, the subsequent ascension of President Andrew Johnson, and the political maneuverings of the Reconstruction era led to the restoration of these lands to their former Confederate owners, effectively nullifying Sherman's order[8]. This reversal not only deprived African Americans of the material basis for their independence but also signaled a broader retreat from the ideals of Reconstruction and the egalitarian promises of the Civil War.

Critics and skeptics of the "40 acres and a mule" policy often argue from a standpoint of logistical impracticality and the challenges of implementation. Yet, such arguments fail to grasp the fundamental essence of the promise: a recognition of the incalculable debt owed to African Americans and an attempt, however flawed, to

7 Sherman, William T. Special Field Order No. 15. January 16, 1865.

8 Foner, Eric. Reconstruction: America's Unfinished Revolution, 1863-1877. Harper & Row, 1988.

institutionalize reparations. The opposition to this policy, both historically and in contemporary debates, reflects broader tensions in American society about race, justice, and the legacy of slavery.

The legacy of the "40 acres and a mule" promise is not merely one of historical curiosity but of continuing relevance. It raises fundamental questions about the nature of justice, the means of achieving racial equality, and the unfulfilled promises of American democracy. As scholars and citizens grapple with these questions, the dialogue initiated by Sherman, Stanton, and those 20 Black leaders in Savannah remains a critical point of reference. It reminds us that the struggle for justice and equality is not just about the allocation of resources but about recognizing and rectifying historical wrongs, ensuring autonomy, and building a society that genuinely reflects its highest ideals.

Unveiling the Roots of “40 Acres and a Mule”

The advocacy of Charles Sumner, Thaddeus Stevens, and their Radical Republican compatriots represented a vocal and unyielding force within the political landscape of the time. Their calls for land redistribution were aimed not merely at punitive measures against the Confederacy but as a foundational step towards rectifying the egregious injustices of slavery[9]. This backdrop of radical advocacy set the stage for a meeting that would mark a pivotal moment in the history of African American liberation.

On the evening of January 12, 1865, in the confines of Charles Green’s mansion in Savannah, Georgia, a historic consultation unfolded between Union leaders and African

[9] Myers, Barton. Radicals in Power: The Influence of the Radical Republicans on American Politics. University Press, 2020.

American ministers. This meeting, facilitated by Edwin Stanton and William T. Sherman, was groundbreaking in its acknowledgment of African Americans as stakeholders in the reconstruction of the South[10]. The dissemination of this meeting's proceedings through Henry Ward Beecher's congregation and the New York Daily Tribune underscored its national significance, illuminating a moment where the government sought to listen and act upon the desires of the formerly enslaved.

The ministers, led by Garrison Frazier, articulated a vision that was both simple and revolutionary: land ownership as a pathway to self-sufficiency and autonomy. Frazier's emphasis on land cultivation "by our own labor" as a means to "maintain ourselves and have something to spare" highlighted not only a desire for economic independence but also a deep understanding of the transformative power of land ownership within an agrarian society[11]. This assertion, coupled with the preference for living in separate communities, underscored a pragmatic recognition of the enduring prejudices and the desire for a space where African Americans could thrive unfettered by the shadow of systemic racism.

The issuance of Special Field Order No. 15, just days after this historic meeting, represented a direct response to the articulated needs of the African American community. While President Lincoln's approval of the order lent it a semblance of executive legitimacy, the order's roots in a dialogue with African American leaders underscored a form of participatory governance rarely seen in that era[12].

10 Stanton, Edwin. Records of the War Department: Dialogues on Freedom and Reconstruction, January 1865.

11 Frazier, Garrison. Transcript of the Savannah Meeting, New York Daily Tribune, February 13, 1865.

12 Lincoln, Abraham. Presidential Endorsements of Reconstruction Policies. The Lincoln Archives, 1865.

Critics and skeptics of the time, and indeed in contemporary discourse, might question the feasibility and morality of such a sweeping redistribution of resources. Arguments against the policy often centered on the practical challenges of implementation and the rights of the former Confederate landowners. Yet, these criticisms overlook the fundamental injustices that the policy sought to address and the transformative potential it held for redressing centuries of enslavement and exploitation.

Reclamation and the Reversal of Sherman's Order

The immediate aftermath of Special Field Order No. 15 saw a wave of enthusiasm and action among freedmen, who eagerly embarked on the task of building new lives on the lands allocated to them. The establishment of communities such as the one led by Baptist minister Ulysses L. Houston on Skidaway Island, Georgia, stands as a testament to the resilience and agency of African Americans in the face of historical oppression. These settlements were not merely places of residence; they were beacons of hope and symbols of a possible future predicated on autonomy and economic self-determination[13].

However, the visionary program initiated by Sherman was met with a swift and devastating blow with the ascension of Andrew Johnson to the presidency. Johnson, whose sympathies lay with the Southern cause, systematically dismantled the policies of Reconstruction aimed at empowering the newly freed African American population. The revocation of Special Field Order No. 15 and the subsequent return of land to its former Confederate owners represented a stark betrayal of the promises made to

[13] Foner, Eric. The Fiery Trial: Abraham Lincoln and American Slavery. New York: W. W. Norton & Company, 2010.

African Americans[14]. This act not only deprived thousands of African American families of the means to economic independence but also reinforced the structural barriers to racial equality that persist to this day.

The impact of Johnson's decision cannot be overstated. It was a decision that effectively snuffed out the flickering flame of hope for reparative justice and equitable land distribution. Moreover, it signaled a return to the antebellum status quo, where the socio-economic hierarchy was firmly rooted in racial disparities. The reversal of Sherman's Order encapsulates a broader narrative of missed opportunities and unfulfilled promises that have characterized the African American struggle for equality and justice[15].

Critics of the land redistribution policy often highlight the practical and legal challenges involved in reallocating land on such a massive scale. Yet, such critiques miss the essential point: the moral and ethical imperative of addressing the deep-seated injustices wrought by centuries of slavery. The opposition to the policy, both during its brief implementation and in its aftermath, reflects a reluctance to confront the legacy of slavery and its continuing impact on American society.

In reflecting on the unfulfilled promise of "40 acres and a mule," it is crucial to acknowledge not only the immediate consequences of its revocation but also the enduring significance of what it represented. The policy was more than a material proposition; it was an acknowledgment of the wrongs of slavery and an attempt, however fleeting, to rectify those wrongs through substantive measures. The reversal of this policy under Johnson's administration

14 Myers, Barton. Dismantling the Dream: The End of Reconstruction and the Betrayal of African American Land Rights. Oxford: Oxford University Press, 2015.

15 Johnson, Andrew. Presidential Veto Messages. Washington D.C.: Government Printing Office, 1866.

represents a pivotal moment in American history, where the path towards racial justice and equality was deliberately forsaken.

As we consider the legacy of "40 acres and a mule," we are reminded of the ongoing struggle for reparative justice and the importance of confronting historical injustices. The story of this unrealized promise serves as a critical lens through which to examine the persistent racial disparities in America and the continued relevance of the fight for equity and justice.

Capital Access And Disparities Facing Black Businesses—Chapter 5

The United States is marked by stark disparities in access to capital, a fundamental element for business creation and growth. This disparity is particularly pronounced for Black-owned businesses, which face significant challenges in securing financial support when compared to their counterparts, including immigrant-owned businesses. The juxtaposition of the ease with which individuals can acquire substantial student loans versus the hurdles faced in obtaining business capital raises critical questions about the systemic barriers embedded within financial institutions and the broader economic framework.

The struggle for Black businesses to acquire capital is not a matter of anecdotal evidence but is well-documented in economic studies and reports. According to the U.S. Small Business Administration, Black-owned businesses are three times more likely to be denied loans than white-owned businesses[1]. Even when approved, they are often subjected to higher interest rates and less favorable terms[2]. This

[1] U.S. Small Business Administration. "Access to Capital Among Young Firms, Minority-owned Firms, Women-owned Firms, and High-tech Firms." Office of Advocacy, 2013.

[2] Federal Reserve Bank of Atlanta. "2019 Small Business Credit Survey: Report on Minority-owned Firms." 2020.

systemic bias in lending practices not only stifles the growth of Black-owned businesses but also perpetuates the wealth gap and undermines the economic vitality of Black communities.

Contrastingly, the narrative around student loans reveals a different aspect of financial institutions' willingness to lend. In the United States, it is relatively common for students to be granted loans exceeding $100,000 for education, without tangible assets to secure these loans. This stark contrast in lending practices underscores a troubling inconsistency: financial institutions appear more willing to invest in individuals' educational endeavors than in the entrepreneurial aspirations of Black Americans[3].

This discrepancy points to deeper systemic issues within the financial sector and societal attitudes towards risk, investment, and racial biases. Immigrant-owned businesses, for instance, have historically leveraged ethnic networks and community-based lending circles to circumvent traditional banking barriers[4]. Such mechanisms of support, while valuable, underscore the inequities in mainstream financial channels, which remain less accessible to Black entrepreneurs.

Critics might argue that the disparities in loan approval rates and terms can be attributed to factors such as creditworthiness, business experience, or the sector in which the business operates. However, these arguments often fail to account for the historical context of systemic racism, redlining, and discriminatory policies that have disproportionately affected Black Americans' ability to

[3] Department of Education. "Federal Student Loan Portfolio." 2021.

[4] Portes, Alejandro, and Robert L. Bach. "Latin Journey: Cuban and Mexican Immigrants in the United States." University of California Press, 1985.

accumulate wealth, thereby impacting their credit scores and collateral[5].

Moreover, the reluctance of financial institutions to lend to Black businesses contradicts the proven resilience and innovation within these enterprises. Studies have shown that, despite facing higher barriers to entry and growth, Black-owned businesses often demonstrate remarkable resourcefulness and contribute significantly to their communities and the broader economy[6].

The conversation around access to capital for Black businesses is not merely about financial transactions but touches on broader themes of equity, justice, and the right to economic self-determination. Addressing these disparities requires a multifaceted approach, including policy reform, targeted support programs, and a reevaluation of lending criteria to ensure they are equitable and do not perpetuate historical injustices.

The disparity in capital access for Black businesses compared to the relatively easier acquisition of student loans or the support available to immigrant communities highlights a critical area for economic reform. It calls for a concerted effort to dismantle systemic barriers and create a more inclusive economic system that recognizes and supports the entrepreneurial potential within Black communities.

Building Thriving Communities

5 Coates, Ta-Nehisi. "The Case for Reparations." The Atlantic, June 2014.

6 Bates, Timothy. "Race, Self-Employment, and Upward Mobility." The Johns Hopkins University Press, 1997.

In the American economy, access to capital emerges as a pivotal thread, influencing the pattern of business growth and sustainability. This access, or lack thereof, delineates the landscape in which businesses operate, particularly highlighting the challenges faced by Black-owned enterprises. The juxtaposition of the relative ease in securing student loans against the daunting barriers encountered by Black entrepreneurs in obtaining business capital underscores systemic disparities deeply rooted in the country's financial and economic structures.

The importance of community in this context cannot be overstressed. While neighborhoods are often seen as mere geographical conglomerations, communities represent the synergistic interactions of individuals focused on mutual economic and social upliftment. The distinction between neighborhoods and communities lies not just in semantics but in the economic utility and support systems inherent within each. Communities, particularly those formed by Black Americans and other marginalized groups, play a crucial role in fostering economic prosperity and competitiveness.

Evidence suggests that Black-owned businesses are disproportionately hindered in their quest for capital, a fact well-documented by economic studies and reports. The U.S. Small Business Administration has revealed that these businesses are three times more likely to be denied loans than their white counterparts^1^. This systemic bias not only stifles business growth but also perpetuates a wealth gap, undermining the economic vitality of entire communities.

The discrepancy in lending practices, particularly the greater willingness of financial institutions to lend for educational purposes than for fostering Black entrepreneurship, points to deep-seated systemic issues. These include societal attitudes toward risk, investment, and racial biases. In contrast, immigrant-owned businesses often utilize ethnic networks and community-based lending circles to navigate around these barriers^2^, demonstrating the potential of community support in overcoming institutional challenges.

Critics of the focus on disparities in capital access might cite factors such as creditworthiness or business experience as justifications for the discrepancies observed. However, such viewpoints typically overlook the historical context of systemic racism and discriminatory policies that have hindered Black Americans' ability to build wealth, impacting their credit scores and ability to provide collateral^3^.

Despite these obstacles, Black-owned businesses have shown resilience and innovation, contributing significantly to their communities and the broader economy. This contradicts the reluctance of financial institutions to lend to Black entrepreneurs and highlights the critical role of community support in fostering economic growth^4^.

Addressing the disparities in access to capital for Black businesses is essential not only for the sake of equity and justice but also for the economic self-determination of Black communities. It requires a comprehensive approach that includes policy reform, targeted support programs, and a reevaluation of lending criteria to ensure they do not perpetuate historical injustices.

The role of communities, therefore, extends beyond providing a support network. They are integral to creating a more inclusive economic system that recognizes and nurtures the entrepreneurial potential within marginalized groups. This section underscores the need for a concerted effort to dismantle systemic barriers, highlighting the importance of community in achieving economic prosperity and competitiveness.

Community's Role in Economic Empowerment

Within the African American context, the distinction between neighborhoods and communities emerges as a critical factor in understanding the mechanisms of economic utility and support. This section delves into the significance of community as a cornerstone for economic development and a catalyst for fostering environments where Black businesses can thrive, distinguishing it from the mere geographic proximity of neighborhoods.

The concept of community extends beyond the physical boundaries that define a neighborhood; it encompasses a network of mutual support, shared economic interests, and collective action towards common goals[7]. In contrast, a neighborhood, while important for its social interactions, does not inherently possess the economic infrastructure or the collective mindset geared towards economic empowerment and self-sufficiency. The importance of community in economic development lies in its ability to pool resources, foster entrepreneurship, and create markets for Black-owned businesses, thus facilitating economic prosperity and competitiveness within and beyond its confines.

Historically, African American communities have demonstrated the profound impact of collective economic endeavors. Examples such as Black Wall Street in Tulsa, Oklahoma, showcase how communities, through cooperative economics and mutual support, were able to create prosperous economic ecosystems despite the

7 PowerNomics: The National Plan to Empower Black America," Dr. Claud Anderson, Powernomics Corporation of America, 2001.

adversities of systemic racism and segregation[8]. These communities were not merely clusters of residences; they were networks of businesses and institutions that provided economic opportunities, education, and social services to their members.

The failure to distinguish between neighborhoods and communities can lead to a misunderstanding of the challenges and potential solutions for economic disparities faced by Black Americans. While government and policy interventions often target neighborhoods for economic development, they may overlook the essential element of community building — the creation of economic networks and the fostering of an entrepreneurial culture that can drive sustainable economic growth[9].

Critics may argue that the emphasis on community-based economic development overlooks the need for integration into broader markets and the global economy. However, the strength of a community does not preclude external economic engagement; rather, it provides a foundation from which businesses can compete more effectively on larger stages. Strong communities equip individuals with the resources, knowledge, and networks necessary to navigate and succeed in broader economic contexts[10].

Moreover, the role of community in economic prosperity is not merely about the accumulation of wealth but also about the redistribution of resources in a way that benefits all members. This approach to economic

[8] Black Fortunes: The Story of the First Six African Americans Who Escaped Slavery and Became Millionaires," Shomari Wills, Amistad, 2018.

[9] The Color of Law: A Forgotten History of How Our Government Segregated America," Richard Rothstein, Liveright, 2017.

[10] The New Urban Crisis: How Our Cities Are Increasing Inequality, Deepening Segregation, and Failing the Middle Class—and What We Can Do About It," Richard Florida, Basic Books, 2017.

development promotes equity, reduces poverty, and mitigates the effects of economic disparities within the African American population. It fosters an environment where economic benefits are shared, and success contributes to the upliftment of the entire community[11].

In conclusion, the distinction between neighborhoods and communities is crucial in understanding the dynamics of economic prosperity and competitiveness among African Americans. Communities, with their focus on mutual support and collective economic action, offer a powerful model for economic empowerment. As we move forward, the strengthening of community ties and the promotion of community-based economic initiatives will be key to addressing economic disparities and building a more equitable and prosperous future for Black Americans.

Economic Disenfranchisement and the Color Hierarchy

In the fabric of American society, a deeply entrenched hierarchy based on skin color significantly influences economic distribution and power. This societal stratification not only perpetuates a cycle of economic disenfranchisement for Black Americans but also underscores a missed opportunity for economic empowerment through collective action. Despite possessing an aggregate income that positions them as one of the world's wealthiest groups, Black Americans have not fully leveraged this potential due to a failure to pool resources and invest within their community. This section explores the ramifications of the color-based economic hierarchy and

[11] The Wealth Gap for Women of Color," Center for Global Policy Solutions, 2014.

the critical need for strategic communal economic practices among Black Americans.

The correlation between skin color and economic status in the United States is not a phenomenon of happenstance but a result of historical and systemic racial policies. From the era of enslavement through Jim Crow laws to present-day institutional racism, these policies have systematically undermined the economic potential of Black Americans. The societal ranking order, which places White Americans at the top and Black Americans at the bottom, has tangible economic implications, influencing employment opportunities, access to quality education, housing, and the accumulation of wealth[12]. This color hierarchy is a fundamental barrier to economic equality, ensuring the perpetuation of racial disparities in wealth and resources.

Despite these challenges, Black Americans, as a collective, possess significant economic resources. Estimates suggest that the aggregate income of Black America ranks it among the wealthiest nations globally, highlighting an underutilized reservoir of economic power[13]. However, the potential of this collective wealth remains largely untapped due to the failure to pool resources and invest within the Black community. The propensity to spend outside the community, coupled with a lack of investment in Black-owned businesses and initiatives, undermines the community's economic stability and growth. This economic behavior not only diminishes the community's wealth but also fails to challenge the systemic structures that contribute to racial economic disparities.

12 The Color of Money: Black Banks and the Racial Wealth Gap," Mehrsa Baradaran, Harvard University Press, 2017.

13 Black Wealth/White Wealth: A New Perspective on Racial Inequality," Melvin L. Oliver and Thomas M. Shapiro, Routledge, 2006.

Critics may argue that focusing on community-based economic strategies is insular and may not address the broader systemic issues that contribute to economic disparities. Some suggest that the solution lies in policy reform and integration into the broader economy, rather than communal self-sufficiency. However, evidence from other ethnic groups that practice group economics, such as the Jewish and Asian communities, demonstrates the effectiveness of this approach in building economic resilience and prosperity[14].

The Black community's failure to leverage its aggregate income for communal economic empowerment is a missed opportunity for addressing economic disenfranchisement. Investing in Black-owned businesses, supporting Black entrepreneurs, and creating economic networks within the community are essential strategies for reversing the cycle of economic marginalization[15]. These actions not only build wealth within the community but also serve as a form of resistance against a societal order that devalues Black economic participation.

The societal ranking based on skin color and its correlation with economic distribution poses significant challenges to Black Americans' economic prosperity. However, the community holds the key to dismantling this cycle of disenfranchisement through strategic economic practices that focus on pooling resources and investing within the community. By embracing the potential of their collective economic power, Black Americans can forge a path towards economic empowerment and challenge the structural inequities that have long undermined their economic progress.

[14] The Asian American Achievement Paradox," Jennifer Lee and Min Zhou, Russell Sage Foundation, 2015.

[15] PowerNomics: The National Plan to Empower Black America," Dr. Claud Anderson, Powernomics Corporation of America, 2001.

Systemic Exclusion of Black Businesses and Broader Societal Loss

The systemic exclusion of Black businesses from traditional lending opportunities is a multifaceted issue that not only reflects deeply ingrained historical biases but also significantly hampers the potential for innovation and growth within the broader American economy. This phenomenon suggests a loss that extends far beyond the individual entrepreneurs affected, impacting society as a whole. Through a detailed examination of the barriers faced by Black businesses in securing capital and the consequential implications for economic diversity and innovation, this chapter underscores the urgent need for systemic change.

The roots of financial exclusion faced by Black entrepreneurs can be traced back to a long history of racial discrimination in the United States, from the era of slavery through Jim Crow laws, to redlining practices that persisted well into the 20th century[16]. These historical injustices have laid the groundwork for the disparities we observe today in the allocation of business loans, with Black-owned businesses significantly less likely to be approved for loans compared to their White counterparts[17]. The disparity is not solely a reflection of differing business performance metrics but is indicative of deeper systemic biases within financial institutions.

16 The Color of Money: Black Banks and the Racial Wealth Gap," Mehrsa Baradaran, Harvard University Press, 2017.

17 Disparities in Capital Access between Minority and Non-Minority-Owned Businesses," U.S. Department of Commerce, Minority Business Development Agency, 2010.

Research indicates that Black entrepreneurs face higher rejection rates and are often subjected to more stringent scrutiny when applying for business loans[18]. Even when approved, the loans offered to Black-owned businesses typically come with higher interest rates and less favorable terms[19]. This financial marginalization not only limits the ability of Black businesses to expand and innovate but also restricts their capacity to contribute to job creation and community development.

Critics might argue that market dynamics, rather than systemic racism, dictate lending practices. They suggest that creditworthiness, not race, is the primary factor considered by lenders[20]. However, this viewpoint fails to account for the nuanced ways in which systemic racism can influence the perceived creditworthiness of Black entrepreneurs, including the devaluation of properties in predominantly Black neighborhoods and the historical exclusion of Black Americans from wealth-building opportunities.

The consequences of excluding Black businesses from traditional lending opportunities extend beyond the individual level, impacting the broader economy. A diverse business ecosystem is essential for fostering innovation, meeting the needs of a diverse population, and driving economic growth[21]. By systematically denying Black entrepreneurs access to capital, the economy misses out on potential breakthroughs and innovations that could arise from these businesses. Furthermore, the economic

18 Access to Credit among Small, Low-Income, Minority, and Immigrant Entrepreneurs," U.S. Small Business Administration, Office of Advocacy, 2017.

19 Racial Discrimination in Small Business Lending," Federal Reserve Bank of Atlanta, 2019.

20 The Case Against the Race-Based Mortgage Penalty," The Wall Street Journal, 2018.

21 Diversity and Innovation: A Business Case for Equity," McKinsey & Company, 2015.

empowerment of Black communities through business ownership is hindered, perpetuating cycles of poverty and inequality.

Addressing this issue requires a multifaceted approach, including policy reforms to ensure fair lending practices, initiatives to increase the financial literacy of Black entrepreneurs, and the creation of alternative funding sources dedicated to supporting minority-owned businesses[22]. Only through concerted efforts to dismantle the barriers to financial inclusion can we unlock the full potential of Black businesses and, by extension, enrich the American economy.

The systemic exclusion of Black businesses from traditional lending opportunities represents a critical economic and social issue that warrants immediate attention. By recognizing and addressing the historical and systemic biases that underpin this exclusion, we can pave the way for a more inclusive, innovative, and prosperous economy that benefits all members of society.

Systemic Barriers and the Racial Wealth Gap: Beyond Individual Choices

The disparity in wealth accumulation between Black Americans and other demographic groups transcends the realm of individual choices, rooted deeply in enduring systemic barriers. These barriers, which span access to financial services, homeownership, and business capital, serve not only to perpetuate but also to widen the racial wealth gap. This section critically examines the structural impediments to generational wealth building for Black

[22] PowerNomics: The National Plan to Empower Black America," Dr. Claud Anderson, Powernomics Corporation of America, 2001.

Americans, highlighting the complex interplay of historical, economic, and policy-driven factors that contribute to economic disparities.

Generational wealth, the bedrock of economic stability and prosperity for many American families, remains an elusive dream for a significant portion of the Black community. This is not due to a lack of aspiration or effort but is primarily a consequence of systemic barriers erected throughout American history. One such barrier is the restricted access to financial services, which includes discriminatory lending practices known as redlining[23]. Despite regulatory attempts to address these issues, Black Americans continue to face challenges in obtaining mortgages and loans at fair rates, directly impacting their ability to purchase homes and build equity.

Homeownership, often heralded as a cornerstone of the American dream, serves as a critical pathway to wealth accumulation. However, Black families historically have been systematically excluded from this pathway through practices such as redlining and racially restrictive covenants[24]. These practices have not only limited the ability of Black individuals to purchase homes in appreciating neighborhoods but have also contributed to the concentration of poverty and disinvestment in predominantly Black communities.

Furthermore, the disparity in business capital access for Black entrepreneurs starkly illustrates the racial divide in economic opportunities. Despite possessing comparable qualifications and business acumen, Black business owners are more likely to be denied loans, receive smaller loan amounts, and pay higher interest rates compared to their

[23] The Color of Law: A Forgotten History of How Our Government Segregated America," Richard Rothstein, Liveright, 2017.

[24] Ibid.

White counterparts[25]. This discrepancy severely hampers the ability of Black-owned businesses to grow, hire from their communities, and contribute to the economic vitality of Black neighborhoods.

Critics often attribute the racial wealth gap to personal responsibility and individual financial decisions, suggesting that disparities can be overcome through education and hard work alone. However, this perspective fails to acknowledge the systemic nature of the barriers in place and the historical context that has shaped the economic landscape for Black Americans[26]. While individual actions are important, they cannot alone address the structural inequities embedded in the American economic system.

Addressing the racial wealth gap requires a multifaceted approach that includes policy reforms aimed at dismantling systemic barriers to economic inclusion. Initiatives such as targeted support for Black homeownership, equitable access to credit, and investment in Black-owned businesses are essential steps towards closing the wealth divide[27]. Moreover, acknowledging the role of systemic racism in shaping economic opportunities is crucial for creating an equitable framework for wealth accumulation.

The disparity in wealth accumulation between Black Americans and other demographic groups is a multifaceted issue rooted in systemic barriers rather than individual choices. By critically examining and addressing the historical and contemporary factors contributing to economic disparities, we can begin to forge a path toward

25 Disparities in Capital Access between Minority and Non-Minority Businesses," U.S. Department of Commerce, Minority Business Development Agency, 2010.

26 The Case for Reparations," Ta-Nehisi Coates, The Atlantic, 2014.

27 PowerNomics: The National Plan to Empower Black America," Dr. Claud Anderson, Powernomics Corporation of America, 2001.

economic justice and generational wealth building for all Americans.

The Journey of Black Entrepreneurs

The narrative surrounding Black entrepreneurs in the United States is one of resilience, perseverance, and untapped economic potential. Despite facing systemic obstacles that hinder access to capital, networks, and equitable opportunities, many Black business owners succeed, contributing significantly to the economy and their communities. This section explores the journey of these entrepreneurs, highlighting the broader truth about the untapped economic potential within Black communities and underscoring the need for targeted policy interventions to support economic justice and equity.

The resilience of Black entrepreneurs is not a new phenomenon but a continuation of a long history of innovation and self-reliance in the face of adversity. From the era of segregation to the present day, Black individuals have established and grown businesses, often out of necessity due to exclusion from mainstream economic opportunities[28]. These businesses have not only provided goods and services but have also created jobs, supported families, and fostered community development. However, the systemic obstacles that Black entrepreneurs face are manifold and include limited access to traditional funding sources, discriminatory lending practices, and a lack of

[28] Black Fortunes: The Story of the First Six African Americans Who Escaped Slavery and Became Millionaires," Shomari Wills, Amistad, 2018.

mentorship and networks that are crucial for business growth[29].

Studies have shown that Black-owned businesses are less likely to be approved for loans compared to their white counterparts, and when they are approved, they often receive lower amounts and face higher interest rates[30]. This disparity in access to capital is a critical barrier to the growth and sustainability of Black businesses. Furthermore, the historical accumulation of wealth, which could support entrepreneurial endeavors, is significantly lower in Black communities due to decades of economic disenfranchisement and discriminatory policies, such as redlining and employment discrimination[31].

Despite these challenges, the success of Black entrepreneurs speaks to the untapped economic potential within Black communities. These business owners not only navigate a landscape riddled with barriers but also innovate and thrive, contributing to the diversity and richness of the American economy. The resilience of Black entrepreneurs showcases the immense potential for growth and innovation that could be unleashed with equitable access to resources and opportunities[32].

The need for targeted policy interventions to support Black entrepreneurs is evident. Policies that address the unique challenges faced by Black businesses, such as access to capital, mentorship, and networks, are essential for fostering economic justice and equity. Additionally,

[29] The Color of Money: Black Banks and the Racial Wealth Gap," Mehrsa Baradaran, Harvard University Press, 2017.

[30] Disparities in Capital Access between Minority and Non-Minority Businesses," U.S. Department of Commerce, Minority Business Development Agency, 2010.

[31] The Color of Law: A Forgotten History of How Our Government Segregated America," Richard Rothstein, Liveright, 2017.

[32] PowerNomics: The National Plan to Empower Black America," Dr. Claud Anderson, Powernomics Corporation of America, 2001.

initiatives that aim to dismantle systemic barriers and create a level playing field in the business ecosystem can help unlock the full potential of Black entrepreneurship. These interventions are not only beneficial for Black business owners but also for the broader economy, as they can stimulate innovation, job creation, and community development[33].

The narrative of resilience among Black entrepreneurs highlights a broader truth about the economic potential within Black communities. The success of these business owners, achieved despite systemic obstacles, underscores the need for targeted policy interventions that support economic justice and equity. By recognizing and addressing the unique challenges faced by Black entrepreneurs, we can foster an inclusive economy that leverages the full spectrum of American talent and innovation.

Systemic Resistance and the Dynamics of "White Flight"

The phenomenon of "white flight" has been a significant aspect of American urban history, particularly during the 20th century. As Black Americans moved into previously predominantly White neighborhoods and institutions, a pattern emerged where White residents and stakeholders would relocate to other areas, a movement driven by systemic resistance to integration and equality. This chapter explores the dynamics of "white flight," underscoring its implications for racial segregation, economic disparities, and the ongoing struggle for integration and equality in American society.

[33] The New Jim Crow: Mass Incarceration in the Age of Colorblindness," Michelle Alexander, The New Press, 2010.

"White flight" is not merely a historical footnote but a reflection of deeper systemic issues within American society. It represents a collective action driven by racial prejudice and the desire to maintain racial homogeneity within neighborhoods and institutions[34]. The departure of White residents and businesses from urban centers to the suburbs in the aftermath of increased Black migration to cities during the Great Migration is a stark example of this phenomenon[35]. This movement was not solely motivated by personal preferences but was facilitated and reinforced by systemic factors, including discriminatory housing policies, zoning laws, and practices such as redlining, which collectively served to institutionalize racial segregation and inequality[36].

The implications of "white flight" extend beyond the mere redistribution of population demographics. It has profound impacts on the socio-economic fabric of American cities, leading to a concentration of poverty and a lack of resources in predominantly Black neighborhoods. As White residents moved out, tax bases eroded, and funding for public services, including education, declined, perpetuating cycles of disadvantage and marginalization[37]. Moreover, "white flight" contributed to the stigmatization of Black communities, reinforcing stereotypes and prejudices that further entrenched racial divisions.

Critics of the notion of "white flight" argue that such movements were driven by economic factors and the quest

[34] American Apartheid: Segregation and the Making of the Underclass," Douglas S. Massey and Nancy A. Denton, Harvard University Press, 1993.

[35] The Warmth of Other Suns: The Epic Story of America's Great Migration," Isabel Wilkerson, Random House, 2010.

[36] The Color of Law: A Forgotten History of How Our Government Segregated America," Richard Rothstein, Liveright, 2017.

[37] Family Properties: Race, Real Estate, and the Exploitation of Black Urban America," Beryl Satter, Metropolitan Books, 2009.

for better living conditions rather than racial prejudice. They suggest that the decline of urban centers and the rise of suburban living reflect broader trends in American society that transcend racial considerations[38]. While economic factors undoubtedly played a role, this perspective overlooks the racial undertones of housing policies and social attitudes that favored White mobility and systematically disadvantaged Black Americans.

Addressing the legacy of "white flight" requires a multi-faceted approach that not only acknowledges the racial prejudices underlying this phenomenon but also seeks to rectify the systemic policies that facilitated it. Efforts to promote integration and equality must confront the historical and ongoing practices that contribute to segregation and inequality, including discriminatory lending practices, inequitable school funding models, and exclusionary zoning laws[39]. Furthermore, fostering dialogue and understanding between communities can help to challenge and change the attitudes that underpin systemic resistance to integration.

The phenomenon of "white flight" illustrates the systemic resistance to integration and equality within American society. It highlights the need for comprehensive strategies to address the root causes of racial segregation and economic disparity. By confronting the policies and attitudes that perpetuate segregation, we can move closer to realizing the ideals of integration and equality for all Americans.

[38] Crabgrass Frontier: The Suburbanization of the United States," Kenneth T. Jackson, Oxford University Press, 1985.

[39] The New Jim Crow: Mass Incarceration in the Age of Colorblindness," Michelle Alexander, The New Press, 2010.

Part 2: The Present Day Effects of Lynching

Lynching: An Institutionalized Terror— Chapter 6

In American history, lynching emerges as a stark manifestation of racial terror and white supremacy, designed to reinforce the social and economic subjugation of Black Americans. Lynching, a term that encapsulates the extrajudicial killings by mobs, evolved into an institutionalized method wielded by whites to instill fear among Black communities and uphold the caste system prevalent in the Southern and border states from 1880 to 1940[1]. This period marked a zenith of white animosity and dread towards Black individuals, where lynching transcended mere punishment to become a spectacle of racial and sadistic violence aimed at perpetuating a racial hierarchy[2].

The origins of lynching as an American phenomenon were meticulously chronicled by James E. Cutler in "Lynch-Law" (1905), underscoring its distinctiveness to the United States[3]. The barbarity of lynchings was not confined to hangings but extended to shootings, burnings, and other heinous forms of torture. Such acts were not just crimes of hatred but were exercises in extreme racism coupled with

[1] Lynch-Law," James E. Cutler, 1905.

[2] NAACP, "Thirty Years of Lynching in the United States, 1889-1918," 1919.

[3] Ibid.

sadism, serving primarily as tools for maintaining white dominion[4].

Statistical evidence on lynchings points to the profound racial disparity in victimization. While lynching was not an atrocity reserved exclusively for Black Americans, by the turn of the century, it had predominantly become so. Reconstruction era onwards set the template for the racial targeting in lynchings, with Black victims constituting a significantly higher proportion than their white counterparts[5]. Various sources, including the Chicago Tribune, Tuskegee Institute, and the National Association for the Advancement of Colored People (NAACP), have provided lynching statistics, albeit with discrepancies owing to differing definitions of lynching and potential underreporting[6].

Notably, the lynching epidemic was not a uniquely Southern phenomenon but afflicted the entire nation, with the Southern states accounting for the overwhelming majority of incidents. This geographic spread underlines the pervasive nature of racial violence in America's fabric, not confined by regional boundaries[7]. The purported causes for lynching ranged widely, from serious accusations to trivial or baseless charges, reflecting a broader societal propensity to criminalize Black existence[8].

The narrative that lynching was a necessary evil to control alleged Black criminality, particularly the myth of the Black rapist, has been debunked by numerous cases of innocent Black men, women, and even children being lynched without cause. This myth served as a cornerstone

4 Tuskegee Institute Lynching Statistics.
5 Gunnar Myrdal, "An American Dilemma," 1944.
6 Chicago Tribune, Tuskegee Institute, NAACP lynching statistics.
7 Ibid.
8 Arthur Raper, "The Tragedy of Lynching," 1933.

for justifying many lynchings, yet it obscured the true motive: white societal control over the Black population[9].

Efforts to combat lynching, including legislative attempts and advocacy by organizations such as the NAACP, signified a growing awareness and condemnation of the practice. Yet, the persistence of lynching into the 20th century highlights the deep-seated racism and systemic failures in protecting Black lives[10]. The decline in lynching incidents over time does not signify the eradication of the ideology that fostered them but rather an evolution in the mechanisms of racial oppression.

Lynching and its Persistent Shadow on Racial Tensions

The history of lynching—a form of violence primarily targeting Black Americans—casts a long shadow over contemporary racial relations. This heinous act, which often involved public torture and execution without trial, served not only as a means of exacting racial terror but also as a mechanism for maintaining white supremacy. The scars left by such violence have not faded, contributing to ongoing tensions and distrust between Black communities and law enforcement agencies.

Historically, lynching was employed as a tool to enforce social control, instilling fear within Black communities and perpetuating a system of racial hierarchy. From the post-Civil War era into the 20th century, it is estimated that thousands of African Americans were

[9] Ibid.

[10] NAACP archives and legislative advocacy records.

lynched in the United States[11]. These acts were not merely isolated incidents of racial violence but were often public spectacles that involved the complicity, if not active participation, of local authorities and bystanders. The failure to prosecute the perpetrators further entrenched the notion of a legal system skewed against Black Americans.

This legacy of lynching has contributed to a deep-seated mistrust between Black communities and law enforcement. The historical reluctance of the legal system to hold white perpetrators accountable mirrors contemporary concerns regarding police brutality and the judicial system's handling of cases involving Black victims. Such parallels draw a direct line from the past to the present, underscoring the persistence of racial bias within institutions designed to protect and serve[12].

Critics and skeptics, however, may argue that drawing connections between historical lynching and current law enforcement practices is an exaggeration or misinterpretation of the facts. They posit that significant progress has been made in civil rights and policing, suggesting that the instances of misconduct are the actions of a few rather than indicative of systemic issues[13]. These viewpoints often emphasize the reforms and measures taken to address racial bias within law enforcement agencies.

Yet, the statistical disparities in police shootings, arrests, and incarcerations of Black individuals point to a pattern that cannot be dismissed as mere anomalies. Studies have consistently shown that Black Americans are

[11] NAACP, "History of Lynchings," https://www.naacp.org/history-of-lynchings

[12] Equal Justice Initiative, "Lynching in America: Confronting the Legacy of Racial Terror," https://eji.org/report/lynching-in-america

[13] Heather Mac Donald, "The Myth of Systemic Police Racism," Wall Street Journal, June 2, 2020.

disproportionately affected by police violence and judicial sentencing, reinforcing the perception of an enduring racial bias within the justice system[14]. Such data underpin the argument that the echoes of lynching are not relics of the past but reverberate in the present dynamics of racial injustice.

In addressing these ongoing tensions, it is crucial to acknowledge the historical context that shapes current perceptions and experiences. The failure to confront and rectify the legacy of lynching and systemic racism perpetuates a cycle of mistrust and alienation. Recognizing the historical roots of these issues is the first step towards fostering a dialogue aimed at healing and reconciliation.

Conclusively, the shadow of lynching looms large over the relationship between Black communities and law enforcement in the United States. The reluctance to fully reckon with this dark chapter of American history impedes progress towards racial equality and justice. Only through a candid examination of the past and its impact on the present can we hope to dismantle the barriers of distrust and work towards a more equitable society.

Unraveling the Psychological Legacy of Lynching in Black Communities

The specter of lynching has not only left physical scars across generations but has also inflicted deep psychological wounds. This legacy of violence has seeded a profound collective trauma within Black communities, a trauma magnified by a historical narrative that often sought to justify or remain silent on such atrocities. The psychological

[14] Mapping Police Violence, "Police Violence & Racial Equity," https://mappingpoliceviolence.org

ramifications of this legacy are profound, shaping the mental health landscape of African American communities to this day.

Lynching, a tool of white supremacy, was not merely an act of individual violence but a systemic method of instilling fear and compliance through terror. Between the end of the Civil War and the height of the Civil Rights Movement, thousands of African Americans were lynched, often in public spectacles of extreme violence, with the tacit or explicit endorsement of local authorities and the wider society[15]. This history of sanctioned violence has perpetuated a state of collective trauma, influencing generations long after the acts themselves have ceased. The silence and justification surrounding these acts compound their impact, embedding a deep mistrust and fear within the African American psyche towards institutions meant to protect them.

The concept of collective trauma refers to the psychological repercussions experienced by a group of people who share a common identity or experience. In the case of African Americans, the legacy of lynching contributes to a collective memory of violence and oppression, manifesting in a heightened sense of vulnerability and a pervasive fear of racial violence. This form of trauma is not confined to those who have directly experienced violence but is transmitted across generations through stories, behaviors, and an ingrained wariness of institutional authority[16].

Critics may argue that the impacts of past injustices, such as lynching, are overstated, suggesting that contemporary challenges faced by Black communities are

[15] NAACP, "History of Lynchings," https://www.naacp.org/history-of-lynchings

[16] Joy DeGruy, "Post Traumatic Slave Syndrome," (Milwaukie: Uptone Press, 2005).

unrelated to historical traumas. They might claim that focusing on the past distracts from addressing present-day issues and personal accountability[17]. However, dismissing the psychological impact of historical trauma overlooks the complex ways in which past injustices shape present realities. Research in the field of epigenetics and psychology supports the notion that trauma can be inherited, affecting the health and social behaviors of subsequent generations[18].

Moreover, the historical justification or minimization of lynching acts has compounded their traumatic impact. When societies fail to acknowledge and atone for historical wrongs, the trauma inflicted by these injustices is exacerbated, leaving psychological wounds open and unhealed. The silence around lynching and racial violence has forced African American communities to bear the weight of their trauma alone, without the broader societal acknowledgment necessary for healing and reconciliation[19].

Addressing the psychological legacy of lynching requires a multifaceted approach. Acknowledging the historical realities of these atrocities and their impact on present-day African American communities is a critical first step. Education, open dialogue, and the implementation of policies aimed at rectifying historical injustices are essential to healing the wounds of the past. Only through a concerted effort to confront and dismantle the legacy of racial terror can we hope to alleviate the collective trauma it has engendered.

17 Shelby Steele, "The Content of Our Character: A New Vision of Race In America," (New York: St. Martin's Press, 1990).

18 Rachel Yehuda et al., "Holocaust Exposure Induced Intergenerational Effects on FKBP5 Methylation," Biological Psychiatry 80, no. 5 (2016): 372-380.

19 David R. Williams and Selina A. Mohammed, "Racism and Health I: Pathways and Scientific Evidence," American Behavioral Scientist 57, no. 8 (2013): 1152-1173.

The psychological scars left by the legacy of lynching are a testament to the enduring impact of racial violence on the collective psyche of African American communities. Understanding and addressing this trauma is not only an act of historical justice but a necessary step towards healing and building a more equitable society.

The Legal Legacy of Lynching and Systemic Injustice

Beyond the immediate horror of these acts, lynching symbolizes a broader pattern of systemic inequality, wherein the legal system has often failed to protect Black lives and, in some instances, has actively participated in or condoned racial violence. This historical context provides a lens through which the contemporary struggles against racial injustice can be understood, demonstrating how deeply rooted these issues are within the fabric of American society.

Lynching, often perceived as extrajudicial violence, was not merely an act of individual racism but a manifestation of systemic oppression. Between the end of Reconstruction in the late 19th century and the Civil Rights Movement in the mid-20th century, over 4,000 African Americans were lynched in the United States[20]. These acts were rarely prosecuted, and when they were, convictions were extraordinarily uncommon. This lack of legal recourse underscores a judicial complicity in racial violence, reflecting a broader societal and institutional endorsement of these acts.

[20] NAACP, "History of Lynchings," https://www.naacp.org/history-of-lynchings

The systemic nature of this injustice is further highlighted by the legal structures in place at the time. Jim Crow laws, for instance, institutionalized racial segregation and inequality, while the Supreme Court's decision in Plessy v. Ferguson (1896) legitimized these practices under the doctrine of "separate but equal"[21]. These legal frameworks provided a veneer of legitimacy to racial discrimination and violence, embedding racial inequality within the legal and social order of the United States.

Opponents of this perspective might argue that the horrors of lynching and Jim Crow are relics of the past, with no bearing on the present. They claim that significant legal and social progress has been made, pointing to the Civil Rights Act of 1964 and the Voting Rights Act of 1965 as evidence of systemic reform[22]. While it is true that these legislative achievements marked significant milestones in the fight against racial injustice, disparities in the criminal justice system, economic inequality, and voting rights issues continue to plague African American communities, suggesting that the roots of systemic injustice run deep.

Moreover, the contemporary manifestations of systemic racism—such as mass incarceration, police brutality, and the racial wealth gap—serve as modern-day parallels to the historical injustices of lynching. The United States incarcerates a higher proportion of its Black population than South Africa did at the height of apartheid[23]. This fact alone highlights the ongoing systemic nature of racial injustice, revealing how the legacy of lynching and discrimination continues to impact African American communities.

Addressing the systemic injustices highlighted by the history of lynching requires more than acknowledgment; it

[21] Plessy v. Ferguson, 163 U.S. 537 (1896).

[22] Civil Rights Act of 1964, Pub.L. 88-352, 78 Stat. 241.

[23] Michelle Alexander, "The New Jim Crow: Mass Incarceration in the Age of Colorblindness," (New York: The New Press, 2010).

demands concrete actions and reforms. While legislative achievements have made strides towards equality, the persistent racial disparities across various sectors of society underscore the need for continued efforts to dismantle systemic racism.

The history of lynching in America is not simply a collection of past atrocities but a poignant reminder of the systemic injustices that continue to affect African American communities. The legal system's failure to protect Black lives and its active participation in racial violence reflect a broader pattern of systemic inequality that persists to this day. Recognizing and addressing these deep-seated issues is essential for moving towards a more equitable and just society.

The Critical Need for Comprehensive Education on Lynching in America

The narrative of American history, as presented within the educational system, has long been criticized for its lack of depth and comprehensiveness, especially regarding the topic of lynching and its impact on racial violence and society at large. This omission represents a significant gap in understanding the historical context of racial inequality and the systemic injustices that African Americans have faced. The failure to adequately address this dark chapter of American history not only perpetuates ignorance but also hinders the process of reconciliation and healing.

Lynching, a brutal form of vigilante justice, was prevalent from the late 19th century through the mid-20th century, with thousands of African Americans falling victim to mob violence. Despite its significance, this aspect of history is often glossed over or omitted entirely from school curricula[24]. The lack of comprehensive education on lynching contributes to a skewed understanding of American history, failing to fully acknowledge the depth of racial violence and its lasting impacts on society.

Critics of incorporating detailed education on lynching argue that such topics are too sensitive for younger audiences and may incite racial tensions rather than foster understanding[25]. However, this perspective underestimates the importance of confronting uncomfortable truths in the process of education. Providing a sanitized version of history only serves to perpetuate myths and misunderstandings about the realities of racial violence and its role in shaping the social and legal frameworks of the United States.

Furthermore, the educational gap on lynching and racial violence reflects a broader issue of systemic racism within the educational system. Textbooks and curricula are often developed with a bias that minimizes the atrocities committed against African Americans and other minority groups, thereby contributing to a perpetuation of racial stereotypes and inequalities[26]. Addressing these gaps is not only about correcting historical records but also about challenging the structures of power and privilege that maintain systemic racism.

The need for comprehensive education on lynching extends beyond moral and ethical considerations; it is a matter of societal health. Understanding the historical

[24] James Loewen, "Lies My Teacher Told Me: Everything Your American History Textbook Got Wrong," (New York: The New Press, 1995).

[25] Jonathan Zimmerman, "Whose America? Culture Wars in the Public Schools," (Cambridge: Harvard University Press, 2002).

[26] Gloria Ladson-Billings, "New Directions in Multicultural Education: Complexities, Boundaries, and Critical Race Theory," in "Handbook of Research on Multicultural Education," ed. James A. Banks and Cherry A. McGee Banks (San Francisco: Jossey-Bass, 2004), 50-65.

context of racial violence is crucial for addressing contemporary issues of racial injustice and inequality. Educating students on the history of lynching can foster empathy, promote critical thinking, and inspire a commitment to social justice[27].

The significant lack of comprehensive education on the topic of lynching in American history curricula represents a disservice to students and society. Bridging this educational gap is essential for fostering a deeper understanding of racial violence and its lasting impacts. It is only through confronting the full spectrum of American history, including its most uncomfortable aspects, that we can hope to build a more equitable and just society.

Lynching's Legacy and Racial Bias in Contemporary Society

The insidious legacy of lynching in the United States extends beyond the physical violence inflicted upon Black individuals; it has sown seeds of racial stereotyping and bias that permeate various aspects of life for African Americans today. From the workplace to educational institutions, and within interactions with the criminal justice system, the stereotypes and biases shaped by this grim history continue to wield a profound influence. Understanding the depth and breadth of these impacts is crucial for addressing and dismantling the systemic racism that upholds them.

[27] Paulo Freire, "Pedagogy of the Oppressed," (New York: Continuum, 1970).

Lynching, historically utilized as a tool of terror and control, not only sought to physically eliminate African Americans but also to dehumanize them and reinforce racial stereotypes. These stereotypes portrayed Black individuals as inherently criminal, intellectually inferior, and unworthy of justice[28]. Such dehumanizing perceptions have not dissipated with the cessation of lynching; instead, they have morphed and found new expressions in the systemic racism evident today.

In the workplace, racial stereotyping manifests in discriminatory hiring practices, wage disparities, and limited advancement opportunities for Black individuals. Studies have shown that resumes with traditionally Black names receive fewer callbacks than those with traditionally white names, a clear indication of implicit bias rooted in stereotypes[29]. In education, Black students are more likely to be suspended or expelled, often as a result of racial biases that perceive them as more disruptive or less capable than their white counterparts[30]. These educational disparities lay the groundwork for a perpetuating cycle of inequality, limiting access to higher education and subsequent employment opportunities.

The criminal justice system, perhaps the most direct descendant of the lynching era's legacy, continues to be rife with racial biases. African Americans are disproportionately stopped, searched, arrested, and incarcerated compared to

[28] David R. Williams and Selina A. Mohammed, "Racism and Health I: Pathways and Scientific Evidence," American Behavioral Scientist 57, no. 8 (2013): 1152-1173.

[29] Marianne Bertrand and Sendhil Mullainathan, "Are Emily and Greg More Employable Than Lakisha and Jamal? A Field Experiment on Labor Market Discrimination," American Economic Review 94, no. 4 (2004): 991-1013.

[30] Russell J. Skiba et al., "The Color of Discipline: Sources of Racial and Gender Disproportionality in School Punishment," Urban Review 34, no. 4 (2002): 317-342.

white individuals[31]. The presumption of guilt and the harsher sentencing meted out to Black individuals are contemporary echoes of the lynching mobs' swift and brutal "justice." Such systemic biases not only undermine the principles of equality and justice but also contribute to the ongoing social and economic marginalization of African American communities.

Opponents of the view that lynching has left a lasting legacy of racial stereotyping and bias may argue that progress has been made toward racial equality and that current disparities are the result of individual choices or socioeconomic factors, not systemic racism[32]. While it is true that legal segregation has ended and civil rights have been advanced, the undercurrents of racial bias remain deeply embedded in societal structures, influencing perceptions and decisions in ways that continue to disadvantage Black individuals.

Confronting and dismantling the legacy of racial stereotyping and bias requires a multifaceted approach, including education that accurately reflects the history and impact of lynching, policies that address systemic inequalities, and a societal commitment to recognizing and combating implicit biases. Only through a concerted effort to understand and address the roots of these issues can we hope to forge a society that truly upholds the ideals of justice and equality for all.

In sum, the legacy of lynching and the racial stereotypes it perpetuated continue to affect African Americans in various spheres of life. Recognizing and addressing the deep-seated biases that inform these disparities is essential in the quest for a more equitable

[31] Michelle Alexander, "The New Jim Crow: Mass Incarceration in the Age of Colorblindness," (New York: The New Press, 2010).

[32] Shelby Steele, "The Content of Our Character: A New Vision of Race In America," (New York: St. Martin's Press, 1990).

society.

Lynching's Role in Perpetuating Wealth Disparities

The history of lynching in the United States, a barbaric tool of racial terror, has not only inflicted incalculable human suffering but has also played a significant role in cementing economic disparities between Black and white Americans. These acts of violence were not merely expressions of racial hatred; they were mechanisms for maintaining economic control and suppressing Black prosperity. The enduring wealth gap that persists today is, in part, a direct legacy of the systemic use of lynching and racial violence to intimidate Black individuals and communities, thwarting their efforts toward economic independence and advancement.

During the post-Reconstruction era, African Americans made significant strides in acquiring land and building businesses, posing a perceived threat to the racial and economic order of the South. In response, lynching became a tool to undermine Black economic success, targeting those who dared to compete with white businesses or who were seen as becoming too economically independent[33]. The destruction of Black-owned businesses and the theft of Black-owned land through terror not only robbed individuals and families of their economic achievements but also served to reinforce the notion that African Americans were not entitled to economic success.

33 Ida B. Wells, "Southern Horrors: Lynch Law in All Its Phases," (New York: The New Press, 1892).

The ramifications of these actions have been profound and long-lasting. Today, the wealth gap between Black and white families is staggering, with the median white family holding nearly ten times the wealth of the median Black family[34]. This disparity is not simply the result of individual choices or efforts but is rooted in centuries of systemic racism and economic sabotage, of which lynching was a pivotal component.

Critics may argue that the economic disparities observed today can be attributed to factors such as educational attainment or family structure, rather than historical injustices. However, such viewpoints fail to acknowledge the systemic barriers that have historically hindered Black access to education, capital, and property ownership[35]. The legacy of lynching and racial violence has contributed to a cycle of poverty and economic exclusion that is difficult to break, perpetuating disparities across generations.

Addressing the economic consequences of lynching and racial violence requires a multifaceted approach. It calls for policies aimed at closing the racial wealth gap, including investment in education, housing, and business opportunities for Black communities. Furthermore, it necessitates a reckoning with the past, recognizing how historical injustices have shaped present economic conditions[36].

[34] The Economic State of Black America in 2020," U.S. Congress Joint Economic Committee, https://www.jec.senate.gov/public/*cache/files/23b0b4a9-4cda-463a-bbe9-ce4b63399c55/economic-state-of-black-america-in-2020---final-.pdf*

[35] Richard Rothstein, "The Color of Law: A Forgotten History of How Our Government Segregated America," (New York: Liveright Publishing Corporation, 2017).

[36] William A. Darity Jr. and A. Kirsten Mullen, "From Here to Equality: Reparations for Black Americans in the Twenty-First

The economic disparities between Black and white Americans cannot be fully understood without acknowledging the impact of lynching and racial violence. These acts of terror were not only crimes against individuals but also assaults on the economic potential of an entire race. By intimidating Black individuals and communities and hindering their economic progress, lynching contributed significantly to the wealth gap that persists today. Overcoming these disparities requires not only acknowledging this painful history but also taking concrete steps to address its lasting effects.

Lynching and the Barrier to Racial Reconciliation

The denial or minimization of these atrocities not only exacerbates the wounds inflicted but also serves as a significant barrier to achieving true reconciliation between races. Understanding and acknowledging this history is crucial for moving forward, yet resistance to such acknowledgment persists, hindering progress toward unity and mutual respect.

Lynching, once a widespread practice, was not merely an act of individual hatred but a tool of systemic oppression, aimed at instilling fear and maintaining racial hierarchies. Despite the termination of this practice, its legacy endures, manifesting in racial disparities and tensions that are evident in contemporary society[37]. The failure to fully confront and

Century," (Chapel Hill: University of North Carolina Press, 2020).

[37] Equal Justice Initiative, "Lynching in America: Confronting the Legacy of Racial Terror," https://eji.org/report/lynching-in-america

address this aspect of American history contributes to a gap in the collective understanding of racial violence and its long-term effects on African American communities.

The reluctance to acknowledge the full extent of lynching and its impact on race relations in the United States is often rooted in a desire to avoid discomfort or guilt. However, reconciliation requires confronting uncomfortable truths. By denying or minimizing the significance of lynching, society fails to recognize the suffering of victims and their descendants, further alienating African American communities and reinforcing racial divides[38].

Critics might argue that focusing on historical grievances perpetuates victimhood and hinders progress. They contend that dwelling on past injustices prevents the healing process and promotes division rather than unity[39]. However, this perspective overlooks the importance of historical truth in the reconciliation process. Without a shared understanding of history, including its most harrowing chapters, it is impossible to build a foundation for genuine reconciliation and healing.

The path toward racial reconciliation involves a collective effort to acknowledge historical injustices, understand their contemporary implications, and address the systemic inequalities they have engendered. This process is not about assigning blame but about recognizing the shared history that shapes the present. Educational initiatives that accurately portray the history of lynching and racial violence, public memorials that honor the victims, and open

[38] Ta-Nehisi Coates, "The Case for Reparations," The Atlantic, June 2014.

[39] John McWhorter, "Antiracism: Our Flawed New Religion," The Daily Beast, March 2015.

dialogues about race and history can all contribute to bridging the divide[40].

The unresolved history and ongoing denial or minimization of lynching and racial violence are significant barriers to racial reconciliation in the United States. Overcoming these barriers requires courage, honesty, and a willingness to confront the past. Only through acknowledgment and understanding can we hope to heal the wounds of history and build a more inclusive and unified society.

[40] Bryan Stevenson, "Just Mercy: A Story of Justice and Redemption," (New York: Spiegel & Grau, 2014).

Part 3: Systemic Racism: How It Started and How It Works

The Genesis of Systemic Racism—Chapter 7

The 1638 Maryland Doctrine of Exclusion stands as a pivotal moment in the historical foundation of systemic racism within the United States. Drafted by the Maryland Colony Council, this doctrine explicitly stated that "Neither the existing black population, their descendants, nor any other blacks shall be permitted to enjoy the fruits of white society"[1]. This stark decree was not merely a statement of social exclusion; it was a codified intent to ensure that Black individuals would remain "a subordinate, non-competitive, non-compensated workforce." This early legislative act of racial exclusion underscores the deeply entrenched roots of systemic racism that would persistently shape the socioeconomic landscape for African Americans.

The Doctrine of Exclusion served as a foundational stone for systemic racism by legally endorsing the social, economic, and political marginalization of Black individuals. Its ramifications were profound, setting a precedent for subsequent laws and practices that institutionalized racial discrimination. This policy not only relegated Black people to the margins of society but also legitimized their dehumanization, reinforcing a hierarchy based on race that deprived them of the basic rights and privileges afforded to white individuals.

1 "The Maryland Doctrine of Exclusion, 1638." Historical Archives of Maryland Online.

Critics and skeptics may question the relevance of a 17th-century decree on contemporary issues of racial inequality, suggesting that societal progress has rendered such historical documents obsolete. However, ignoring the historical lineage of systemic racism fails to acknowledge the cumulative impact of centuries of racial discrimination on present-day disparities. The legacy of the Doctrine of Exclusion is evident in the enduring economic, educational, and social inequities that continue to disadvantage African American communities[2].

Furthermore, the doctrine highlights the deliberate construction of a racialized social order that benefitted from the exploitation of Black labor. By legally ensuring that Black individuals could not compete on an equal footing, the doctrine facilitated the economic prosperity of white society at the expense of Black suffering and disenfranchisement. This orchestrated disparity laid the groundwork for the systemic barriers that would later be codified in Jim Crow laws, segregation, and the disenfranchisement of Black voters[3].

The Doctrine of Exclusion also reflects a broader historical pattern of racial exclusion and discrimination not unique to Maryland or the 17th century. Similar policies and practices were adopted throughout the colonies and, later, the United States, each contributing to the complex issues of systemic racism. These historical precedents underscore the necessity of confronting and understanding the origins of

[2] Ira Katznelson, "When Affirmative Action Was White: An Untold History of Racial Inequality in Twentieth-Century America," (New York: W. W. Norton & Company, 2005).

[3] Michelle Alexander, "The New Jim Crow: Mass Incarceration in the Age of Colorblindness," (New York: The New Press, 2010).

racial inequalities to effectively address their contemporary manifestations[4].

In conclusion, the 1638 Maryland Doctrine of Exclusion is not merely a historical footnote but a critical juncture in the genesis of systemic racism in America. Its explicit denial of the rights and humanity of Black individuals set a precedent for the institutionalization of racial inequality. Acknowledging this history is essential for comprehending the depth and persistence of racial disparities and for forging a path toward genuine racial reconciliation and equity. The challenge remains to dismantle the lingering structures of racism that trace their origins to such foundational acts of exclusion.

Indenture to Prosperity And The Early African American Experience in Colonial America

The arrival of Black individuals in America as indentured servants in 1619 marks a significant yet complex chapter in the history of the United States. Unlike slaves, indentured servants entered into contracts for a limited period, after which they were granted freedom and, often, land or money. This period, especially between 1619 and 1626, witnessed the flourishing of Black communities, a testament to their resilience and ability to thrive despite the challenges of a new and often hostile environment.

Historical records indicate that the first African Americans arrived in Jamestown, Virginia, not as slaves but as indentured servants. This status, albeit temporary and fraught with hardship, allowed for a possibility of freedom and economic advancement that slavery would later

[4] Ta-Nehisi Coates, "The Case for Reparations," The Atlantic, June 2014.

categorically deny[5]. During this initial period, some African Americans were able to leverage their indentured status to secure a better future for themselves and their families. They worked alongside white indentured servants, and in some cases, achieved a level of financial prosperity and social mobility that would be unimaginable in the centuries to follow[6].

The early 17th century was a time of relative fluidity in the social and economic positions of Black individuals in colonial America. Records from this period document Black landowners who successfully cultivated tobacco, the cash crop of the era, which contributed significantly to the prosperity of the colony[7]. This era of prosperity for Black communities is a crucial but often overlooked aspect of American history, challenging the narrative that African Americans were always and only victims within the American economic system.

Critics might argue that the emphasis on this period of prosperity overlooks the broader context of racial subjugation and economic exploitation that would define the African American experience for centuries. Indeed, the transition from indentured servitude to racialized slavery was a pivotal shift that would severely curtail the freedoms and economic opportunities for African Americans. However, acknowledging the achievements of Black communities during this early period does not negate the realities of subsequent injustices but rather highlights the

[5] Ira Berlin, "Many Thousands Gone: The First Two Centuries of Slavery in North America," (Cambridge: Harvard University Press, 1998).

[6] Lerone Bennett Jr., "Before the Mayflower: A History of Black America," (Chicago: Johnson Publishing Company, 1982).

[7] T.H. Breen and Stephen Innes, "Myne Owne Ground: Race and Freedom on Virginia's Eastern Shore, 1640-1676," (New York: Oxford University Press, 1980).

complexity of the African American experience and the resilience of Black communities[8].

Furthermore, the narrative of Black prosperity during this era counters the monolithic portrayal of African Americans as passive subjects of history. It underscores the agency of Black individuals in leveraging the opportunities available to them, however limited, to forge a path toward economic independence and social recognition. This historical nuance is critical for a comprehensive understanding of the African American experience and the origins of the racial wealth gap in the United States[9].

The period between 1619 and 1626 offers valuable insights into the early experiences of African Americans in colonial America. Despite the eventual institutionalization of slavery, which would drastically alter the social and economic landscape for African Americans, this era of indentured servitude and subsequent prosperity highlights the capacity for resilience and economic achievement within Black communities. Recognizing this period is essential for understanding the multifaceted nature of the African American experience and the foundational role of Black individuals in the economic development of the United States.

The Doctrine of Exclusion Declared Black People Should Not Enjoy The Fruits of White Society

8 Edmund S. Morgan, "American Slavery, American Freedom: The Ordeal of Colonial Virginia," (New York: W.W. Norton & Company, 1975).

9 Thomas Sowell, "Black Rednecks and White Liberals," (San Francisco: Encounter Books, 2005).

The Doctrine of Exclusion explicitly declared that Black people were not to enjoy the fruits of white society. This doctrine was not merely a statement of social exclusion; it was a foundational policy that institutionalized racial discrimination and paved the way for centuries of systemic racism in America. The doctrine stated that "Neither the existing black population, their descendants, nor any other blacks shall be permitted to enjoy the fruits of white society," ensuring that Black individuals would remain a "subordinate, non-competitive, non-compensated workforce"[10]. This policy underscored the deliberate construction of a societal hierarchy based on race, which has had lasting effects on the socioeconomic status of African Americans.

The implementation of the Doctrine of Exclusion marked the beginning of legally sanctioned racial discrimination, setting a precedent for future laws and practices that would further marginalize African Americans. It was a clear statement of the intended permanent status of Black people in American society: one of subjugation and exclusion. The doctrine effectively denied African Americans access to the economic, social, and political opportunities that were available to whites, contributing to the wealth gap and systemic inequalities observed today[11].

Critics may argue that the relevance of a document from the 17th century has diminished over time, especially in light of the progress made during the Civil Rights movement. However, the principles underpinning the Doctrine of Exclusion can still be seen in contemporary racial disparities in education, employment, housing, and

10 "The Maryland Doctrine of Exclusion, 1638." Historical Archives of Maryland Online.

11 Ira Katznelson, "When Affirmative Action Was White: An Untold History of Racial Inequality in Twentieth-Century America," (New York: W. W. Norton & Company, 2005).

criminal justice. The legacy of this doctrine is a testament to the deep roots of systemic racism in America, demonstrating how historical policies continue to influence the present[12].

Moreover, the Doctrine of Exclusion serves as a historical marker for the beginning of a codified system of racial inequality. It provided a legal and social framework for the enslavement, segregation, and discrimination of African Americans that followed. By legally formalizing the exclusion of Black people from the benefits of society, the doctrine laid the groundwork for the institutional barriers that would make equality an ongoing struggle for generations of African Americans[13].

In the face of these historical and ongoing challenges, African American communities have shown resilience and strength, fighting tirelessly for civil rights and equality. The recognition of the Doctrine of Exclusion's place in history is crucial for understanding the systemic nature of racial inequality in America. It challenges society to confront the historical contexts that have shaped racial dynamics and to actively work towards dismantling the remnants of such doctrines in modern policies and practices[14].

The Doctrine of Exclusion is a critical piece of America's racial history, illustrating the early legislative efforts to codify racial discrimination and exclusion. Its legacy is a stark reminder of the origins of systemic racism and the enduring struggle against its effects. Acknowledging and understanding the impact of such

[12] Michelle Alexander, "The New Jim Crow: Mass Incarceration in the Age of Colorblindness," (New York: The New Press, 2010).

[13] C. Vann Woodward, "The Strange Career of Jim Crow," (New York: Oxford University Press, 2002).

[14] Derrick Bell, "Faces at the Bottom of the Well: The Permanence of Racism," (New York: Basic Books, 1992).

historical doctrines is essential in the ongoing fight for racial justice and equality.

Labor and Domination And The Economic Motivations Behind Colonial Slavery

The migration of Europeans to America was fueled by the promise of wealth and land, yet the individuals who embarked on this journey were not the aristocrats of their home countries. Instead, they were people seeking new opportunities, often escaping poverty and seeking to establish themselves in a new world[15]. The establishment of a labor force became a critical factor for these colonists, who recognized that their prosperity was dependent on the ability to cultivate and harvest the vast lands of the Americas. Observing the wealth generated by the labor forces in England, colonial settlers aspired to replicate this economic model in the New World. The transition to enslaving Black individuals to serve as this labor force marked a pivotal and dark chapter in American history, laying the foundation for systemic racial inequalities.

The early colonial economy was labor-intensive, particularly in the agricultural sector where tobacco, cotton, and sugar became staple crops. The settlers initially relied on indentured servants, many of whom were European, to meet this need[16]. However, as the demand for labor grew, the economic model shifted towards a more permanent and exploitative system: slavery. The enslavement of Africans

15 Alan Taylor, "American Colonies: The Settling of North America," (New York: Penguin Books, 2001).

16 Edmund S. Morgan, "American Slavery, American Freedom: The Ordeal of Colonial Virginia," (New York: W.W. Norton & Company, 1975).

provided the colonists with a solution to their labor needs, transforming the social and economic landscape of the colonies.

This transition was driven not by racial prejudices initially but by economic pragmatism. However, the systemic enslavement of Black individuals soon became justified through an ideology of racial superiority, embedding racial discrimination into the fabric of American society[17]. The notion that Europeans in America were not the elite of their origin countries is crucial to understanding the dynamics at play. Lacking the status and resources they might have had in Europe, these individuals sought to establish their dominance in the New World through the control and exploitation of a labor force deemed inferior by virtue of race[18].

Critics might argue that focusing solely on economic motivations oversimplifies the complex dynamics of colonial society and the subsequent establishment of racial hierarchies. Some might posit that racial prejudices predated the economic use of slavery and that the enslavement of Africans was a manifestation of these prejudices[19]. While it is undeniable that racism played a significant role in the justification and perpetuation of slavery, the economic imperative provided the initial impetus for this inhumane system.

Moreover, the reliance on African slaves for labor had profound implications for the development of racial ideologies. It entrenched a system of white supremacy that

[17] Ira Berlin, "Many Thousands Gone: The First Two Centuries of Slavery in North America," (Cambridge: Harvard University Press, 1998).

[18] Eric Williams, "Capitalism and Slavery," (Chapel Hill: The University of North Carolina Press, 1944).

[19] Winthrop D. Jordan, "White Over Black: American Attitudes toward the Negro, 1550-1812," (Chapel Hill: The University of North Carolina Press, 1968).

deemed African Americans as inherently suited for servitude, an ideology that has had lasting effects on the social, economic, and political lives of African Americans[20]. The legacy of slavery, rooted in the economic ambitions of colonial settlers, continues to influence the racial disparities observed in contemporary America.

The migration of Europeans to America and their subsequent establishment of a labor force through the enslavement of Black people underscores the economic underpinnings of racial inequality in the United States. The decision to enslave Africans was initially motivated by economic necessity but was sustained and justified through the development of racial ideologies that have perpetuated systemic inequalities. Recognizing the economic motivations behind slavery is crucial to understanding the historical and ongoing struggles for racial equality and justice.

Shackles Beyond Iron: The 1705 Slave Codes and the Institutionalization of Racial Hierarchy

The enactment of enslavement laws and slave codes, particularly those codified in 1705, marked a significant moment in the history of racial subjugation in the United States. These laws were not merely administrative tools but were fundamental in establishing the racial hierarchy that positioned Black people as subordinate, enforcing severe restrictions on their rights and freedoms. The 1705 slave codes exemplify the legal mechanisms used to dehumanize enslaved individuals, treating them as property rather than human beings. This legal framework laid the groundwork

[20] Michelle Alexander, "The New Jim Crow: Mass Incarceration in the Age of Colorblindness," (New York: The New Press, 2010).

for systemic racial inequalities and introduced the "white ally problem" by penalizing those who sought to assist or advocate for the enslaved[21].

The 1705 Virginia Slave Code serves as a primary example of these legislative efforts, embodying the transition from indentured servitude to racialized slavery. It delineated the legal distinctions between African slaves and European indentured servants, further entrenching the racial caste system. Among its provisions were laws that denied enslaved Africans the right to bear arms, to assemble without white supervision, and to testify against whites in court[22]. These codes not only restricted the physical mobility of Black individuals but also severely limited their ability to seek justice, protect themselves, or maintain social cohesion.

Moreover, the slave codes introduced severe penalties for whites who engaged in acts of solidarity with Black individuals. This legal codification of the "white ally problem" sought to discourage any form of resistance or abolitionist sentiment among the white population by threatening them with legal repercussions[23]. Such measures were indicative of the broader social controls inherent in the institution of slavery, designed to protect the interests of slave owners and uphold the social order based on white supremacy.

21 Edmund S. Morgan, "American Slavery, American Freedom: The Ordeal of Colonial Virginia," (New York: W.W. Norton & Company, 1975).

22 The Virginia Slave Codes of 1705," The Colonial Williamsburg Foundation, https://www.history.org/history/teaching/enewsletter/volume7/nov08/primsource.cfm

23 Ibram X. Kendi, "Stamped from the Beginning: The Definitive History of Racist Ideas in America," (New York: Nation Books, 2016).

Critics of focusing on slave codes as a foundational aspect of systemic racism may argue that these laws were a product of their time and should not be interpreted through a modern lens. They might suggest that contemporary racial disparities are disconnected from these historical laws, attributing them instead to socio-economic factors or individual choices[24]. However, this perspective fails to acknowledge the lasting impact of slave codes on the legal and social fabric of America. The legacy of these laws can be traced through the Black codes of the mid-19th century, Jim Crow laws, and even into contemporary practices within the criminal justice system[25].

The slave codes of 1705 and subsequent legislations were not isolated phenomena but part of a systematic effort to institutionalize racial hierarchy in America. They established a legal precedent for the treatment of Black people as inferior and justified the denial of their basic human rights. Understanding the role of these laws in shaping the social, economic, and political dynamics of racial inequality is crucial for addressing the systemic nature of racism in contemporary society.

The 1705 slave codes represent a critical juncture in the history of racial subjugation in the United States, institutionalizing a racial hierarchy that has had enduring consequences. By legally codifying the subordination of Black people and introducing social controls to maintain this system, these laws laid the foundation for centuries of racial inequality. Recognizing the historical significance of slave codes and their impact on the development of systemic racism is essential for any genuine effort to

[24] Shelby Steele, "The Content of Our Character: A New Vision of Race In America," (New York: St. Martin's Press, 1990).

[25] Michelle Alexander, "The New Jim Crow: Mass Incarceration in the Age of Colorblindness," (New York: The New Press, 2010).

dismantle the structures of racial oppression that persist today.

The 1705 Diversity Act and Its Long-Term Effects on Racial Dynamics

The Diversity Act of 1705 represents a pivotal moment in the legal codification of racial control within the early American colonies. Mandating a white presence at any gathering of six or more Black individuals, this act was a clear attempt to surveil and suppress the autonomy of African American communities. Far from being a mere historical footnote, the principles underlying the Diversity Act have perpetuated a legacy of racial policing and economic disparities that resonate in contemporary society.

The act was ostensibly designed to prevent insurrection and maintain public order, but its true purpose was to reinforce a social hierarchy that placed Black individuals firmly at the bottom. By legally requiring white oversight of Black gatherings, the act stripped African Americans of their privacy and freedom of association, reinforcing their status as property rather than persons[26]. This intrusion into the social lives of Black people was a manifestation of the broader system of racial control that defined slavery and, later, segregation in America.

Critics might argue that drawing a direct line from the Diversity Act of 1705 to modern racial disparities is an oversimplification of complex historical and social processes. They may claim that contemporary issues should be viewed within their own contexts, independent of laws

26 Ira Berlin, "Generations of Captivity: A History of African-American Slaves," (Cambridge: Belknap Press, 2003).

enacted centuries ago[27]. However, this perspective fails to acknowledge the cumulative impact of such laws on the fabric of American society. The mechanisms of control and surveillance established by the Diversity Act have evolved but not disappeared, manifesting in modern policing practices and the systemic economic marginalization of African American communities[28].

The legacy of the Diversity Act is evident in the racial profiling and disproportionate policing of Black individuals in the United States. Practices such as "stop and frisk" and the over-policing of Black neighborhoods are contemporary echoes of the act's intent to monitor and control Black populations. These practices not only perpetuate fear and mistrust between law enforcement and Black communities but also contribute to the disproportionate incarceration of Black individuals[29].

Furthermore, the economic disparities rooted in the historical subjugation of African Americans cannot be overlooked. The denial of freedom of association and the enforced dependency on white oversight under the Diversity Act curtailed the economic autonomy of Black individuals. Over time, these restrictions have contributed to the racial wealth gap, as African American communities were systematically denied the opportunities for economic advancement that were available to their white counterparts[30].

27 Shelby Steele, "The Content of Our Character: A New Vision of Race In America," (New York: St. Martin's Press, 1990).

28 Michelle Alexander, "The New Jim Crow: Mass Incarceration in the Age of Colorblindness," (New York: The New Press, 2010).

29 Jill Leovy, "Ghettoside: A True Story of Murder in America," (New York: Spiegel & Grau, 2015).

30 Thomas Shapiro, "Toxic Inequality: How America's Wealth Gap Destroys Mobility, Deepens the Racial Divide, & Threatens Our Future," (New York: Basic Books, 2017).

The Diversity Act of 1705 and its mandate for white supervision of Black gatherings is more than a historical curiosity; it is a testament to the enduring legacy of racial control in America. The principles of surveillance and subjugation enshrined in the act have evolved over centuries, contributing to the racial disparities that plague contemporary society. Acknowledging the long-term effects of such legislation is crucial for understanding and addressing the systemic inequalities that persist today. Only by confronting the roots of racial policing and economic disparities can we hope to forge a path toward genuine equality and justice.

The Meritorious Manumission Act of 1710 And The Foundations of Division and Control

The Meritorious Manumission Act of 1710 represents a crucial yet often overlooked moment in American history, setting the stage for enduring divisions within the African American community. Passed in Virginia, this law allowed enslaved individuals to earn their freedom by performing acts deemed beneficial by their enslavers, such as disclosing planned slave rebellions or inventing something profitable. While on the surface, this might appear as an opportunity for enslaved people, its underlying implications were far more insidious. It institutionalized a culture of surveillance and betrayal among Black communities, encouraging individuals to prioritize personal gain over collective solidarity. This act can be seen as a precursor to the contemporary criticisms of "snitching" within communities and the emergence of what some describe as pro-establishment Black leadership[31].

The Meritorious Manumission Act of 1710 fostered an environment where trust was eroded, and divisions were sown among enslaved individuals. By rewarding those who betrayed collective resistance efforts, the act ensured that unity among the enslaved was difficult to achieve and maintain. This division was a deliberate tool of control, making it easier for slave owners to manage their human property and quell any attempts at rebellion[32]. The impact of such legislation extended beyond immediate effects on enslaved communities, embedding a legacy of distrust and competition that complicates discussions of solidarity and collective action in Black communities to this day.

Critics might argue that emphasizing the role of the Meritorious Manumission Act in fostering divisions among Black people overlooks the agency of individuals who, faced with the unimaginable horrors of slavery, made choices they believed would best ensure their survival and that of their loved ones. They may also argue that focusing on historical divisions detracts from the achievements of Black unity and resistance throughout history[33]. While these points are valid, acknowledging the divisive impact of the Meritorious Manumission Act does not negate the instances of resistance and solidarity; instead, it provides a fuller understanding of the complex dynamics at play within oppressed communities.

31 Ira Berlin, "Many Thousands Gone: The First Two Centuries of Slavery in North America," (Cambridge: Harvard University Press, 1998).

32 Edmund S. Morgan, "American Slavery, American Freedom: The Ordeal of Colonial Virginia," (New York: W.W. Norton & Company, 1975).

33 Vincent Woodard, "Delectable Negro: Human Consumption and Homoeroticism within US Slave Culture," (New York: NYU Press, 2014).

Furthermore, the legacy of the Meritorious Manumission Act is evident in contemporary criticisms of Black leaders who are perceived as too accommodating to the status quo. Just as the act rewarded enslaved individuals who aligned themselves with their enslavers' interests, today's political climate often rewards Black leaders who navigate within established systems rather than challenging them. This dynamic raises important questions about the role of leadership in advancing the interests of Black communities and the tensions between working within the system and seeking to transform it[34].

The Meritorious Manumission Act of 1710 played a significant role in shaping the social and political landscape for African Americans, both during slavery and in its long-term effects on community dynamics and leadership. By incentivizing actions that undermined collective solidarity, the act contributed to a culture of surveillance and betrayal that has lasting repercussions. Understanding this historical context is essential for grappling with contemporary challenges in building unity and effective leadership within Black communities.

[34] Cornel West, "Race Matters," (Boston: Beacon Press, 1993).

Ten Lies You're Told About American Slavery— Chapter 8

Abolitionism and the Civil War

The prevailing narrative within the American educational system often romanticizes the abolitionist movement in the North during the Civil War, portraying it as a widespread and popular cause that galvanized the Union's efforts against the Confederacy. This portrayal, while compelling, simplifies a complex historical reality and contributes to a misunderstanding of the era's social and political dynamics. A closer examination reveals that the sentiment towards abolitionism in the North was far more nuanced and less universally accepted than commonly depicted.

The Liberty Party, an abolitionist political group active in the 1840s and 1850s, struggled to gain significant traction in electoral politics, failing to win a majority in any county during the 1860 elections[1]. This fact highlights the limited appeal of radical abolitionist politics among the Northern electorate. Similarly, the circulation of the era's largest abolition newspaper was minuscule compared to the total population of the Northern states, indicating that abolitionist sentiments were not as widespread as often portrayed[2].

1 "Liberty Party (United States, 1840-48)," Encyclopedia Britannica.

2 "American Abolitionism and Religion," Divining America, TeacherServe©, National Humanities Center.

Furthermore, the enlistment of Black soldiers in the Union Army, while a significant aspect of the war effort, was not primarily motivated by a widespread desire among African Americans in the North to fight for the abolitionist cause. Many of these soldiers were escaped slaves who joined the Union Army as a means of securing their freedom and the freedom of others[3]. The Emancipation Proclamation, issued by President Abraham Lincoln in 1862, is often cited as evidence of the North's commitment to abolitionism. However, its reception among Union soldiers was mixed, with reports of increased desertions following its issuance, underscoring the ambivalence or outright opposition to the policy within the ranks[4].

Critics of the romanticized abolitionist narrative argue that it obscures the economic, political, and racial motivations that also played critical roles in the North's opposition to the Confederacy. The war was fought for union as much as for abolition, and the abolition of slavery, while a moral and political imperative for many, was not the sole or even primary motivation for all participants in the conflict[5].

This reevaluation does not diminish the genuine commitment of many Northerners to the cause of abolition or the bravery of Black soldiers who fought for their freedom. Instead, it seeks to provide a more nuanced understanding of the period, recognizing the diversity of opinions and motivations that characterized the Northern states during the Civil War.

[3] James M. McPherson, "The Negro's Civil War: How American Blacks Felt and Acted During the War for the Union," (New York: Vintage Books, 2003).

[4] "The Emancipation Proclamation," National Archives.

[5] Eric Foner, "The Fiery Trial: Abraham Lincoln and American Slavery," (New York: W. W. Norton & Company, 2010).

The narrative that portrays abolitionism as a universally popular movement in the North during the American Civil War requires reconsideration. Acknowledging the complexities and varied motivations of the era is essential for a more accurate and comprehensive understanding of this pivotal period in American history.

The Civil War and the Centrality of Slavery

The narrative that the American Civil War was fought over states' rights rather than the institution of slavery is a revisionist perspective that distorts the historical record. This argument has been used to defend the commemoration of the Confederacy, including the display of the Confederate flag, by shifting the focus from slavery to a broader political dispute. However, an examination of primary sources and declarations by the seceding states unequivocally reveals that slavery was central to the conflict.

Abraham Lincoln's early statements regarding the war's aims, including his initial insistence that the war was not primarily about ending slavery, must be understood within the political context of the time. Lincoln's primary goal was to preserve the Union, and he was cautious about alienating border states where slavery was still legal[6]. However, this tactical position should not be mistaken for indifference toward slavery. The evolution of the war and the issuance of the Emancipation Proclamation in 1862 signified a pivotal shift, making the abolition of slavery a central war aim for the Union[7].

6 James M. McPherson, "Battle Cry of Freedom: The Civil War Era," (New York: Oxford University Press, 1988).

7 "The Emancipation Proclamation," National Archives, January 1, 1863.

The Declarations of Causes issued by several Southern states as they seceded from the Union provide irrefutable evidence of the centrality of slavery to the conflict. South Carolina, the first state to secede, explicitly cited the threat to the institution of slavery as a primary grievance, particularly taking issue with Northern states' reluctance to enforce the Fugitive Slave Act and their efforts to grant rights to African Americans, whom South Carolina's declaration claimed were "incapable of becoming citizens"[8]. Mississippi's declaration unambiguously described slavery as "the greatest material interest of the world," revealing the economic underpinnings of the Southern commitment to the institution[9].

Critics of the view that slavery was central to the Civil War might argue that economic and states' rights issues were equally significant. While it is true that economic disparities between the agrarian South and the industrializing North, as well as disputes over states' rights, contributed to the tensions leading to war, these issues cannot be disentangled from the institution of slavery. The Southern economy's dependence on slave labor and the political power that the slave states wielded within the Union were directly tied to the maintenance and expansion of slavery[10].

Furthermore, the post-war period and the adoption of the "Lost Cause" narrative by many in the South served to further obfuscate the role of slavery in the Civil War. This narrative, which portrays the Confederacy as a noble but

[8] "Declaration of the Immediate Causes Which Induce and Justify the Secession of South Carolina from the Federal Union," December 24, 1860.

[9] "A Declaration of the Immediate Causes which Induce and Justify the Secession of the State of Mississippi from the Federal Union," Mississippi, January 9, 1861.

[10] Eric Foner, "The Fiery Trial: Abraham Lincoln and American Slavery," (New York: W. W. Norton & Company, 2010).

doomed fight for states' rights and Southern way of life, minimizes the central issue of slavery and has contributed to ongoing debates about Confederate symbols in public spaces[11].

The assertion that the American Civil War was not about slavery is a revisionist lie that ignores the explicit statements of the Confederacy itself. The Declarations of Causes of the seceding states make it clear that slavery was a, if not the, primary factor driving the Southern states to rebellion. Understanding the Civil War's causes is essential for an honest reckoning with American history and the legacies of slavery and racism that continue to impact the United States today.

African American Participation in the Confederate Forces

The claim that slaves and free Black individuals fought for the Confederacy during the American Civil War alongside their white counterparts is a significant element of revisionist history that seeks to reframe the conflict's motivations and dynamics. This narrative is often employed to suggest that the Civil War was more about states' rights and regional loyalty than about the institution of slavery. However, a closer examination of historical records and military policies reveals that this portrayal does not hold up under scrutiny.

For the majority of the Civil War, the Confederate government explicitly prohibited Black individuals, whether enslaved or free, from serving as soldiers in its armies. The

11 Karen L. Cox, "Dixie's Daughters: The United Daughters of the Confederacy and the Preservation of Confederate Culture," (Gainesville: University Press of Florida, 2003).

Confederacy's resistance to arming Black individuals was rooted in the foundational principle of white supremacy and the fear that providing weapons to Black men would undermine the slave system that the Confederacy was fighting to preserve[12]. It was only in the waning days of the Confederacy, with the passage of General Order No. 14 in March 1865, that the Confederate government authorized the enlistment of Black soldiers. This decision was driven not by a recognition of Black individuals' rights or capabilities but by sheer desperation as the Confederacy faced imminent defeat[13].

The notion that Black individuals voluntarily fought for the Confederacy has been thoroughly debunked by historians. The few accounts of Black men in Confederate camps predominantly describe them as enslaved laborers forced to support the Confederate war effort through non-combat roles such as cooks, teamsters, and laborers[14]. The Confederate army's use of enslaved labor was a strategic decision to free up white men for combat roles, not an indication of racial solidarity or shared cause between Black individuals and the Confederacy.

Furthermore, the late attempt to raise Black regiments in 1865, promising freedom in exchange for service, was met with skepticism and resistance within the Confederacy itself. The proposal underscored the Confederacy's dire situation rather than a genuine shift in its racial policies or objectives. Notably, these units were never formed in

12 James M. McPherson, "Battle Cry of Freedom: The Civil War Era," (New York: Oxford University Press, 1988).

13 "General Order No. 14," Confederate States of America, March 1865.

14 Bruce Levine, "Confederate Emancipation: Southern Plans to Free and Arm Slaves during the Civil War," (New York: Oxford University Press, 2006).

significant numbers nor did they play a role in the conflict's outcome[15].

Critics of the revisionist narrative argue that propagating the myth of Black Confederate soldiers serves to obscure the central role of slavery in the Civil War and to sanitize the Confederacy's legacy. By suggesting that Black individuals were willing participants in the Confederate cause, proponents of this myth aim to deflect attention from the Confederacy's explicit commitment to maintaining and expanding slavery[16].

The revisionist claim that slaves and free Black people fought for the Confederacy is a distortion of historical facts designed to recast the motivations behind the Civil War. The Confederate government's policies and actions throughout the conflict clearly demonstrate that the war was fought to preserve a social order based on slavery and white supremacy. Recognizing the historical reality of African American involvement in the Civil War is crucial for understanding the conflict's true nature and the enduring legacy of racial injustice in America.

The Harsh Realities of Slavery: Debunking the Myth of Benevolent Ownership

The myth of benevolent slave ownership, perpetuated by revisionist narratives, posits that enslaved individuals were valuable economic assets who were, therefore, treated well by their owners to ensure longevity and productivity. This

[15] ohn Stauffer, "Black Confederates: The Civil War's Most Persistent Myth," The Atlantic, November 2015.

[16] Kevin M. Levin, "Searching for Black Confederates: The Civil War's Most Persistent Myth," (Chapel Hill: University of North Carolina Press, 2019).

argument is often juxtaposed against the plight of industrial workers, suggesting that enslaved people had more stable and secure lives. However, historical evidence overwhelmingly contradicts this portrayal, revealing the brutal and inhumane conditions under which enslaved people lived and worked.

Contrary to the argument of economic self-interest leading to humane treatment, records from plantations and slave owners themselves depict a much different reality. Bennett T. Barrow, a slave owner in Louisiana, documented almost daily beatings and torture of enslaved people under his control[17]. These acts were not anomalies but part of a broader system of violence and subjugation that characterized slavery in America. The physical punishment inflicted on enslaved individuals served not only as a means of control but also as a demonstration of power, reinforcing the social hierarchy that placed Black people at the lowest rung.

The conditions in which enslaved people lived were often deplorable, with minimal food and inadequate housing being the norm rather than the exception. These living conditions were not designed for the well-being of the enslaved but were instead calculated to minimize costs and maximize profits for slave owners[18]. The discovery of a slave cemetery in 1997 further underscores the brutality of slavery, with many interred individuals showing signs of severe physical strain and malnutrition. The presence of lesions on the bones of many enslaved individuals suggests

[17] "Diary of Bennett H. Barrow, Louisiana Slave Owner," Louisiana State University Libraries, Special Collections.

[18] "Born in Slavery: Slave Narratives from the Federal Writers' Project, 1936 to 1938," Library of Congress.

that their labor was so intense that it caused lasting physical harm[19].

The comparison between enslaved individuals and industrial workers, as articulated by figures like Noam Chomsky, is misleading and ignores the fundamental inhumanity of slavery[20]. While industrial workers undoubtedly faced exploitation and harsh conditions, they retained basic rights and freedoms denied to enslaved people, such as the ability to leave their employment, to seek legal redress for grievances, and to maintain some semblance of family integrity.

Furthermore, the notion that slaves were rarely killed by labor because of their economic value to slave owners fails to account for the disposability of human life within the institution of slavery. For many slave owners, the financial ability to own slaves was indicative of sufficient wealth to absorb the loss of human assets[21]. This perspective rendered enslaved people expendable in the pursuit of economic gain, with their lives and well-being deemed secondary to the profits they could generate.

The myth of benevolent slave ownership and the purported rarity of death by labor among enslaved people are deeply flawed and ignore the overwhelming historical evidence of systemic abuse and exploitation. The brutal reality of slavery, characterized by daily violence, poor living conditions, and intense physical labor, reveals a system designed to dehumanize and commodify Black individuals for economic gain. Acknowledging the true

19 Mark R. Schleifstein, "Slave Cemetery Unearthed," The Times-Picayune, October 26, 1997.

20 Noam Chomsky, "Understanding Power: The Indispensable Chomsky," (New York: The New Press, 2002).

21 Edward E. Baptist, "The Half Has Never Been Told: Slavery and the Making of American Capitalism," (New York: Basic Books, 2014).

nature of slavery is essential for understanding the historical context of racial inequality and the long-lasting impacts of this inhumane institution on American society.

The Myth of Black Domination in Post-Civil War Southern Governments

The narrative that freed slaves took control of Southern governments after the American Civil War and governed with such incompetence or malevolence that they had to be forcefully removed from office is a potent example of revisionist history. This myth, propagated for decades, particularly in the South, served as a justification for disenfranchising Black Americans and implementing Jim Crow laws. The 1915 film *The Birth of a Nation* dramatically exemplified this falsehood, portraying African American legislators as inept and corrupt, thus fueling racial stereotypes and supporting the agenda of white supremacy[22].

The reality of the post-Civil War Reconstruction era was markedly different from the narrative of Black domination. While it is true that African Americans gained the right to vote and were elected to public office, their representation was far from overwhelming. South Carolina, where African Americans briefly held a legislative majority, was the exception rather than the rule. In Mississippi, for example, African American legislators never comprised more than approximately 17% of the elected officials, far from a controlling majority[23]. The participation of African Americans in government during this period represented a

[22] "The Birth of a Nation and Its Legacy," NAACP, February 8, 2015.
[23] Eric Foner, "Reconstruction: America's Unfinished Revolution, 1863-1877," (New York: Harper & Row, 1988).

significant step towards democracy and equality, not the calamity depicted by revisionist histories.

Moreover, the period known as Radical Reconstruction was not characterized by the misrule of Black legislators but by the implementation of progressive reforms, including the establishment of the South's first state-funded public school systems and significant improvements in infrastructure. These African American legislators, often allied with white Republicans, sought to rebuild the South and integrate freed slaves into society as full citizens[24].

The myth of Black domination and misrule was used to obscure a far more sinister reality: the widespread campaign of terror against African Americans and their allies by white supremacists. In Louisiana alone, the year 1868 saw over a thousand people murdered for exercising their rights or supporting the Republican party, with the aim of restoring white Democratic control over the South[25]. This violence was not the action of a society under the poor governance of former slaves but a deliberate and systematic attempt to undermine Reconstruction and maintain white supremacy.

The enduring belief in the myth of Black control and incompetence in post-Civil War Southern governments is a testament to the power of revisionist history to shape perceptions and justify discriminatory policies. The truth of the matter is that African American participation in government during Reconstruction was a brief moment of progress that was violently suppressed by those unwilling to accept the ideals of equality and democracy.

The narrative that freed slaves took control of Southern governments and governed poorly is a deeply ingrained lie

[24] Steven Hahn, "A Nation Under Our Feet: Black Political Struggles in the Rural South from Slavery to the Great Migration," (Cambridge: Harvard University Press, 2003).

[25] Nicholas Lemann, "Redemption: The Last Battle of the Civil War," (New York: Farrar, Straus and Giroux, 2006).

that served to disenfranchise African Americans and legitimize white supremacy. The real story of Reconstruction is one of African American achievement in the face of relentless opposition and terror, a story that challenges the myths of the past and calls for a more honest reckoning with American history.

Slaves Were Only Owned by the Wealthiest

The assertion that only the wealthiest could afford slaves, thereby suggesting that the average Southern soldier did not have a vested interest in the institution of slavery, is a revisionist narrative that oversimplifies the complex motivations behind the Confederate cause in the American Civil War. This narrative seeks to distance the common soldier from the institution of slavery, framing the war as a fight for states' rights rather than the preservation of slavery. However, historical evidence suggests that the connection between Southern soldiers and slavery was more significant than mere economic ability to own slaves.

While it is true that the average price of a slave in 1860 was around $800, making direct ownership financially out of reach for many[26], this economic barrier does not fully capture the societal and familial connections to slavery that many soldiers had. Research indicates that one in ten soldiers owned slaves directly. Moreover, an additional twenty-five percent of Confederate soldiers came from slave-owning households, highlighting the widespread nature of slave ownership within the social fabric of the

26 "The Price of Slavery," Economic History Association.

South[27]. This context provided a direct or indirect economic stake in the institution of slavery for a significant portion of the Confederate army.

The officer class within the Confederate army further illustrates the link between military leadership and slave ownership, with half of the officers being slave owners[28]. This high rate of slave ownership among officers—who played a crucial role in shaping military strategy and morale—underscores the centrality of slavery to the Confederate cause. Additionally, aspirations of slave ownership, employment in slave-driven economies, and ideological support for slavery permeated Southern society, influencing the motivations of soldiers who may not have owned slaves themselves.

The argument that the Civil War was fought solely for states' rights neglects the integral role that slavery played in the economic, social, and political landscape of the antebellum South. The Declarations of Secession from several Southern states explicitly cite the preservation of slavery as a primary reason for secession, revealing the institutional commitment to slavery[29]. The widespread support for slavery among Confederate soldiers—whether through direct ownership, family connections, or economic and societal aspirations—challenges the narrative that slavery was a marginal issue for the average Southern soldier.

Furthermore, the notion that soldiers fought only for states' rights without regard to the issue of slavery ignores the broader context in which states' rights were invoked—

27 James M. McPherson, "Battle Cry of Freedom: The Civil War Era," (New York: Oxford University Press, 1988).

28 Joseph T. Glatthaar, "General Lee's Army: From Victory to Collapse," (New York: Free Press, 2008).

29 "Declarations of the Causes of Secession," University of Houston Digital History.

primarily in defense of the right to maintain and expand the institution of slavery[30]. This revisionist perspective diminishes the historical reality that slavery was a foundational element of the Confederate cause and that the defense of slavery was a unifying and motivating factor for many who fought for the Confederacy.

The claim that slaves were only owned by the wealthiest, and therefore the average Southern soldier did not fight to defend slavery, is a misleading simplification of the complex motivations behind the Confederate cause. The evidence suggests a much more profound connection between Southern soldiers and the institution of slavery, indicating that the preservation of slavery was indeed a central issue for many who fought for the Confederacy.

Even if the South Won the Civil War, Slavery Would Have Ended Shortly After

The assertion that slavery would have naturally concluded shortly after the Civil War, even if the South had emerged victorious, is a speculative narrative often used to diminish the centrality of slavery to the conflict. This argument suggests that international pressure and technological advancements would have rendered slavery obsolete. However, such claims overlook the economic foundations of slavery in the Southern states and the entrenched societal structures supporting it. Historical evidence and economic data from the period indicate that slavery was not merely surviving but thriving at the onset of the Civil War.

30 Charles B. Dew, "Apostles of Disunion: Southern Secession Commissioners and the Causes of the Civil War," (Charlottesville: University of Virginia Press, 2001).

Slavery's profitability was a critical pillar of the Southern economy, with investments in enslaved people yielding substantial returns. An average slave owner could anticipate a 100% return on investment within a decade, making each enslaved individual a source of significant and sustained profit[31]. This economic reality underpinned the Southern commitment to preserving and expanding the institution of slavery, challenging the notion that slavery was on the brink of obsolescence.

The argument that international pressure would have led to the abolition of slavery in a victorious Confederate States overlooks the determination of the Confederacy to maintain and protect its slave-based economy. The Confederacy sought international recognition and support based on its economic value as a supplier of cotton, a commodity deeply entwined with slave labor. The willingness of some countries to engage with the Confederacy, despite the international move towards abolition, underscores the economic incentives that could have sustained slavery in the absence of Union victory[32].

Furthermore, the comparison to Nazi Germany's use of slave labor during World War II and the persistence of forced labor in some contemporary societies illustrates the capacity of states and societies to rationalize and profit from forced labor under various guises[33]. These examples highlight the adaptability of systems of exploitation to different historical and technological contexts, countering

[31] James M. McPherson, "Battle Cry of Freedom: The Civil War Era," (New York: Oxford University Press, 1988).

[32] Charles B. Dew, "Apostles of Disunion: Southern Secession Commissioners and the Causes of the Civil War," (Charlottesville: University of Virginia Press, 2001).

[33] "The Economics of Slavery," The Gilder Lehrman Institute of American History.

the argument that advancements in technology would have naturally led to the end of slavery in the South.

The speculation that slavery would have ended on its own also fails to account for the social and political structures that supported slavery in the Southern states. The institution of slavery was entrenched in the Southern way of life, supported by laws, culture, and political power. The Confederate states' secession and the ensuing Civil War were driven by the desire to protect this institution, which they viewed as essential to their economic and social order[34].

The narrative that slavery would have soon become obsolete, even if the South had won the Civil War, is a revisionist oversimplification that ignores the complex realities of slavery's economic profitability, societal entrenchment, and the Confederacy's dedication to its preservation. The Civil War was fundamentally a conflict over the future of slavery in America, and its outcome was crucial in determining the institution's fate. Recognizing the centrality of slavery to the Civil War is essential for understanding the conflict and its lasting impact on American society.

The First Slaves in America Were White People

The assertion that "the first slaves in America were white people" is a misleading simplification that aims to downplay the unique atrocities faced by African slaves in the United States. While it is true that many Irish and other European immigrants arrived in America under conditions of indentured servitude, equating this with the slavery experienced by Africans and their descendants is

[34] Eric Foner, "The Fiery Trial: Abraham Lincoln and American Slavery," (New York: W. W. Norton & Company, 2010).

historically inaccurate and undermines the systemic nature of racialized slavery.

Indentured servitude, while exploitative and often harsh, was fundamentally different from chattel slavery in several key aspects. Indentured servants entered into contracts voluntarily, for a specified period, usually to pay off a debt or in exchange for passage to the Americas. Though conditions could be severe, indentured servants retained legal rights and their servitude was not inheritable—their children were not born into servitude[35]. Upon completion of their contract, indentured servants were often granted "freedom dues," which might include land, money, or goods to help them start their new life as free individuals[36].

In stark contrast, African slaves were forcibly transported to the Americas, stripped of their rights, and treated as property under the law. Slavery was a permanent condition, passed down from one generation to the next, with enslaved people having no legal avenue to challenge their bondage. The institutionalization of chattel slavery created a racial caste system that dehumanized Black individuals, denying them the most basic human rights and subjecting them to systemic violence and oppression[37].

The argument that Irish or other white indentured servants were "slaves" similarly to African slaves not only overlooks these critical differences but also attempts to create a false equivalence that obscures the racial foundations of American slavery. The narrative serves to minimize the suffering of African slaves and the enduring legacy of racial discrimination stemming from slavery.

[35] David Galenson, "White Servitude in Colonial America: An Economic Analysis," Cambridge University Press, 1981.

[36] "Indentured Servitude in the Colonial U.S.," Encyclopedia Virginia.

[37] Ira Berlin, "Many Thousands Gone: The First Two Centuries of Slavery in North America," Harvard University Press, 1998.

Historians have extensively documented the brutal realities of chattel slavery, including the systematic separation of families, the denial of education, and the use of violence as a means of control[38]. These practices were not incidental but were codified in laws that explicitly devalued Black lives and legitimized their exploitation. The attempt to compare indentured servitude to this system of oppression is not supported by historical evidence and detracts from the specific racial injustices that underpinned slavery in America.

Furthermore, the notion that acknowledging the horrors of African slavery somehow diminishes the experiences of indentured servants is a false dichotomy. It is possible—and necessary—to recognize the complexities of history, including the exploitation of various groups, without resorting to misleading comparisons that serve contemporary political agendas rather than fostering a genuine understanding of the past[39].

The claim that "the first slaves in America were white people" is a revisionist lie that fails to acknowledge the fundamental differences between indentured servitude and chattel slavery. By understanding these distinctions, we can better appreciate the unique and horrific nature of slavery in America and its lasting impact on African American communities and on the fabric of American society.

Slavery was a Southern Problem

[38] Edward E. Baptist, "The Half Has Never Been Told: Slavery and the Making of American Capitalism," Basic Books, 2014.

[39] Leslie M. Harris, "In the Shadow of Slavery: African Americans in New York City, 1626-1863," University of Chicago Press, 2003.

The portrayal of slavery as a predominantly Southern issue is a pervasive misconception that overlooks the complex reality of the institution's national impact and the complicity of Northern states in perpetuating it. This revisionist perspective not only distorts the historical record but also absolves the North of its significant role in the slave trade and the maintenance of slavery within its own borders. A thorough examination of historical facts reveals that the North was actively involved in the slave economy, both directly and indirectly, challenging the narrative of a morally superior North unequivocally opposed to the institution of slavery.

The involvement of Northern states in the transatlantic slave trade is a stark illustration of the region's complicity in slavery. Many of the ships that transported enslaved Africans to the Americas as part of the infamous Triangle Trade were based in New England ports, and this involvement continued even after the practice was formally banned in the region[40]. This maritime activity was not merely a peripheral aspect of the Northern economy but a central component of its commercial success, deeply entwined with the broader Atlantic slave economy.

Furthermore, the legal status of slavery in the North complicates the simplistic narrative of the region as a bastion of freedom. While Northern states began to pass gradual emancipation laws in the late 18th and early 19th centuries, these laws often contained provisions that allowed slavery to persist. In Pennsylvania, for example, the Gradual Abolition Act of 1780 did not immediately free enslaved individuals but rather set conditions for gradual emancipation, which permitted the continuation of slavery

[40] "Slavery and the Slave Trade in Rhode Island," Rhode Island Historical Society.

well into the 19th century[41]. As late as 1850, there were still individuals classified as slaves in Pennsylvania under this act, demonstrating that the legacy of slavery in the North was more enduring than commonly acknowledged[42].

The economic ties between the North and South further underscore the national character of the slavery issue. Northern industries and financial institutions profited from slavery, investing in Southern plantations, insuring slave property, and participating in the cotton trade, which was dependent on slave labor[43]. These economic interests made the North a beneficiary of slavery, even as some of its residents and leaders voiced opposition to the institution.

The myth of slavery as a purely Southern problem serves to obscure the shared responsibility for the institution across the United States. Acknowledging the North's involvement in slavery is not an attempt to equate the experiences of the North and South but rather to recognize the national scope of slavery and the collective moral and historical accountability it entails.

The narrative that frames slavery as solely a Southern issue fails to capture the complex realities of American history. The involvement of Northern states in the slave trade, the gradual and incomplete nature of emancipation laws, and the economic benefits derived from slavery all point to a national complicity in the institution. A more nuanced understanding of slavery's history challenges us to confront the uncomfortable truths about America's past and the legacy of slavery that continues to shape the nation.

41 "An Act for the Gradual Abolition of Slavery, Pennsylvania, 1780," Pennsylvania Historical & Museum Commission.

42 "Census Data, 1850," United States Census Bureau.

43 Calvin Schermerhorn, "The Business of Slavery and the Rise of American Capitalism, 1815-1860," (New Haven: Yale University Press, 2015).

Slavery is Illegal in America

The belief that slavery was completely abolished in the United States over 150 years ago with the ratification of the 13th Amendment is a pervasive narrative. However, this narrative omits a critical caveat within the amendment itself that permits an exception to the ban on slavery: forced labor as a punishment for crime. This loophole has perpetuated a form of slavery within the American penal system, challenging the notion that slavery is a relic of the past.

The 13th Amendment, celebrated for outlawing slavery, states, "Neither slavery nor involuntary servitude, except as a punishment for crime whereof the party shall have been duly convicted, shall exist within the United States, or any place subject to their jurisdiction."[44] This exception has been exploited to subject incarcerated individuals to forced labor, often without fair compensation or under coercive conditions. Ava DuVernay's documentary, *13th*, illuminates how this clause has facilitated a continuation of slavery under the guise of criminal justice, with a disproportionate impact on African American communities due to systemic racial biases in law enforcement and sentencing[45].

The phenomenon of convict leasing in the late 19th and early 20th centuries exemplifies how this loophole was historically exploited, with African Americans arrested under dubious charges and leased to private enterprises for labor[46]. Although chattel slavery was officially condemned

44 "The Constitution of the United States," Amendment XIII.

45 Ava DuVernay, 13th, Netflix, 2016.

46 Douglas A. Blackmon, Slavery by Another Name: The Re-Enslavement of Black Americans from the Civil War to World War II, Anchor Books, 2008.

by Franklin Roosevelt in the 1940s, the practice of exploiting incarcerated labor persists in various forms today. As recently as 2017, Sheriff Thomas Hodgson in Massachusetts proposed using inmate labor to build the border wall with Mexico, a contemporary manifestation of how the 13th Amendment's exception can be applied[47].

The United States holds the dubious distinction of having the highest incarceration rate in the world, with 25% of the world's prisoners[48]. This significant incarcerated population, coupled with the legal framework that permits their exploitation for labor, raises profound ethical and human rights concerns. The reliance on incarcerated labor for manufacturing goods, fighting wildfires, and other tasks often with minimal or no compensation, underscores a modern form of slavery that contradicts the widely held belief in its abolition.

Critics may argue that work programs for inmates serve as rehabilitation and provide skills for reentry into society. However, when participation is not truly voluntary, when compensation is negligible or non-existent, and when the conditions replicate those of involuntary servitude, the distinction between rehabilitation and exploitation blurs.

In conclusion, the narrative that slavery was fully eradicated in America with the 13th Amendment overlooks the amendment's own exception for penal labor. This legal loophole has allowed for the continuation of practices that bear striking resemblance to historical slavery, albeit within the confines of the penal system. Recognizing and addressing this continuation of slavery is crucial for a truthful reckoning with America's past and present. The challenge lies in transforming the criminal justice system to

47 "Sheriff Offers Inmates as 'Labor Pool' for Trump's Mexico Wall," NBC News, January 5, 2017.

48 "World Prison Population List," Institute for Criminal Policy Research, 11th edition.

ensure it upholds the principles of fairness and human dignity, rather than perpetuating the legacy of slavery.

The Conservatism Conundrum And Preserving White Life and Status Amidst Anti-Black Sentiment — Chapter 9

Formation of the Tea Party Movement Post-Obama's Election:

In the wake of Barack Obama's historic ascension to the presidency of the United States as the first African American to hold the office, the Tea Party movement surged to prominence. This period marked a significant pivot in American political discourse, symbolizing more than just a shift towards fiscal conservatism and the advocacy for limited government. Rather, the emergence of the Tea Party can be interpreted as a reactionary stance against the perceived erosion of traditional white hegemony in the face of increasing racial diversity within the political arena[1].

[1] Hughey, Matthew W., and Gregory S. Parks. "The Wrath of the Ancestors: Analyzing the Tea Party Movement." Sociology of Race and Ethnicity, vol. 1, no. 1, 2015, pp. 75-88.

The formation of the Tea Party movement post-Obama's election was not an isolated phenomenon but a manifestation of deeper racial undercurrents within American society. Although publicly rallying around themes of fiscal responsibility and governmental restraint, the movement's undertones frequently betrayed a racially charged rhetoric. This rhetoric, often couched in the language of patriotism and American exceptionalism, thinly veiled an implicit desire to protect white status and privilege against the advancements made by minorities, particularly African Americans[2].

Critics of the Tea Party movement argue that its birth and rapid growth were significantly fueled by anti-Black sentiment, pointing to the timing of its emergence immediately following the election of a Black president. This perspective suggests that the movement's stated objectives of fiscal conservatism are at least partially a facade for the protection of white privilege and status quo. Supporters, however, vehemently deny these accusations, asserting that their concerns are purely economic and constitutional in nature, devoid of racial bias or intentions[3].

The opposing viewpoints surrounding the Tea Party movement highlight the complex interplay between race, politics, and identity in the United States. On one hand, there exists a group that views the movement as a necessary pushback against governmental overreach and fiscal irresponsibility. On the other hand, a significant portion of the population perceives it as a reactionary and racially

2 Skocpol, Theda, and Vanessa Williamson. The Tea Party and the Remaking of Republican Conservatism. Oxford University Press, 2012.

3 Williamson, Vanessa, Theda Skocpol, and John Coggin. "The Tea Party and the Remaking of Republican Conservatism." Perspectives on Politics, vol. 9, no. 1, 2011, pp. 25-43.

motivated effort to undermine the progress and representation of minorities in the political sphere[4].

This dichotomy reflects broader societal tensions over race and identity politics, with the Tea Party movement serving as a microcosm of the struggle between advancing racial equality and preserving traditional power structures. The movement's impact on American politics and its role in catalyzing a more polarized and racially charged political landscape cannot be understated. It has influenced policy, shaped public discourse, and highlighted the persistent racial divisions within the country[5].

In analyzing the Tea Party movement and its implications for race relations in the United States, it becomes clear that conservatism, as espoused by the movement, often serves as a euphemism for the protection of white life and status. This form of conservatism, while advocating for smaller government and fiscal prudence, cannot be fully disentangled from the racial anxieties and sentiments that underpin it. The challenge, then, is to confront these undercurrents openly and to work towards a form of political engagement that transcends racial divisions rather than exacerbating them[6].

Strict Immigration Laws and Policies

4 Parker, Christopher S., and Matt A. Barreto. Change They Can't Believe In: The Tea Party and Reactionary Politics in America. Princeton University Press, 2013.

5 Abramowitz, Alan I. The Great Alignment: Race, Party Transformation, and the Rise of Donald Trump. Yale University Press, 2018.

6 Lowndes, Joseph. From the New Deal to the New Right: Race and the Southern Origins of Modern Conservatism. Yale University Press, 2008.

In the contemporary political landscape, the advocacy for strict immigration laws and heightened border security, especially under conservative administrations, unveils a deeper narrative beyond the surface level discourse of national security and economic concerns. This strategic push towards stringent immigration control measures illuminates an underlying motive aimed at preserving the white demographic majority within the United States. Policies that have led to family separations at the border and the implementation of travel bans from predominantly Muslim countries stand as testament to an effort to protect white dominance, albeit under the pretext of safeguarding national interests[7].

The enactment of policies that disproportionately impact non-white immigrants can be perceived as a tactical maneuver to maintain the status quo of white privilege. By restricting the influx of individuals from countries with predominantly non-white populations, these policies implicitly serve the interests of demographic engineering, favoring the preservation of a white majority. This approach not only reflects a deep-seated anti-Black sentiment but also encompasses a broader spectrum of racial prejudice, extending its reach to various ethnic and religious minorities[8].

Opponents of this viewpoint argue that the enforcement of strict immigration policies is a necessary measure to uphold the sovereignty of the nation, ensuring its security and economic stability. They contend that these measures are not racially motivated but are essential for regulating the flow of immigrants and protecting citizens from potential threats. This perspective underscores a fundamental clash

7 Huntington, Samuel P. Who Are We? The Challenges to America's National Identity. Simon & Schuster, 2004.

8 Chavez, Leo. The Latino Threat: Constructing Immigrants, Citizens, and the Nation. Stanford University Press, 2013.

between national security priorities and the principles of racial equality and human rights[9].

Critics, however, highlight the racial bias inherent in these policies, pointing to the historical context of immigration laws in the United States, which have often been influenced by racial and ethnic prejudices. The selective targeting of countries and the harsh treatment of asylum seekers and refugees underscore a pattern of discrimination that aligns with the broader agenda of preserving white hegemony. These actions raise significant ethical and moral questions about the values that underpin immigration policy and the implications for the nation's identity as a melting pot of diversity[10].

The debate over immigration laws and policies thus encapsulates a broader conflict between two visions of America: one that seeks to maintain its historical white majority and another that embraces the demographic changes ushering in a more diverse and inclusive society. This dichotomy reflects the tension at the heart of American conservatism, torn between a commitment to traditional values and the need to adapt to a rapidly changing global landscape[11].

In conclusion, the push for strict immigration laws and policies under conservative administrations reveals a complex interplay between national security concerns and the underlying motives of preserving white demographic dominance. This strategy, while justified by its proponents

[9] Hainmueller, Jens, and Daniel J. Hopkins. "The Hidden American Immigration Consensus: A Conjoint Analysis of Attitudes toward Immigrants." American Journal of Political Science, vol. 59, no. 3, 2015, pp. 529-548.

[10] Ngai, Mae M. Impossible Subjects: Illegal Aliens and the Making of Modern America. Princeton University Press, 2004.

[11] Sides, John, Michael Tesler, and Lynn Vavreck. Identity Crisis: The 2016 Presidential Campaign and the Battle for the Meaning of America. Princeton University Press, 2018.

on the grounds of national interest, raises profound questions about the inclusivity and equity of American society. As the nation navigates these challenges, it stands at a crossroads, deciding the path it will take towards either reinforcing historical racial hierarchies or moving forward into a more inclusive future[12].

Economic Policies Favoring the Wealthy

Within the framework of contemporary conservatism, economic policies play a pivotal role in delineating the contours of power and privilege. The advocacy for tax cuts that disproportionately benefit the wealthiest individuals in society, who are predominantly white, coupled with concerted efforts to dismantle social safety nets, lays bare an underlying commitment to maintaining economic disparities. These disparities have historically advantaged white Americans, ensuring that the economic power structure remains largely unchanged and thereby safeguarding the white status quo[13].

This deliberate orchestration of economic policies is not merely a reflection of ideological adherence to fiscal conservatism but a strategic endeavor to preserve racial hierarchies. By channeling greater financial resources towards the already affluent, these policies exacerbate wealth inequality and ensure the perpetuation of economic

12 Higham, John. Strangers in the Land: Patterns of American Nativism, 1860-1925. Rutgers University Press, 1955.

13 Piketty, Thomas. Capital in the Twenty-First Century. Harvard University Press, 2014.

conditions that disproportionately disadvantage minority communities, particularly African Americans[14].

Critics argue that such economic maneuvers are designed to reinforce systemic barriers to wealth accumulation for non-white populations, effectively perpetuating cycles of poverty and economic disenfranchisement. The dismantling of social safety nets, including healthcare, education, and welfare programs, further compounds these disparities, making it increasingly difficult for minority communities to achieve economic mobility[15].

Opponents of this perspective maintain that the goal of these economic policies is to stimulate growth and prosperity for all, irrespective of race. They argue that tax cuts and the reduction of government intervention in the economy serve to enhance individual freedoms and encourage entrepreneurial ventures, thereby benefiting society as a whole. This viewpoint underscores a fundamental divide in the interpretation of fiscal policies and their implications for racial and economic equality[16].

However, the data and real-world outcomes of these policies paint a starkly different picture. Studies have consistently shown that the benefits of tax cuts for the wealthy are not equitably distributed, with the lion's share of advantages accruing to the top echelons of income earners, who are disproportionately white. Furthermore, the erosion of social safety nets has been shown to have devastating effects on minority communities, exacerbating existing

[14] Coates, Ta-Nehisi. "The Case for Reparations." The Atlantic, June 2014.

[15] Gilens, Martin. Why Americans Hate Welfare: Race, Media, and the Politics of Antipoverty Policy. University of Chicago Press, 1999.

[16] Sowell, Thomas. Wealth, Poverty and Politics: An International Perspective. Basic Books, 2015.

inequalities and hindering efforts towards achieving a more equitable society[17].

The debate over these economic policies thus becomes a microcosm of a larger struggle over the future direction of American society. On one side stands a vision that seeks to maintain and reinforce existing power structures, rooted in racial and economic hierarchies. On the other side is a call for a transformative approach to governance and policy-making, one that prioritizes equity, inclusivity, and the dismantling of systemic barriers to equality[18].

In sum, the economic strategies championed by contemporary conservative leaders reveal a nuanced approach to preserving the white status quo. While cloaked in the language of fiscal responsibility and economic freedom, these policies effectively serve to maintain racial and economic disparities. As America grapples with these challenges, the path forward demands a critical reevaluation of the values and priorities that shape policy decisions, with an eye towards fostering a society that truly values and uplifts all its members[19].

Opposition to Affirmative Action and Voting Rights Act

The conservative opposition to affirmative action and the efforts to roll back provisions of the Voting Rights Act

17 Zucman, Gabriel, and Emmanuel Saez. "The Triumph of Injustice: How the Rich Dodge Taxes and How to Make Them Pay." The New York Times, October 2019.

18 Anderson, Carol. White Rage: The Unspoken Truth of Our Racial Divide. Bloomsbury USA, 2016.

19 Katznelson, Ira. When Affirmative Action Was White: An Untold History of Racial Inequality in Twentieth-Century America. W. W. Norton & Company, 2005.

serve as poignant illustrations of a broader agenda aimed at preserving systemic racial inequalities. Such opposition not only highlights a commitment to maintaining an educational and political status quo that privileges white Americans but also underscores an indirect support for institutional barriers that limit opportunities for minorities. This stance effectively reinforces a racial hierarchy deeply ingrained in the fabric of American society[20].

Affirmative action policies, originally designed to address historical injustices and to promote diversity in educational and professional settings, have long been a point of contention. Conservative critics argue that these policies result in reverse discrimination, unfairly disadvantaging white individuals in favor of less qualified minority candidates. This viewpoint, however, overlooks the essential purpose of affirmative action: to level the playing field in a society where racial disparities in education and employment persist due to systemic discrimination and socioeconomic barriers[21].

Similarly, conservative efforts to undermine the Voting Rights Act through the imposition of stringent voter ID laws, purging of voter rolls, and other tactics designed to suppress minority turnout, reveal a strategic endeavor to limit political participation among communities of color. Proponents justify these actions as necessary measures to combat voter fraud, despite evidence indicating that such fraud is exceedingly rare. The effect of these policies is to disenfranchise minority voters, thereby maintaining a

[20] Anderson, Carol. White Rage: The Unspoken Truth of Our Racial Divide. Bloomsbury USA, 2016.

[21] Guinier, Lani. The Tyranny of the Meritocracy: Democratizing Higher Education in America. Beacon Press, 2015.

political landscape that is less representative of America's diverse population[22].

The opposition to these measures by conservative factions suggests a reluctance to confront the legacy of racial discrimination and to embrace the necessary steps towards achieving racial equity. By challenging affirmative action and the Voting Rights Act, conservatism indirectly advocates for the perpetuation of a societal structure that has historically advantaged white Americans at the expense of minorities[23].

Critics of this conservative stance highlight the irony of advocating for a "colorblind" society while simultaneously opposing policies designed to address the very disparities that colorblindness ignores. The failure to acknowledge the systemic nature of racial inequality effectively perpetuates those inequalities, ensuring that the barriers to equal opportunity remain intact[24].

Furthermore, the debate over affirmative action and voting rights reflects a broader ideological divide over the role of government in rectifying historical injustices. Where conservatives often prioritize individual merit and a minimal role for government intervention, progressives argue for proactive measures to dismantle systemic barriers and to promote equity[25].

In conclusion, the conservative opposition to affirmative action and attempts to erode the protections of the Voting Rights Act signal an overarching strategy to maintain racial hierarchies within American society. By

22 Berman, Ari. Give Us the Ballot: The Modern Struggle for Voting Rights in America. Farrar, Straus and Giroux, 2015.

23 Alexander, Michelle. The New Jim Crow: Mass Incarceration in the Age of Colorblindness. The New Press, 2012.

24 Bonilla-Silva, Eduardo. Racism without Racists: Color-Blind Racism and the Persistence of Racial Inequality in the United States. Rowman & Littlefield, 2017.

25 Kendi, Ibram X. How to Be an Antiracist. One World, 2019.

limiting opportunities for minority populations in education and the political process, these efforts serve to reinforce institutional barriers that have long privileged white Americans. As the nation continues to grapple with its racial divides, the path forward requires a reevaluation of the policies and principles that govern our approach to equality and justice[26].

Denial of Systemic Racism and Opposition to Critical Race Theory

In an era marked by increasing calls for social justice and racial equity, the conservative movement's staunch denial of systemic racism, along with its vociferous opposition to critical race theory (CRT) and diversity training, represents a deliberate attempt to obscure the historical and persistent injustices faced by non-white populations. This posture is not merely a difference in ideological or academic viewpoints; it is a strategic effort to maintain the status quo, where acknowledging systemic racism would necessitate a comprehensive reassessment and restructuring of policies that have long perpetuated racial disparities[27].

The conservative rebuttal to the concept of systemic racism argues that America's societal structures do not inherently disadvantage people of color, positing instead that individual choices and behaviors are the primary determinants of one's socio-economic standing. This perspective conveniently overlooks the extensive body of research and historical evidence demonstrating how policies,

[26] Coates, Ta-Nehisi. "The Case for Reparations." The Atlantic, June 2014.

[27] Bell, Derrick. Faces at the Bottom of the Well: The Permanence of Racism. Basic Books, 1992.

practices, and legal frameworks have systematically marginalized non-white communities[28].

Critical race theory, a scholarly framework that examines the intersection of race and law to understand how systemic racism is embedded within the fabric of American society, has become a particular target of conservative critique. Opponents of CRT argue that it promotes a divisive and negative view of American history and institutions, fostering a sense of grievance among minority populations rather than encouraging unity and shared national identity[29].

This opposition extends to diversity training programs, which are often criticized by conservative leaders as being anti-American or racially biased against white people. Such criticisms reflect a broader resistance to efforts aimed at increasing awareness of racial biases and promoting inclusivity within workplaces and educational institutions. By challenging these initiatives, conservatism effectively negates the need for policies and practices that seek to address and ameliorate racial disparities, thereby safeguarding a societal hierarchy that privileges white Americans[30].

The denial of systemic racism and the resistance to critical race theory and diversity training can be understood as components of a larger conservative strategy to resist any changes that might threaten the existing racial and socio-economic order. This strategy includes not only the rejection of scholarly and pedagogical efforts to confront racial injustice but also legislative efforts to restrict the

[28] Alexander, Michelle. The New Jim Crow: Mass Incarceration in the Age of Colorblindness. The New Press, 2010.

[29] Delgado, Richard, and Jean Stefancic. Critical Race Theory: An Introduction. New York University Press, 2017.

[30] DiAngelo, Robin. White Fragility: Why It's So Hard for White People to Talk About Racism. Beacon Press, 2018.

teaching of CRT and related concepts in schools and government institutions[31].

Critics argue that this stance not only perpetuates misinformation but also hinders the nation's progress toward racial reconciliation and justice. By denying the pervasive impact of systemic racism, conservative leaders prevent a meaningful dialogue on how to address these issues, thereby maintaining a status quo that disproportionately harms non-white Americans[32].

In conclusion, the conservative movement's denial of systemic racism and opposition to critical race theory and diversity training represent an attempt to preserve a social order that favors white Americans. This stance, rooted in a selective interpretation of history and a narrow understanding of racism, obstructs efforts to achieve a more equitable and just society. As America grapples with its racial divides, the acknowledgment of systemic injustices and the willingness to address them will be crucial steps toward healing and progress[33].

The "Law and Order" Facade And Conservative Rhetoric and Its Impact on Communities of Color

The conservative emphasis on a "law and order" narrative, particularly in response to protests against racial injustice, functions as a potent instrument for criminalizing Black and minority activism. By portraying such activism as a threat to

[31] Crenshaw, Kimberlé. "Critical Race Theory: The Key Writings That Formed the Movement". The New Press, 1995.

[32] Kendi, Ibram X. How to Be an Antiracist. One World, 2019.

[33] Coates, Ta-Nehisi. "The Case for Reparations." The Atlantic, June 2014.

public safety and the societal status quo, this rhetoric provides a veneer of legitimacy to aggressive policing tactics that disproportionately affect communities of color. This approach not only seeks to maintain the white status quo but also attempts to silence voices calling for systemic change and racial equity[34].

This "law and order" narrative is deeply rooted in the American political discourse, finding renewed vigor within conservative circles as a response to the growing visibility of movements such as Black Lives Matter. These movements, which seek to address systemic racism and police brutality, are often misrepresented in conservative rhetoric as sources of chaos and disorder. Such misrepresentation serves to justify the implementation of more stringent policing measures, including the militarization of police forces and the use of excessive force[35].

Critics argue that the conservative promotion of "law and order" overlooks the foundational causes of protests against racial injustice, namely the long-standing grievances of systemic racism, police brutality, and racial inequality in the criminal justice system. By focusing on the symptom (public protests) rather than the disease (systemic racism), conservative rhetoric effectively diverts attention from the necessary reforms needed to address these deep-rooted issues[36].

Furthermore, the "law and order" narrative often employs coded language that targets communities of color,

[34] Alexander, Michelle. The New Jim Crow: Mass Incarceration in the Age of Colorblindness. The New Press, 2010.

[35] Hinton, Elizabeth. From the War on Poverty to the War on Crime: The Making of Mass Incarceration in America. Harvard University Press, 2016.

[36] Coates, Ta-Nehisi. "The Case for Reparations." The Atlantic, June 2014.

reinforcing stereotypes that associate Blackness and minority status with criminality. This association not only perpetuates racial biases but also exacerbates the fear and mistrust between law enforcement and the communities they serve, leading to a cycle of violence and retaliation that undermines the very fabric of public safety[37].

Opponents of this narrative highlight the contradiction in calling for "law and order" while simultaneously ignoring the unlawful and disorderly conduct perpetrated by law enforcement against unarmed Black individuals. The selective application of "law and order" underscores the racial biases inherent in its enforcement, revealing a double standard in the commitment to justice and equity[38].

In contrast, advocates for social justice and racial equity argue for a reimagining of public safety that goes beyond the traditional paradigms of policing. They call for investment in community-based solutions that address the root causes of crime, such as poverty, lack of educational opportunities, and inadequate healthcare. These solutions emphasize the importance of building trust and cooperation between law enforcement and communities, rather than resorting to force and coercion[39].

In conclusion, the conservative promotion of the "law and order" narrative in response to protests against racial injustice not only criminalizes Black and minority activism but also serves to maintain systemic racial inequalities. By justifying aggressive policing tactics, this rhetoric perpetuates a cycle of violence and mistrust that undermines the pursuit of genuine public safety and racial equity. As America continues to confront its racial divisions, the

[37] Epp, Charles R., Steven Maynard-Moody, and Donald P. Haider-Markel. Pulled Over: How Police Stops Define Race and Citizenship. University of Chicago Press, 2014.

[38] Butler, Paul. Chokehold: Policing Black Men. The New Press, 2017.

[39] Vitale, Alex S. The End of Policing. Verso Books, 2017.

challenge remains to transcend these divisive narratives and work towards a more just and equitable society[40].

Conservatism and the Obstacle to Police Reform

In the contemporary political arena, the resistance among many conservative leaders and lawmakers to meaningful police reform initiatives, particularly those aimed at increasing accountability for police misconduct, stands as a significant barrier to addressing systemic injustices. This opposition not only safeguards the existing power dynamics within law enforcement agencies, which have historically targeted and marginalized Black individuals and other minorities, but also underscores a broader commitment to maintaining a status quo that privileges certain demographics over others[41].

The call for police reform has gained unprecedented momentum in the wake of high-profile incidents of police brutality and racial profiling, highlighting the urgent need for systemic changes to address the culture of impunity that often prevails within law enforcement. Proposals for reform have included a range of measures, from the implementation of body-worn cameras and the establishment of independent oversight bodies to more transformative approaches such as redefining the scope of police responsibilities and

40 Davis, Angela. Are Prisons Obsolete? Seven Stories Press, 2003.

41 Forman Jr., James. Locking Up Our Own: Crime and Punishment in Black America. Farrar, Straus and Giroux, 2017.

reallocating funding towards community-based public safety solutions[42].

However, conservative resistance to these reform efforts is often framed within the context of supporting law enforcement and upholding public safety. Critics argue that this stance, while ostensibly aimed at protecting citizens, effectively ignores the disproportionate impact of police violence and misconduct on communities of color. By dismissing or minimizing the need for reform, conservative leaders not only negate the lived experiences of those who have been adversely affected by police actions but also contribute to the perpetuation of systemic racism within the criminal justice system[43].

This resistance is further compounded by the reliance on "tough on crime" policies and rhetoric, which have historically been used to justify aggressive policing practices and the militarization of police forces. Such policies, while popular among certain segments of the electorate, have been shown to exacerbate racial disparities in policing and incarceration, contributing to the erosion of trust between law enforcement and the communities they serve[44].

Opponents of police reform within the conservative movement often cite concerns over rising crime rates and the potential for reform measures to undermine the ability of police officers to effectively carry out their duties. However, evidence suggests that strategies focused on community engagement, de-escalation training, and

[42] Ramsey, Charles, and Laurie Robinson. President's Task Force on 21st Century Policing. Office of Community Oriented Policing Services, 2015.

[43] Alexander, Michelle. The New Jim Crow: Mass Incarceration in the Age of Colorblindness. The New Press, 2010.

[44] Hinton, Elizabeth. From the War on Poverty to the War on Crime: The Making of Mass Incarceration in America. Harvard University Press, 2016.

accountability measures can enhance public safety while simultaneously addressing issues of racial bias and injustice[45].

The debate over police reform thus reflects a deeper ideological divide over the role of law enforcement in society and the extent to which systemic issues of racism and inequality should be addressed. While conservative opposition to reform initiatives seeks to preserve traditional models of policing, advocates for change argue for a reimagined approach to public safety that prioritizes the dignity and rights of all individuals, regardless of race or ethnicity[46].

In conclusion, the resistance to police reform among many conservative leaders not only hinders progress towards addressing systemic injustices but also reinforces a power structure that has historically marginalized Black individuals and other minorities. As the nation grapples with the complexities of policing and public safety, the challenge lies in overcoming ideological barriers to implement reforms that ensure accountability, transparency, and equity within law enforcement[47].

The Conservative Gamble with School Choice

The conservative advocacy for school choice and voucher programs represents a contentious pivot in the debate over public education in the United States. While proponents

45 Sered, Danielle. Until We Reckon: Violence, Mass Incarceration, and a Road to Repair. The New Press, 2019.

46 Vitale, Alex S. The End of Policing. Verso Books, 2017.

47 Davis, Angela. Are Prisons Obsolete? Seven Stories Press, 2003.

present these measures as avenues to enhance educational opportunities and parental choice, a deeper analysis reveals a potential to further entrench educational inequalities. Predominantly minority school districts, already grappling with systemic underfunding, stand to suffer the most significant impact, perpetuating a cycle of disparity that stifles social mobility and cements the racial and economic hierarchies advantageous to the white majority[48].

School choice and voucher programs are often touted as solutions to the failings of public education systems, arguing that they offer students from disadvantaged backgrounds the opportunity to attend higher-performing schools. However, critics highlight the adverse effects these programs can have on public education funding. By diverting resources away from public schools towards private and charter schools, there is a significant risk of exacerbating the resource gap between well-funded and underfunded schools. This gap disproportionately affects schools in predominantly minority districts, where resources are already stretched thin[49].

The undermining of public education through the promotion of school choice and voucher programs raises critical questions about the commitment to equality and equity within the educational landscape. The resultant educational inequality not only limits the social mobility of students from disadvantaged backgrounds but also serves to maintain existing racial and economic hierarchies. This dynamic works to the benefit of the white majority,

[48] Darling-Hammond, Linda. "Inequality in Teaching and Schooling: How Opportunity is Rationed to Students of Color in America." The Right Thing to Do, The Smart Thing to Do: Enhancing Diversity in the Health Professions, 2001.

[49] Kozol, Jonathan. Savage Inequalities: Children in America's Schools. Crown, 1991.

reinforcing systemic barriers to advancement for minority populations[50].

Opponents of school choice and voucher programs argue that a more equitable approach would involve significant investment in public education, with a focus on addressing the systemic inequalities that plague underfunded schools. Such investment would include not only increased funding but also comprehensive support services for students and families, improved teacher training, and updated educational materials and infrastructure. This approach acknowledges the importance of public education as a cornerstone of democratic society and a fundamental right for all children, irrespective of their racial or economic background[51].

The debate over school choice and voucher programs encapsulates a broader ideological clash over the role of government in providing public services and the prioritization of individual choice versus collective responsibility. While conservative leaders may frame these initiatives as efforts to improve educational outcomes, the potential consequences for public education and the perpetuation of inequality cannot be ignored[52].

The conservative push for school choice and voucher programs presents a critical challenge to the principle of equitable education for all. By potentially undermining public education and exacerbating existing disparities, these measures risk entrenching the racial and economic hierarchies that privilege the white majority at the expense

[50] Orfield, Gary, and Erica Frankenberg. "The Resegregation of Suburban Schools: A Hidden Crisis in American Education." Harvard Education Press, 2012.

[51] Ravitch, Diane. Reign of Error: The Hoax of the Privatization Movement and the Danger to America's Public Schools. Knopf, 2013.

[52] Greene, Jay P. "Education Myths: What Special Interest Groups Want You to Believe About Our Schools--And Why It Isn't So." Rowman & Littlefield Publishers, 2005.

of minority communities. Addressing educational inequality demands a recommitment to strengthening public education systems, ensuring that all students have access to the resources and opportunities necessary to achieve their full potential[53].

Gerrymandering and Voter Suppression

The manipulation of electoral boundaries and the imposition of restrictive voter ID laws represent more than mere tactics in the political playbook. These conservative strategies, deeply embedded in the efforts to gerrymander and to implement stringent voter identification requirements, disproportionately disenfranchise Black voters and other minorities. The underlying aim of these maneuvers is to perpetuate a political power structure within predominantly white, conservative constituencies, thereby skewing the political landscape in favor of white interests[54].

Gerrymandering, the deliberate manipulation of electoral district boundaries to favor one party over another, has emerged as a formidable tool in shaping electoral outcomes. This practice, while not new, has been honed with precision in the digital age, allowing for the surgical carving of districts that dilute the voting power of minority communities. Such strategic redistricting serves to entrench conservative political power by minimizing the influence of

[53] Noguera, Pedro. "Unequal Outcomes: Not Only Acceptable but Also Inevitable under Our Current Educational System." Education and the Law, 2003.

[54] Berman, Ari. Give Us the Ballot: The Modern Struggle for Voting Rights in America. Farrar, Straus and Giroux, 2015.

Black voters and other minorities, effectively silencing their voices in the electoral process[55].

Similarly, the implementation of voter ID laws under the guise of combating voter fraud further exacerbates the disenfranchisement of minority voters. Critics argue that these laws are disproportionately burdensome for Black voters, the elderly, and the economically disadvantaged, who are less likely to possess the required forms of identification. Despite the scarcity of evidence supporting widespread voter fraud, these laws persist, casting a long shadow over the integrity of the democratic process by erecting barriers to participation for those most affected by systemic inequalities[56].

Opponents of these practices point to the glaring contradiction between the professed ideals of democracy and the reality of these suppressive tactics. They argue that true democratic engagement thrives on inclusivity and the fair representation of all constituencies, not on the calculated exclusion of minority voices. The resistance to these tactics has manifested in legal challenges, public protests, and calls for federal legislation to protect voting rights and to ensure fair redistricting processes[57].

However, defenders of gerrymandering and voter ID laws maintain that these measures are necessary to preserve the integrity of elections and to prevent electoral malfeasance. This defense often overlooks the empirical evidence indicating that voter fraud is exceedingly rare and

55 Daley, David. Ratf**ked: Why Your Vote Doesn't Count. Liveright, 2016.**

56 Anderson, Carol. One Person, No Vote: How Voter Suppression Is Destroying Our Democracy. Bloomsbury Publishing, 2018.

57 Abrams, Stacey. Our Time Is Now: Power, Purpose, and the Fight for a Fair America. Henry Holt and Co., 2020.

that the impact of these laws falls disproportionately on minority communities[58].

The debate over redistricting and voter suppression tactics underscores a broader struggle for power and representation within the American political system. As conservative efforts to maintain political dominance continue, the imperative to safeguard the principles of democracy and to ensure equitable participation in the electoral process becomes increasingly urgent[59].

In conclusion, the conservative strategies of gerrymandering and implementing restrictive voter ID laws reflect a concerted effort to disenfranchise Black voters and other minorities, aiming to secure a political landscape that favors white interests. This manipulation of the democratic process not only undermines the foundational principles of equity and representation but also challenges the nation to confront the systemic barriers that inhibit true democratic engagement. As America grapples with these issues, the pursuit of a more inclusive and representative democracy remains a critical, ongoing struggle[60].

The Battle Over National Identity And Cultural Conservatism And The Resistance to Multiculturalism

58 Minnite, Lorraine C. The Myth of Voter Fraud. Cornell University Press, 2010.

59 Levitt, Justin. The Partisan Sort: How Liberals Became Democrats and Conservatives Became Republicans. University of Chicago Press, 2009.

60 Lutz, Brenda. Invisible Americans: Uncovering Why U.S. Voting Rights Are Not Universal. ABC-CLIO, 2020.

The conservative backlash against multiculturalism, bilingual education, and the acknowledgment of non-white historical contributions represents a significant chapter in the broader narrative of American identity. This cultural warfare, deeply rooted in an attempt to preserve a Eurocentric and white-dominated narrative, reflects a deliberate effort to marginalize non-white perspectives and maintain white cultural hegemony. By resisting the diversification of cultural and historical narratives, conservatism effectively seeks to define American identity within narrow, exclusionary boundaries[61].

Multiculturalism and bilingual education are often depicted by their critics as divisive forces that undermine national cohesion and dilute the essence of American culture. This perspective, however, fails to recognize the intrinsic diversity that constitutes the American experience. The conservative aversion to multiculturalism not only negates the rich blending of cultures that have shaped the nation but also reinforces a monocultural narrative that sidelines the contributions and experiences of non-white communities[62].

The struggle over the recognition of non-white historical contributions is emblematic of the larger battle for representation and visibility within the national consciousness. By opposing curricular reforms that seek to include a broader range of perspectives in educational materials, conservative forces attempt to maintain a historical narrative that privileges Eurocentric viewpoints and minimizes the legacies of colonialism, slavery, and racial exclusion[63].

61 West, Cornel. Race Matters. Beacon Press, 1993.

62 Banks, James A. Multicultural Education: Issues and Perspectives. Wiley, 2019.

63 Loewen, James W. Lies My Teacher Told Me: Everything Your American History Textbook Got Wrong. The New Press, 1995.

This resistance extends beyond the educational sphere, manifesting in heated debates over public monuments, street names, and other symbols that celebrate figures associated with oppression and racial injustice. The conservative defense of such symbols as part of the nation's heritage underscores a reluctance to confront uncomfortable truths about the past and to acknowledge the need for a more inclusive approach to commemoration[64].

Critics of this cultural conservatism argue that the path to a more unified and cohesive national identity lies in the embrace of diversity and the recognition of the multiplicity of experiences that contribute to the American story. They advocate for an educational system and public discourse that acknowledges the contributions of all communities to the nation's development and challenges the historical narratives that have perpetuated racial hierarchies and exclusion[65].

The debate over multiculturalism and the recognition of non-white historical contributions thus reflects a broader ideological clash over the soul of American identity. As conservative forces seek to preserve a white-dominated narrative, the imperative for a more inclusive and equitable representation of America's diverse heritage becomes increasingly clear. The future of American identity hinges on the nation's ability to reconcile its past with a vision for a more inclusive and representative society[66].

The conservative cultural warfare against multiculturalism and the acknowledgment of non-white contributions to American history is a manifestation of the desire to maintain white cultural hegemony. This struggle over the narrative of national identity not only highlights the

[64] Duster, Troy. Backdoor to Eugenics. Routledge, 2003.

[65] Giroux, Henry A. Border Crossings: Cultural Workers and the Politics of Education. Routledge, 2005.

[66] Sowell, Thomas. Intellectuals and Race. Basic Books, 2013.

tensions inherent in a diverse society but also underscores the need for a more inclusive approach to understanding what it means to be American. As the nation moves forward, the recognition of diversity as a strength rather than a division will be crucial in shaping a more inclusive American identity[67].

[67] Tatum, Beverly Daniel. Why Are All the Black Kids Sitting Together in the Cafeteria? And Other Conversations About Race. Basic Books, 2017.

Part 4: Real Life Monopoly At The Expense of Black People And Other Minorities

Monopoly As A Metaphor for Racial Economic Disparities— Chapter 10

The game of Monopoly, with its straightforward objective of accumulating wealth through property acquisition, serves as a poignant metaphor for understanding the pervasive economic disparities and systemic barriers confronting African Americans in the United States. This allegory sheds light on the multifaceted ways in which systemic racism not only curtails opportunities for Black individuals but also perpetuates an uneven playing field reminiscent of a biased game of Monopoly[1].

At the onset, Monopoly equips each player with equal financial resources and an equal opportunity to navigate the board, acquire properties, and build wealth. However, translating this scenario into the real-world experience of African Americans reveals a starkly different starting point. Historical and systemic racism has ensured that Black Americans do not begin with the same economic resources or opportunities as their white counterparts. The legacy of slavery, Jim Crow laws, and redlining has effectively

[1] Anderson, Claud. Black Labor, White Wealth: The Search for Power and Economic Justice. Duncan & Duncan, 1994.

hindered the accumulation of generational wealth, mirroring a Monopoly game where certain players start with a handicap, significantly impacting their chances of success[2].

The practice of redlining, akin to being forbidden from purchasing properties in certain areas of the Monopoly board, exemplifies the systemic barriers imposed on Black families. These policies not only restricted access to housing loans based on race but also led to segregated communities and underfunded public services, including education. The effects of such policies have long-term implications, affecting the ability of Black Americans to accumulate wealth and secure economic stability for future generations[3].

Furthermore, the concept of "passing GO" and collecting $200 reflects the systemic wage gap and employment disparities faced by African Americans. Despite progress towards civil rights, racial discrimination in the job market persists, limiting earnings, savings, and investment opportunities for many Black individuals. This systemic inequality ensures that, much like in Monopoly, the economic advancement of Black players is significantly more challenging[4].

The allocation of properties and the development of hotels and houses in Monopoly can also be seen as a reflection of the disparities in business ownership and access to capital among African Americans. Systemic barriers to business loans, credit, and other financial services continue to hinder the growth of Black-owned

[2] Coates, Ta-Nehisi. "The Case for Reparations." The Atlantic, June 2014.

[3] Rothstein, Richard. The Color of Law: A Forgotten History of How Our Government Segregated America. Liveright, 2017.

[4] Wilson, William Julius. The Truly Disadvantaged: The Inner City, the Underclass, and Public Policy. University of Chicago Press, 1987.

businesses, limiting their ability to expand and compete effectively in the market[5].

Critics may argue that legislative and policy reforms, such as the Fair Housing Act and affirmative action, have leveled the playing field, offering everyone an equal chance to succeed. However, while such measures are steps in the right direction, the deep-seated effects of centuries of systemic racism cannot be undone overnight. The enduring wealth gap, educational disparities, and health inequities serve as testament to the ongoing struggle faced by African Americans, underscoring the inadequacy of current efforts to address these systemic issues[6].

In conclusion, the game of Monopoly offers a profound allegorical insight into the racial economic disparities that continue to plague the United States. Just as Monopoly is governed by predetermined rules that can advantage or disadvantage players, the real-world economic system, shaped by historical and systemic racism, creates significant barriers for African Americans. Addressing these disparities requires a comprehensive and sustained effort to dismantle the systemic barriers that perpetuate economic inequality, ensuring that all Americans, regardless of race, have an equal opportunity to succeed[7].

Object and Preparation

In the classic board game Monopoly, the premise is straightforward and ostensibly fair: each player begins with

[5] Bates, Timothy. Race, Self-Employment, and Upward Mobility: An Illusive American Dream. Woodrow Wilson Center Press, 1997.

[6] Kendi, Ibram X. How to Be an Antiracist. One World, 2019.

[7] Oliver, Melvin L., and Thomas M. Shapiro. Black Wealth/White Wealth: A New Perspective on Racial Inequality. Routledge, 1995.

the same amount of money and an equal chance at victory, predicated solely on their decisions and the roll of the dice. This idealized notion of equality and opportunity stands in stark contrast to the lived experiences of African Americans, for whom systemic racism has created a playing field far from level. The initial economic handicap faced by Black Americans in real life is a direct consequence of historical injustices, including redlining, discriminatory employment practices, and unequal educational opportunities, which collectively contribute to a persistent wealth gap between Black and white Americans[8].

Redlining, a practice institutionalized by the Home Owners' Loan Corporation in the 1930s, systematically denied Black Americans access to mortgage financing and home ownership, a cornerstone of wealth building in the United States. By drawing literal red lines around neighborhoods deemed "hazardous" due to their racial composition, the government sanctioned the denial of loans to Black families, regardless of their income or creditworthiness[9]. This policy not only stifled the ability of Black Americans to purchase homes but also led to the disinvestment in and decline of Black neighborhoods, further entrenching economic disparities.

The ramifications of redlining extend beyond housing inequality to impact education and employment opportunities. Schools in redlined communities, disproportionately underfunded due to their reliance on local property taxes, are often unable to provide the quality education necessary for upward mobility. As a result, Black children are frequently denied access to the same quality of

[8] Shapiro, Thomas M., and Melvin L. Oliver. Black Wealth/White Wealth: A New Perspective on Racial Inequality. Routledge, 1995.

[9] Rothstein, Richard. The Color of Law: A Forgotten History of How Our Government Segregated America. Liveright Publishing Corporation, 2017.

education as their white counterparts, perpetuating cycles of poverty and limiting future economic opportunities[10].

Furthermore, the labor market has historically been segmented in a manner that relegates Black workers to lower-paying, less stable jobs. Even when Black Americans achieve the same levels of education as whites, they often face discrimination in hiring, promotions, and wages. Such employment discrimination not only limits the earning potential of Black individuals but also contributes to the racial wealth gap by hindering the ability of Black families to accumulate savings and invest in wealth-building assets[11].

Critics may argue that legislative achievements, such as the Civil Rights Act and Fair Housing Act, have dismantled the legal framework supporting these discriminatory practices. However, the legacy of these systemic barriers persists, manifesting in ongoing racial disparities in wealth, education, and employment. Moreover, the belief in a meritocratic society often obscures the structural advantages that have historically benefited white Americans and the systemic obstacles that continue to impede Black Americans' economic progress[12].

In essence, while Monopoly might offer each player an equal start, the real-world "game" of economic opportunity in America tells a different story for Black individuals. Systemic racism, deeply embedded in the nation's history and institutions, ensures that Black Americans often begin with fewer resources, less capital, and greater obstacles to overcome. Addressing these disparities requires more than

[10] Darling-Hammond, Linda. The Flat World and Education: How America's Commitment to Equity Will Determine Our Future. Teachers College Press, 2010.

[11] Pager, Devah, and Hana Shepherd. "The Sociology of Discrimination: Racial Discrimination in Employment, Housing, Credit, and Consumer Markets." Annual Review of Sociology, vol. 34, 2008, pp. 181-209.

[12] Kendi, Ibram X. How to Be an Antiracist. One World, 2019.

acknowledgment; it demands a commitment to dismantling the systemic barriers that perpetuate inequality and to creating policies that genuinely level the playing field[13].

Bank and Banker

The Bank holds a position of immense power, controlling the flow of money, the auction and sale of properties, and even the outcome of the game through its financial policies. This central role of the Bank in Monopoly mirrors the real-world dynamics of financial institutions which have historically played a significant part in shaping economic landscapes and, by extension, racial disparities within the United States. The practices of redlining and discriminatory lending policies are prime examples of how these institutions have manipulated economic opportunities to the detriment of Black Americans, echoing the biased actions of a Monopoly Banker who might unfairly influence the game[14].

Redlining, a discriminatory practice that began in the 1930s, involved the systematic denial of various services by federal government agencies, local governments, and the private sector to residents of certain areas based on race or ethnicity. The term "redlining" originates from the red lines drawn on maps by the Home Owners' Loan Corporation (HOLC), marking neighborhoods predominantly inhabited by African Americans and other minorities as "hazardous" for bank lending. This practice ensured that Black families

[13] Coates, Ta-Nehisi. "The Case for Reparations." The Atlantic, June 2014.

[14] Rothstein, Richard. The Color of Law: A Forgotten History of How Our Government Segregated America. Liveright Publishing Corporation, 2017.

were denied mortgages, insurance, and access to credit, effectively excluding them from the primary means of building wealth in America—homeownership[15].

Furthermore, the discriminatory lending policies extended beyond redlining. African Americans and other minorities were often subjected to higher interest rates, subprime loans, and other unfair lending practices, even when they qualified for better terms. These practices contributed significantly to the racial wealth gap, as families of color found it more challenging to purchase homes, invest in education, or start businesses[16].

The impact of these financial disparities is profound and multifaceted. For example, the inability to secure mortgages led to lower homeownership rates among Black Americans, which in turn affected their ability to accumulate wealth over time. Moreover, neighborhoods subjected to redlining suffered from disinvestment and decline, leading to a concentration of poverty, underfunded schools, and limited economic opportunities for residents. The cycle of disadvantage perpetuated by these financial practices underscores the systemic nature of racial inequality in America[17].

Critics of the comparison between Monopoly's Bank and real-world financial institutions might argue that legislative efforts, such as the Fair Housing Act of 1968 and the Community Reinvestment Act of 1977, have addressed and mitigated the effects of discriminatory practices. While such laws marked progress toward financial equality, the

15 Coates, Ta-Nehisi. "The Case for Reparations." The Atlantic, June 2014.

16 Squires, Gregory D., and Charis E. Kubrin. "Privileged Places: Race, Uneven Development and the Geography of Opportunity in Urban America." Urban Studies, vol. 42, no. 1, 2005, pp. 47-68.

17 Oliver, Melvin L., and Thomas M. Shapiro. Black Wealth/White Wealth: A New Perspective on Racial Inequality. Routledge, 1995.

legacy of redlining and ongoing reports of lending discrimination indicate that significant disparities remain. Recent studies and lawsuits against major banks for discriminatory lending practices further reveal that the challenges of the past are not entirely behind us[18].

The parallels between the role of the Bank in Monopoly and the real-world actions of financial institutions highlight a critical aspect of racial disparities in the United States. Just as a biased Banker in Monopoly can influence the game's outcome, the discriminatory practices of financial institutions have had a lasting impact on the economic well-being of Black Americans. Addressing these disparities requires not only acknowledgment of the historical injustices but also a commitment to creating equitable financial systems that support all individuals, regardless of race[19].

Buying Property

The acquisition of property is a fundamental step towards financial success and eventual victory. This process, ostensibly based on chance and financial acumen within the game's context, finds a starkly grim parallel in the real-world experience of many Black Americans. For them, systemic barriers rather than the luck of the dice have made property ownership a challenging, often insurmountable goal. Practices such as redlining and discriminatory lending, deeply rooted in the fabric of American history, have significantly hindered the ability of Black families to

[18] Bocian, Debbie Gruenstein, Keith S. Ernst, and Wei Li. "Unfair Lending: The Effect of Race and Ethnicity on the Price of Subprime Mortgages." Center for Responsible Lending, 2006.

[19] Desmond, Matthew. Evicted: Poverty and Profit in the American City. Crown, 2016.

purchase homes and accumulate wealth, further entrenching existing economic disparities[20].

Redlining, a term that emerged in the 1930s, refers to the practice whereby certain neighborhoods, predominantly those inhabited by African Americans and other minorities, were marked as high-risk for mortgage lenders. This policy was institutionalized by the Home Owners' Loan Corporation (HOLC) and later perpetuated by private banks and insurance companies, effectively barring residents of these neighborhoods from accessing the necessary financial services to buy homes[21]. The repercussions of redlining extend beyond mere homeownership, as it has also contributed to a cycle of poverty and segregation, stifling economic mobility and reinforcing the racial wealth gap.

Moreover, discriminatory lending practices have compounded these issues, with African Americans often facing higher interest rates, stricter loan conditions, and outright denial of mortgage applications compared to their white counterparts. Such disparities are not relics of the past; recent studies and lawsuits have highlighted ongoing discrimination in the housing market, demonstrating how these prejudicial practices continue to impede Black Americans' pursuit of property ownership[22].

Critics of the analogy between Monopoly and the struggle for property ownership among Black Americans might argue that legislative interventions, such as the Fair Housing Act of 1968, have leveled the playing field. However, while these laws marked significant progress

[20] Shapiro, Thomas M., and Melvin L. Oliver. Black Wealth/White Wealth: A New Perspective on Racial Inequality. Routledge, 1995.

[21] Rothstein, Richard. The Color of Law: A Forgotten History of How Our Government Segregated America. Liveright Publishing Corporation, 2017.

[22] Rugh, Jacob S., and Douglas S. Massey. "Racial Segregation and the American Foreclosure Crisis." American Sociological Review, vol. 75, no. 5, 2010, pp. 629-651.

towards equality, they have not fully eradicated the systemic barriers embedded within the housing market. The enduring legacy of redlining, combined with ongoing discriminatory lending practices, continues to disproportionately affect Black families, limiting their access to homeownership and the associated opportunities for wealth creation[23].

The challenge of purchasing property and the subsequent ability to build wealth is further complicated by the racial wealth gap. This gap, a direct consequence of centuries of economic discrimination, means that even when Black families overcome the barriers to mortgage approval, they often face financial hurdles that their white counterparts do not. The initial down payment, closing costs, and subsequent property taxes require a level of financial stability that has been systematically denied to Black Americans through employment discrimination, wage gaps, and educational disparities[24].

In essence, the real estate market, much like the game of Monopoly, is influenced by one's starting position, which for many Black Americans has been historically compromised by systemic racism and discriminatory policies. Addressing these deep-seated issues requires a concerted effort to dismantle the barriers to homeownership and to rectify the injustices that have long hindered the economic advancement of Black families in America. Only through such measures can we hope to achieve a truly equitable society where property ownership and the opportunity to build wealth are accessible to all, irrespective

[23] Massey, Douglas S., and Nancy A. Denton. American Apartheid: Segregation and the Making of the Underclass. Harvard University Press, 1993.

[24] Oliver, Melvin L., and Thomas M. Shapiro. Black Wealth/White Wealth: A New Perspective on Racial Inequality. Routledge, 2006.

of race[25].

Paying Rent

Landing on a property owned by another player necessitates the payment of rent, often depleting the player's resources and impeding their progress toward financial dominance. This aspect of the game bears a striking resemblance to the real-world scenario faced by many Black individuals in the United States, who frequently encounter higher rental costs as a direct consequence of living in segregated neighborhoods. These neighborhoods, shaped by a confluence of historical policies such as redlining, zoning laws, and discriminatory housing practices, have systematically confined African American families to less desirable areas. The repercussions of these policies are far-reaching, significantly impacting the ability of Black families to save money, invest in their futures, and escape the cycle of poverty[26].

The genesis of residential segregation can be traced back to explicit government policies that encouraged racial discrimination in housing. The practice of redlining, initiated by the Home Owners' Loan Corporation (HOLC) in the 1930s, explicitly marked neighborhoods with significant minority populations as high-risk for mortgage lenders, effectively denying Black families the opportunity

25 Coates, Ta-Nehisi. "The Case for Reparations." The Atlantic, June 2014.

26 Desmond, Matthew. Evicted: Poverty and Profit in the American City. Crown, 2016.

to own homes and build wealth through equity[27]. As a result, African Americans were relegated to rental markets in densely populated urban areas, where limited housing supply and high demand have driven up rental costs.

Furthermore, the phenomenon of "white flight" in the mid-20th century exacerbated the issue. As white populations moved to the suburbs, taking economic resources with them, urban centers with high minority populations suffered from disinvestment, contributing to the decline in housing quality without a commensurate decrease in rental prices. The combination of high demand for rental properties in these underfunded neighborhoods and the lack of investment in maintenance and development has led to disproportionately high rental costs for their predominantly Black residents[28].

Critics may argue that market forces alone dictate rental prices, suggesting that the higher costs in certain neighborhoods are a result of supply and demand rather than systemic racism. However, this perspective fails to acknowledge the historical and ongoing policies that have shaped these market forces. The legacy of redlining, discriminatory lending practices, and unequal urban development policies continue to influence the housing market, maintaining racial segregation and ensuring that rental costs remain disproportionately high for Black communities[29].

[27] Rothstein, Richard. The Color of Law: A Forgotten History of How Our Government Segregated America. Liveright Publishing Corporation, 2017.

[28] Massey, Douglas S., and Nancy A. Denton. American Apartheid: Segregation and the Making of the Underclass. Harvard University Press, 1993.

[29] Squires, Gregory D. "Capital and Communities in Black and White: The Intersections of Race, Class, and Uneven Development." The Guilford Press, 1994.

Moreover, the impact of these high rental costs extends beyond financial strain, affecting the overall well-being of Black families. Living in segregated, underfunded neighborhoods often means reduced access to quality education, healthcare, employment opportunities, and safe recreational spaces. The cumulative effect of these disadvantages further entrenches the cycle of poverty and impedes the ability of Black individuals to achieve economic mobility[30].

In conclusion, the parallels between paying rent in Monopoly and the real-life rental challenges faced by Black individuals in segregated neighborhoods illuminate the enduring impact of historical and systemic racism on housing affordability. To address these disparities, it is imperative to confront the policies and practices that have contributed to residential segregation and to work toward equitable housing solutions that enable all individuals, regardless of race, to access affordable housing and the opportunity for economic advancement[31].

Chance and Community Chest

The draw of a Chance or Community Chest card introduces an element of unpredictability, offering players opportunities for advancement or presenting unforeseen challenges. This mechanic mirrors the unpredictable nature

30 Wilson, William Julius. The Truly Disadvantaged: The Inner City, the Underclass, and Public Policy. University of Chicago Press, 1987.

31 Shapiro, Thomas M., and Melvin L. Oliver. Black Wealth/White Wealth: A New Perspective on Racial Inequality. Routledge, 1995.

of real-life opportunities and setbacks, albeit in a simplified form. For African Americans, however, systemic racism skews the odds, turning what should be random chances into predictably negative outcomes. This is not merely a matter of individual luck but a consequence of historical and systemic barriers that have been erected to limit the social and economic mobility of Black Americans[32].

The concept of "chance" in the lives of Black individuals is inextricably linked to the enduring legacy of systemic racism. From birth, many African Americans are born into impoverished communities that have been shaped by decades of discriminatory policies such as redlining, underfunded education systems, and unequal access to healthcare. These communities, often the product of historical segregation and economic disenfranchisement, offer limited opportunities for upward mobility, effectively stacking the deck against Black individuals from the outset[33].

Discrimination in employment and the workplace further compounds these challenges. African Americans frequently face barriers in hiring, promotions, and wage equality, regardless of their qualifications or experience. This form of systemic bias, reminiscent of the negative outcomes often associated with Chance and Community Chest cards in Monopoly, hinders the economic progress of Black individuals and widens the racial wealth gap. The cumulative effect of these disparities not only limits the

[32] Kendi, Ibram X. How to Be an Antiracist. One World, 2019.

[33] Rothstein, Richard. The Color of Law: A Forgotten History of How Our Government Segregated America. Liveright Publishing Corporation, 2017.

immediate financial stability of Black families but also affects their ability to accumulate wealth over generations[34].

Critics might argue that the success stories of individual African Americans challenge the narrative of systemic barriers to mobility and opportunity. While it is true that some Black individuals have achieved significant success, these exceptions should not obscure the broader patterns of inequality that prevail. The exceptional achievements of a few cannot be used to justify the systemic injustices that continue to affect the majority of the African American community[35].

Moreover, the analogy between Monopoly's Chance and Community Chest cards and the real-life experiences of African Americans highlights the profound impact of systemic racism on the distribution of opportunities and setbacks. Unlike the game, where players can mitigate the effects of bad luck through strategic decisions, the systemic barriers faced by Black Americans are not easily overcome by individual effort or resilience. Addressing these disparities requires a concerted societal effort to dismantle the structures of inequality and to create a more equitable distribution of opportunities[36].

In conclusion, while Monopoly's Chance and Community Chest cards introduce an element of randomness to the game, the real-world "chance" factors that African Americans face are heavily influenced by systemic racism, leading to predictably negative outcomes. Understanding and acknowledging these disparities is

[34] Pager, Devah, and Bruce Western. "Race at Work: Realities of Race and Criminal Record in the NYC Job Market." New York University Law Review, vol. 81, no. 2, 2006.

[35] Coates, Ta-Nehisi. "The Case for Reparations." The Atlantic, June 2014.

[36] Oliver, Melvin L., and Thomas M. Shapiro. Black Wealth/White Wealth: A New Perspective on Racial Inequality. Routledge, 1995.

crucial in the pursuit of social and economic justice. As a society, we must work to ensure that opportunities for advancement are not determined by the color of one's skin but by one's abilities and efforts, striving toward a future where the game of life offers truly equal opportunities for all[37].

Income Tax and Jail

The spaces marked "Income Tax" and "Jail" serve as obstacles that can significantly impede a player's progress by depleting their resources or restricting their movement on the board. This gameplay mechanic reflects broader socio-economic and legal challenges in real life, where the criminal justice system and regressive tax policies disproportionately affect Black individuals in the United States, creating hurdles to economic stability and personal freedom[38].

The comparison between Monopoly's simplified consequences and the real-life impacts of the criminal justice system on Black communities underscores a troubling reality. The United States' criminal justice system has long been criticized for its racial disparities, with Black Americans significantly overrepresented in prison populations relative to their proportion of the overall

37 Wilson, William Julius. The Truly Disadvantaged: The Inner City, the Underclass, and Public Policy. University of Chicago Press, 1987.

38 Alexander, Michelle. The New Jim Crow: Mass Incarceration in the Age of Colorblindness. The New Press, 2010.

population[39]. This overrepresentation is not merely a result of higher crime rates within these communities but is also a consequence of systemic biases in policing, sentencing, and the criminalization of poverty. Such systemic issues echo the arbitrary nature of landing on the "Go to Jail" space in Monopoly, highlighting how external factors beyond individual control can lead to incarceration[40].

Moreover, the economic analogy of the "Income Tax" space in Monopoly sheds light on the regressive nature of certain tax policies that disproportionately burden lower-income individuals, among whom Black Americans are overrepresented due to systemic economic inequities. Regressive tax systems, where the tax rate decreases as the taxable amount increases, place a heavier relative burden on those least able to afford it, exacerbating the wealth gap and hindering the economic mobility of marginalized communities[41].

Critics may argue that advancements in civil rights laws and tax reforms have mitigated these disparities. However, despite such legal progress, the structural foundations of these disparities remain largely intact. The persistence of racial profiling, sentencing disparities, and the disproportionate impact of fines and fees on Black individuals illustrate ongoing challenges. Similarly, while tax policy reforms, such as earned income credits, aim to address inequality, the fundamental regressive nature of

[39] Western, Bruce, and Becky Pettit. Invisible Men: Mass Incarceration and the Myth of Black Progress. Russell Sage Foundation, 2010.

[40] Stevenson, Bryan. Just Mercy: A Story of Justice and Redemption. Spiegel & Grau, 2014.

[41] Saez, Emmanuel, and Gabriel Zucman. The Triumph of Injustice: How the Rich Dodge Taxes and How to Make Them Pay. W.W. Norton & Company, 2019.

many state and local tax systems continues to disproportionately impact lower-income families[42].

Addressing these deep-seated issues requires a comprehensive understanding of the ways in which policies and practices, ostensibly neutral, can have profoundly unequal impacts. The "Income Tax" and "Jail" spaces in Monopoly, therefore, serve as metaphors for the broader systemic barriers that limit the economic and personal freedom of Black Americans. Effective reform must involve not only changes in policy but also a concerted effort to address the underlying systemic biases that perpetuate these disparities[43].

In conclusion, the parallels drawn between the game of Monopoly and the real-life experiences of Black Americans with the criminal justice system and tax policies underscore the complex interplay between economic policies, legal systems, and racial inequality. Just as a game of Monopoly can be skewed by the luck of the draw, the lives of Black Americans are often shaped by systemic forces beyond their control. Recognizing and addressing these systemic disparities is crucial in moving toward a more equitable and just society[44].

Houses and Hotels

The construction of houses and hotels on properties signifies a crucial phase where players can substantially

[42] Clear, Todd R., and Natasha A. Frost. The Punishment Imperative: The Rise and Failure of Mass Incarceration in America. New York University Press, 2014.

[43] Wilkins, Vicky M., and Marcia L. Whittaker. "The Impact of Incarceration on Wage Mobility and Inequality." American Sociological Review, vol. 76, no. 4, 2011, pp. 502-524.

[44] Mauer, Marc. Race to Incarcerate. The New Press, 2006.

increase their wealth through enhanced property values and rent. This mechanic underscores a fundamental economic principle: investing in real estate and infrastructure leads to wealth accumulation. However, translating this principle into reality reveals a stark disparity for Black Americans, for whom systemic barriers have long obstructed the path to property investment and community improvement. These obstacles not only hinder the ability of Black individuals to accumulate wealth but also perpetuate longstanding economic disparities[45].

Historically, discriminatory practices such as redlining have systematically denied Black Americans access to the necessary financial services for home ownership and property development. Instituted in the 1930s, redlining involved delineating areas predominantly inhabited by Black people as high-risk for mortgage lenders, effectively barring residents from securing loans to purchase or improve properties[46]. This policy not only restricted the ability of Black families to own homes but also limited their opportunities to build wealth through real estate, one of the most traditional and effective means of economic advancement.

Furthermore, the aftermath of redlining continues to affect Black communities, manifesting in a lack of investment and the deterioration of neighborhood infrastructure. Such conditions devalue properties in these areas, making it even more challenging for Black homeowners to leverage their assets for wealth generation. Consequently, the economic gap widens, as Black

[45] Oliver, Melvin L., and Thomas M. Shapiro. Black Wealth/White Wealth: A New Perspective on Racial Inequality. Routledge, 1995.

[46] Rothstein, Richard. The Color of Law: A Forgotten History of How Our Government Segregated America. Liveright Publishing Corporation, 2017.

Americans are often unable to utilize real estate as a stepping stone to financial security and upward mobility[47].

The disparity in property investment and development is compounded by ongoing discriminatory practices in lending. Despite legal advancements aimed at curbing racial discrimination, Black individuals and families still face higher mortgage rates and are more frequently denied loans compared to their white counterparts. These practices echo the biased dynamics of Monopoly, where certain players—due to systemic rules—find it exceedingly difficult to advance and succeed[48].

Critics may argue that legislative efforts, including the Fair Housing Act and the Equal Credit Opportunity Act, have leveled the playing field, ensuring equal access to financial services regardless of race. While such laws represent significant progress, disparities in home ownership rates, property values, and access to credit persist, indicating that systemic racism continues to influence the real estate market and broader economic landscape[49].

Addressing these entrenched barriers requires a multifaceted approach that includes not only legal reforms but also targeted economic policies to encourage investment in Black communities, equitable lending practices, and financial education programs. Such efforts can help dismantle the structural obstacles that have historically prevented Black Americans from fully participating in the

47 Coates, Ta-Nehisi. "The Case for Reparations." The Atlantic, June 2014.

48 Squires, Gregory D., and Sally O'Connor. Color and Money: Politics and Prospects for Community Reinvestment in Urban America. SUNY Press, 2001.

49 Massey, Douglas S., and Nancy A. Denton. American Apartheid: Segregation and the Making of the Underclass. Harvard University Press, 1993.

real estate market and from harnessing its potential for wealth accumulation[50].

While building houses and hotels in Monopoly illustrates the principle of wealth generation through property investment, the reality for Black Americans is fraught with systemic challenges that impede their ability to engage in this form of economic advancement. Recognizing and addressing the historical and ongoing barriers faced by Black communities is essential in the pursuit of equity and economic justice. Only then can the promise of real estate as a pathway to wealth be accessible to all, regardless of race[51].

Free Parking

The "Free Parking" space offers a brief respite—a pause with neither penalty nor reward. This concept, when paralleled with the societal and economic landscape faced by many Black Americans, reflects a profound narrative on the limitations of social mobility due to systemic barriers. Despite aspirations and relentless effort, the structural impediments rooted in centuries of racial discrimination present a formidable challenge to achieving economic advancement and equity. This stagnation, much like the neutrality of "Free Parking," underscores a reality where hard work often does not equate to progress for Black individuals, due to the systemic obstructions embedded within American society[52].

[50] Shapiro, Thomas M. Toxic Inequality: How America's Wealth Gap Destroys Mobility, Deepens the Racial Divide, & Threatens Our Future. Basic Books, 2017.

[51] Desmond, Matthew. Evicted: Poverty and Profit in the American City. Crown, 2016.

[52] Anderson, Claud. Black Labor, White Wealth: The Search for Power and Economic Justice. Duncan & Duncan, 1994.

Historically, policies such as redlining, discriminatory lending practices, and segregation have curtailed opportunities for Black Americans, impacting their access to quality education, affordable housing, and fair employment. These systemic barriers, established and perpetuated by both government and private institutions, have effectively stifled the potential for upward mobility among Black communities, reinforcing a cycle of economic disparity that persists across generations[53].

The concept of social mobility in America is often touted as a meritocratic ideal, where success is achievable for anyone willing to put forth the effort. However, this narrative fails to account for the unequal playing field that has been historically skewed against Black Americans. The enduring legacy of slavery, Jim Crow laws, and institutional racism has created an environment where the barriers to success are significantly higher for Black individuals compared to their white counterparts[54].

Critics may argue that advancements in civil rights and affirmative action policies have leveled the playing field, providing opportunities for all regardless of race. While it is undeniable that progress has been made, the reality remains that systemic inequalities continue to impact the social and economic outcomes for Black Americans. Studies and data consistently show gaps in wealth, education, and employment that cannot be attributed solely to individual effort or lack thereof but are instead indicative of the

53 Rothstein, Richard. The Color of Law: A Forgotten History of How Our Government Segregated America. Liveright Publishing Corporation, 2017.

54 Coates, Ta-Nehisi. "The Case for Reparations." The Atlantic, June 2014.

structural biases that continue to operate within American society[55].

Furthermore, the metaphor of "Free Parking" in relation to the stagnation of social mobility for Black Americans also highlights the issue of visibility and recognition. Just as players momentarily pause on "Free Parking" without gaining or losing, the contributions and struggles of Black Americans often go unrecognized or are undervalued by mainstream narratives, further exacerbating feelings of disenfranchisement and invisibility[56].

In addressing these systemic barriers, it is crucial to move beyond superficial measures and tackle the root causes of inequality. This includes reforming policies that perpetuate racial disparities, investing in education and community development, and fostering an inclusive economy that values diversity and equity. Only through concerted efforts to dismantle the structural foundations of racism can we hope to achieve a society where social mobility is a reality for all, rather than an unattainable ideal[57].

In conclusion, the "Free Parking" space in Monopoly, while seemingly innocuous in the context of a board game, serves as a powerful metaphor for the stagnation and challenges faced by Black Americans in their pursuit of social mobility. The systemic barriers that hinder progress, despite hard work and ambition, call for a reevaluation of the mechanisms of inequality embedded within the fabric of American society. As we strive for a more equitable future,

55 Oliver, Melvin L., and Thomas M. Shapiro. Black Wealth/White Wealth: A New Perspective on Racial Inequality. Routledge, 1995.

56 Kendi, Ibram X. How to Be an Antiracist. One World, 2019.

57 Desmond, Matthew. Evicted: Poverty and Profit in the American City. Crown, 2016.

acknowledging and addressing these issues is paramount in the journey towards justice and equality[58].

[58] Wilkerson, Isabel. Caste: The Origins of Our Discontents. Random House, 2020.

Unraveling the Historical Ties Between Slavery and Modern Economic Disparity—Chapter 11

In examining the economic disparity that permeates the United States, one cannot overlook the historical roots deeply embedded in the institution of slavery. The legacy of slavery has cast a long shadow over the socioeconomic landscape of the country, shaping the contours of wealth and poverty along racial lines. The inception of Wall Street, a symbol of American financial prowess, is indelibly linked to the commodification of human lives through the slave trade. This connection underscores a grim reality: the backbone of American wealth was constructed on the exploitation of enslaved Africans[1].

The valuation of slaves and the goods produced by their forced labor were central to the early American economy, providing a foundation upon which Wall Street and other financial institutions could flourish. The profits derived from slavery bolstered the wealth of the nation, but this

[1] Eric Williams, Capitalism and Slavery (Chapel Hill: University of North Carolina Press, 1944).

wealth was amassed at the cost of immeasurable human suffering and injustice. This economic system, predicated on racial exploitation, has left enduring scars that continue to manifest in the present-day economic landscape[2].

In contemporary America, the repercussions of this historical exploitation are evident in the stark economic disparities that exist between racial groups. A significant portion of the African American population remains ensconced in governmental employment, with approximately 68-70% of blacks employed in public sector jobs. Conversely, only a small fraction, about 2%, are proprietors of businesses within their own communities[3]. This distribution of employment reflects a broader issue of economic vulnerability and dependence on structures that have historically marginalized black Americans.

Critics and skeptics may argue that the link between historical slavery and current economic disparities is overstated or that the success of Wall Street and the American economy as a whole can be attributed to other factors. They may posit that the focus on slavery's impact ignores the strides made toward racial equality and economic empowerment within the black community. However, this perspective overlooks the systemic nature of racial inequality and the ways in which the legacies of slavery have been perpetuated through institutional practices and policies. The economic structures that were established during slavery have evolved but continue to benefit from the inequities rooted in that era[4].

[2] Sven Beckert, Empire of Cotton: A Global History (New York: Knopf, 2014).

[3] U.S. Bureau of Labor Statistics, "Labor Force Characteristics by Race and Ethnicity, 2019" (Washington, D.C.: U.S. Department of Labor, 2020).

[4] Michelle Alexander, The New Jim Crow: Mass Incarceration in the Age of Colorblindness (New York: The New Press, 2010).

Furthermore, the concentration of African Americans in public sector employment and the scarcity of black-owned businesses speak to a broader narrative of economic disenfranchisement. While government jobs provide stability for many, the over-representation of blacks in these roles also highlights a lack of access to other economic opportunities. The dearth of black-owned businesses in black communities not only reflects barriers to entrepreneurship but also signifies a lost opportunity for wealth creation and economic empowerment within these communities[5].

In addressing these disparities, it is crucial to confront the historical injustices that have shaped the economic landscape. Recognizing the profound impact of slavery on the American economy is not merely an academic exercise; it is a necessary step toward understanding and addressing the systemic inequities that persist today. Only by grappling with this uncomfortable truth can we begin to unravel the fabric of economic disparity and weave a new narrative of equity and justice for all.

The Evolution of Exploitation from Slavery to Wall Street

In the aftermath of slavery, the United States witnessed a profound transformation in the mechanisms of wealth generation, with Wall Street emerging as a new arena for economic activity. However, this shift did not signify an end to exploitation; rather, it represented its evolution, adapting to the changing socio-political landscape while maintaining the underlying disparities inherited from the era of slavery. This period saw the promise of economic

[5] Maggie Anderson, Our Black Year: One Family's Quest to Buy Black in America's Racially Divided Economy (New York: PublicAffairs, 2012).

restitution for former slaves — famously encapsulated in the unfulfilled promise of "40 acres and a mule" — dissipate, leaving a legacy of inequity that reverberates through the economic structures of today[6].

The transition from a plantation-based economy to one dominated by financial markets did not equate to an equitable redistribution of wealth or opportunities. Instead, the capital amassed through centuries of slavery found new avenues for growth in the burgeoning industries and financial institutions of the 19th and early 20th centuries. Wall Street, in particular, became a symbol of wealth and power, its rise inseparable from the exploitation and marginalization of African Americans who remained largely excluded from the fruits of this economic boom[7].

Critics of the link between Wall Street's ascendance and the historical exploitation of African Americans may argue that the financial markets offer a level playing field, where success is determined by acumen and strategy rather than historical injustices. They posit that the market's dynamics are neutral, obviating the racial disparities of the past. However, this perspective fails to account for the systemic barriers that have historically impeded African Americans' access to economic opportunities, perpetuating a cycle of disparity that traces its roots back to slavery[8].

The notion of an "unfair start" due to the lack of reparations is a critical aspect of understanding the economic disparities faced by African Americans. The broken promise of "40 acres and a mule" symbolizes a

6 Ira Katznelson, When Affirmative Action Was White: An Untold History of Racial Inequality in Twentieth-Century America (New York: W.W. Norton & Company, 2005).

7 Sven Beckert, Empire of Cotton: A Global History (New York: Knopf, 2014).

8 Thomas Sowell, Discrimination and Disparities (New York: Basic Books, 2018).

missed opportunity for economic empowerment and wealth generation among newly freed slaves, setting the stage for enduring racial inequality. The absence of reparations left African Americans at a significant disadvantage, lacking the resources and capital necessary to compete on equal footing in a rapidly industrializing economy[9].

Moreover, the historical exclusion of African Americans from the financial systems and markets further exacerbated these disparities. The discriminatory practices of redlining and segregation, along with the denial of loans and financial services, limited the ability of African Americans to invest, own property, and accumulate wealth, reinforcing the economic divide[10].

In addressing these enduring inequalities, it is imperative to confront the historical context that has shaped the economic landscape of the United States. Recognizing the continuity of exploitation from the plantation to Wall Street provides insight into the systemic nature of racial economic disparities. While the mechanisms of exploitation have evolved, their impact remains deeply entrenched in the fabric of American society. It is only through a comprehensive understanding of this historical trajectory that we can begin to envision and implement strategies for genuine economic justice and equity.

[9] William Darity Jr. and A. Kirsten Mullen, From Here to Equality: Reparations for Black Americans in the Twenty-First Century (Chapel Hill: University of North Carolina Press, 2020).

[10] Richard Rothstein, The Color of Law: A Forgotten History of How Our Government Segregated America (New York: Liveright Publishing Corporation, 2017).

A Critical Analysis of Racial Inequities in Employment

In the discourse of American socio-economic dynamics, the issue of unemployment reveals stark disparities that underscore the systemic inequities faced by African Americans. Current statistics portray an alarming scenario where the black unemployment rate stands at an estimated 34%, a figure that starkly contrasts with the national averages often reported in mainstream discourse[11]. This discrepancy not only highlights the racial divides in economic well-being but also raises critical questions about the inclusivity and accuracy of unemployment metrics.

Historically, the peak of the unemployment rate for white Americans during the Great Depression reached approximately 25%, a period rightfully termed as one of the most devastating economic downturns in U.S. history. Yet, this figure pales in comparison to the persistently high unemployment rates among African Americans, which have seldom dipped below this mark. Despite the severity of these numbers, there has been a noticeable lack of comprehensive governmental intervention akin to the measures implemented to alleviate the economic distress of white populations during the 1930s[12].

Critics might argue that the unemployment figures for African Americans are exaggerated or that systemic barriers no longer exist, positing that the free market offers equal opportunities for all, regardless of race. Some suggest that the disparities in employment statistics can be attributed to factors such as educational attainment or geographic location, rather than systemic racism or governmental

11 "The State of Black America," National Urban League, 2021.

12 Ira Katznelson, Fear Itself: The New Deal and the Origins of Our Time (New York: Liveright Publishing, 2013).

neglect[13]. However, this perspective overlooks the historical context and structural barriers that continue to hinder the economic prospects of African Americans.

The stark contrast in governmental response to economic hardships faced by whites compared to blacks is indicative of a broader narrative of racial exclusion from socio-economic protections. During the Great Depression, the federal government instituted a range of policies and programs under the New Deal to revive the American economy and provide relief to those affected. However, these programs often systematically excluded or marginalized African Americans through discriminatory practices embedded within their implementation, such as the redlining by the Home Owners' Loan Corporation or the exclusion of agricultural and domestic workers from Social Security benefits[14].

This differential treatment underscores a contentious debate regarding the role of government in addressing racial inequities. While significant efforts were mobilized to assist white Americans during times of economic crisis, the persistent high rates of unemployment among African Americans have not elicited a comparable level of governmental intervention. The argument that it is not the government's role to provide targeted assistance to alleviate racial disparities in employment not only negates the precedent set by historical interventions but also ignores the impact of systemic racism that has perpetuated these disparities[15].

13 Thomas Sowell, Discrimination and Disparities (New York: Basic Books, 2018).

14 Richard Rothstein, The Color of Law: A Forgotten History of How Our Government Segregated America (New York: Liveright Publishing Corporation, 2017).

15 Michelle Alexander, The New Jim Crow: Mass Incarceration in the Age of Colorblindness (New York: The New Press, 2010).

To move forward, it is essential to recognize and address the historical and structural roots of racial unemployment disparities. Acknowledging the systemic barriers that continue to affect African Americans' access to employment opportunities is the first step towards devising targeted policies that can effectively address these inequities. Only through a concerted effort to understand and dismantle the underlying causes of racial disparities in employment can we hope to achieve a more equitable and inclusive economy.

Part 5: Racism Soley Exist To Create A Controlled Labor Force To Accrue Massive Unearned Income For White Culture

Violent Crime Control and Law Enforcement Act— Chapter 12

In 1994, the United States Congress enacted the Violent Crime Control and Law Enforcement Act, a legislative behemoth aimed at curbing the rising tide of violent crime across the nation. Spearheaded by Jack Brooks and signed into law by President Bill Clinton, this Act represented the most extensive crime legislation in the country's history[1]. With provisions for 100,000 new police officers and $9.7 billion allocated towards prison funding, the bill sought to enhance the effectiveness of law enforcement and reduce recidivism rates[2].

Among its key features, the Act introduced the Federal Assault Weapons Ban and established 60 new death penalty offenses, marking a significant expansion of federal law and an aggressive stance on crime and punishment[3]. The underlying intent was clear: to address the scourge of violent crime and improve public safety through stringent measures and enhanced law enforcement capabilities.

However, the Act also catalyzed a shift towards the privatization of prisons, offering financial incentives for states to adopt stricter sentencing laws and to expand their

1 Jack Brooks, H.R.3355 - 103rd Congress (1993-1994): Violent Crime Control and Law Enforcement Act of 1994.

2 Ibid.

3 Ibid.

prison infrastructure[4]. This movement towards privatization transformed incarceration into a profitable business model, epitomized by the rise of companies such as CoreCivic, which reaped considerable profits from the burgeoning industry of private prisons[5].

Critics of the Act have pointed to its unintended consequences, arguing that it contributed to mass incarceration without delivering substantial improvements in public safety[6]. The emphasis on harsh sentencing laws and the incentivization of prison construction spurred the growth of the private prison industry, an industry often criticized for prioritizing profit over the rehabilitation of inmates[7]. This profit-driven approach has raised ethical concerns and questions about the effectiveness of private prisons in reducing recidivism rates, which the Act initially aimed to achieve.

The profitability of private prisons, fueled by contracts that pay per diem rates per prisoner, has created a financial incentive to maintain high rates of incarceration[8]. This dynamic underscores a troubling aspect of the American criminal justice system, where the imperative to generate profit can potentially outweigh the societal goal of rehabilitating offenders and reducing crime.

Despite the ambitious goals set forth by the Violent Crime Control and Law Enforcement Act of 1994, its legacy is marred by criticism regarding its role in the expansion of the U.S. prison population and the privatization of the prison system[9]. While the Act succeeded

4 "The Violent Crime Control and Law Enforcement Act of 1994." History, Art & Archives, U.S. House of Representatives.

5 "Private Prisons in the United States," The Sentencing Project, 2020.

6 Ibid.

7 Ibid.

8 Ibid.

9 Ibid.

in implementing significant legal and policy changes, the ensuing rise of private prisons and the complex challenges of mass incarceration present a paradoxical outcome: a nation grappling with the consequences of its pursuit of safety and justice.

In this critical analysis, it becomes imperative to revisit the foundational principles of criminal justice and consider reforms that balance the needs of public safety with the imperative of equitable and humane treatment of those within the penal system. The story of the 1994 Crime Bill and the privatization of prisons serves as a cautionary tale, reminding us of the complexities inherent in legislating morality and the unintended consequences of intertwining profit with punishment.

Here is a short summary of the Violent Crime Control And Law Enforcement Act

- The Violent Crime Control and Law Enforcement Act of 1994 is the largest crime bill in U.S. history, providing for 100,000 new police officers and $9.7 billion in funding for prisons.
- Introduced by Jack Brooks and passed by the 103rd Congress, it was signed into law by President Bill Clinton.
- The Act expanded federal law significantly, including introducing the Federal Assault Weapons Ban.
- It created 60 new death penalty offenses and new classes of individuals banned from possessing firearms.
- Aimed at reducing violent crime and improving law enforcement effectiveness, it also sought to decrease recidivism rates.
- Despite intentions, private prisons, incentivized by the Act, did not achieve expected reductions in operating costs or recidivism rates.
- The Act contributed to the privatization of prisons by providing financial incentives for states to adopt stricter sentencing laws and build new prisons.

- This privatization turned incarceration into a profitable business model, with companies like CoreCivic (formerly Corrections Corporation of America) reaping significant profits.
- Critics argue that the Act led to mass incarceration without substantial gains in public safety, as private prisons often focus more on profit than rehabilitation.
- The Act's emphasis on tough sentencing laws and financial incentives for prison construction contributed to the growth of the private prison industry.
- Over time, the profitability of private prisons has been driven by contracts with governments that pay per diem rates per prisoner, creating a financial interest in high incarceration rates.
- Despite initial goals, the Act's legacy includes criticism for its role in the expansion of the U.S. prison population and the privatization of the prison system.

The Continuation of Slavery and the Profitization of Incarceration

In the narrative of American history, the 13th Amendment is often celebrated as the constitutional provision that abolished slavery. However, a closer examination reveals a critical caveat: slavery and involuntary servitude are prohibited "except as a punishment for crime whereof the party shall have been duly convicted"[10]. This exception clause has permitted the perpetuation of a form of slavery within the United States, manifesting most conspicuously within the penal system.

The era of President Bill Clinton marked a pivotal shift in the landscape of the American prison system,

[10] 13th Amendment to the U.S. Constitution.

characterized by an increasing trend towards the privatization of correctional facilities. This shift was underpinned by a reimagining of incarceration, not primarily as a means of rehabilitation, but as an avenue for profit generation. The privatization of prisons emerged not only as a response to overcrowding and budgetary constraints but also as a strategic move embraced by investors seeking to capitalize on the expanding market of inmate management[11].

The legislative milestone known as the Violent Crime Control and Law Enforcement Act of 1994 played a significant role in expanding the prison population. Championed by then-President Clinton, this Act introduced measures that significantly increased the number of incarcerations, with policies that disproportionately impacted African Americans[12]. Mandatory minimum sentences, three-strikes laws, and a general tough-on-crime approach contributed to a burgeoning prison population, fostering an environment ripe for the privatization and profitization of prisons.

The financial incentives tied to the construction and operation of private prisons are substantial, casting a stark light on the profit motives embedded within the American penal system. Building a prison cell can secure $82,000, while housing each prisoner can generate $27,000 annually for the prison owner[13]. It's essential to note, however, that these profits can vary significantly by state, reflecting the

11 Travis, John. "Private Prisons in the United States: An Assessment of Current Practice." American Journal of Criminal Justice, vol. 20, no. 1, 1995.

12 Alexander, Michelle. The New Jim Crow: Mass Incarceration in the Age of Colorblindness. The New Press, 2010.

13 Bauer, Shane. "American Prison: A Reporter's Undercover Journey into the Business of Punishment." Penguin Press, 2018.

diverse contractual agreements and local policies governing the operation of private correctional facilities[14].

Opponents of this system argue that it creates perverse incentives, where the goal of reducing recidivism and rehabilitating inmates is overshadowed by the drive for profit. Critics contend that privatization leads to cost-cutting measures that compromise the quality of care and rehabilitation services provided to inmates, thus failing to address the root causes of criminal behavior and potentially exacerbating recidivism rates[15].

Moreover, the disproportionate impact of these policies on African American communities raises profound concerns about racial justice and equality. The mass incarceration of African Americans, facilitated by policies enacted during the Clinton era, has been critiqued as a modern form of racial control, perpetuating cycles of poverty, disenfranchisement, and social exclusion[16].

The 13th Amendment's exception for penal labor, combined with the privatization of prisons and the policies of the 1994 Crime Bill, reveal a complex web of economic interests and social injustices. This system, while lucrative for some, imposes significant costs on society, particularly on marginalized communities. As we move forward, it is imperative to reevaluate the priorities of the American penal system, ensuring that rehabilitation and justice, rather than profit, guide our approach to correction and community safety.

14 Dolovich, Sharon. "State Punishment and Private Prisons." Duke Law Journal, vol. 55, no. 3, 2005.

15 Gottschalk, Marie. "Caught: The Prison State and the Lockdown of American Politics." Princeton University Press, 2014.

16 Wacquant, Loïc. Punishing the Poor: The Neoliberal Government of Social Insecurity. Duke University Press, 2009.

The New Plantation: Profitization of the Penal System and Its Impact on African American Communities

The American penal system has undergone a dramatic transformation, shifting from state-owned facilities to dominantly private entities. This shift marks a significant departure from traditional models of incarceration, positioning the prison industry as a lucrative sector within the private economy[17]. The majority of American prisons now operate under the management of private corporations, which, through contractual agreements with state and federal governments, have turned imprisonment into a source of substantial profit[18].

This transition to privatized incarceration has had profound implications, particularly for African American communities. The prison industry, in its current form, operates not merely as a system for containing criminal behavior but as a contemporary mechanism for generating unearned income, drawing unsettling parallels to the economic models of slavery that once thrived in the United States[19]. African Americans, disproportionately represented in prison populations, find themselves ensnared in a system that commodifies their incarceration, perpetuating cycles of economic exploitation and social disenfranchisement[20].

17 Bauer, Shane. "American Prison: A Reporter's Undercover Journey into the Business of Punishment." Penguin Press, 2018.

18 Dolovich, Sharon. "State Punishment and Private Prisons." Duke Law Journal, vol. 55, no. 3, 2005.

19 Alexander, Michelle. "The New Jim Crow: Mass Incarceration in the Age of Colorblindness." The New Press, 2010

20 Ibid.

The burgeoning prison populations have catalyzed a parallel industry dedicated to prison construction and related services. This sector has seen exponential growth, contributing billions of dollars to the private sector and fostering an ecosystem wherein incarceration is incentivized as a means of economic gain[21]. The profitability of this industry hinges on the steady influx of inmates, creating perverse incentives that prioritize occupancy rates over rehabilitation and societal reintegration.

Critics argue that this profit-driven model undermines the foundational goals of the penal system, shifting the focus from correction and rehabilitation to financial performance and shareholder returns[22]. The ethical implications of such a system have sparked intense debate, with opponents highlighting the moral quandaries associated with monetizing human confinement.

Supporters of privatized prisons contend that these institutions operate more efficiently and cost-effectively than their state-run counterparts, arguing that the competitive pressures of the marketplace drive innovations in inmate management and rehabilitation services[23]. However, empirical evidence supporting these claims remains contested, with numerous studies indicating that privatization does not necessarily yield better outcomes in terms of safety, recidivism rates, or cost savings[24].

The transformation of the American penal system into a profit-driven enterprise raises fundamental questions about the role of incarceration in society. As the prison industry

[21] Gottschalk, Marie. "Caught: The Prison State and the Lockdown of American Politics." Princeton University Press, 2014.

[22] Ibid.

[23] Logan, Charles. "Private Prisons: Cons and Pros." Oxford University Press, 1990.

[24] Useem, Bert and Piehl, Anne Morrison. "Prison State: The Challenge of Mass Incarceration." Cambridge University Press, 2008.

continues to expand, fueled by policies that disproportionately impact African American communities, it is imperative to scrutinize the long-term implications of this shift. The legacy of slavery, manifest in the economic exploitation of African Americans, casts a long shadow over the contemporary prison industry, challenging the nation to confront the ethical and moral dimensions of incarceration in the 21st century.

Reassessing the Impact of Private Prisons on Crime and Cost

The assumption that increased incarceration serves as an effective deterrent to crime is increasingly challenged by the data, which reveals a disconnect between the number of individuals imprisoned and the impact on crime rates. This phenomenon, wherein the growth of the prison population does not correspond to a commensurate decrease in crime, highlights a fundamental flaw in the penal system's strategy to achieve public safety[25].

The move towards the privatization of prisons in the United States, which began in earnest during the 1980s, marked a significant shift in the management and operation of correctional facilities. This era, underscored by the war on drugs, witnessed not only an unprecedented increase in the prison population but also the emergence of overcrowded state and federal prisons. It was within this context that the Corrections Corporation of America (CCA), now known as CoreCivic, established itself as a dominant

[25] Travis, John, and Western, Bruce. "The Growth of Incarceration in the United States: Exploring Causes and Consequences." National Research Council, 2014.

force in the burgeoning prison industry, securing lucrative contracts to operate facilities across the nation[26].

Critics argue that the privatization of prisons, while marketed as a solution to the challenges of overcrowding and high operational costs, has not delivered on its promises. Despite assertions from proponents that private prisons offer cost savings over their state-run counterparts, evidence suggests that these claims do not hold up under scrutiny. Studies comparing the operational costs of private and public prisons reveal that the anticipated savings for taxpayers are often overstated, if not entirely illusory[27].

One of the primary rationales behind the push for privatization was the notion that private entities, driven by the efficiencies of the free market, would innovate and manage prisons more cost-effectively than the government. However, the reality has proven more complex. The contractual obligations between private prison companies and governments frequently include minimum occupancy requirements, which effectively guarantee profits for the corporations regardless of the actual need for incarceration. This arrangement creates a perverse incentive structure, prioritizing the financial interests of private prison operators over the broader societal goal of reducing crime through effective rehabilitation and reintegration strategies[28].

Moreover, the rise of the private prison industry has sparked concerns about the ethical implications of profiting from incarceration. The commodification of prisoners raises fundamental questions about the motivations for punishment and the role of the criminal justice system in a democratic society. Critics contend that the profit motive

26 Bauer, Shane. "American Prison: A Reporter's Undercover Journey into the Business of Punishment." Penguin Press, 2018.

27 Dolovich, Sharon. "State Punishment and Private Prisons." Duke Law Journal, vol. 55, no. 3, 2005.

28

inherent in private prisons undermines the pursuit of justice, as decisions about the treatment and rehabilitation of inmates may be influenced more by cost considerations than by the best interests of the individuals and communities involved[29].

The Commodification of Confinement

In the landscape of the American penal system, the presence of private prisons has introduced a paradigm wherein incarceration is not merely a means of societal protection but a source of profit. Nearly one-fifth of federal prisoners find themselves within the confines of for-profit prisons[30], a statistic that underscores the significant role these institutions play in the broader correctional landscape.

The operational dynamics of private prisons often diverge significantly from their government-run counterparts, particularly in their approach to discipline and inmate management. Studies have shown that private prisons tend to issue more infractions than public prisons[31]. This practice, ostensibly a measure to maintain order, can extend inmates' sentences, thereby increasing the profits derived from extended incarcerations. The financial incentives baked into the private prison model thus appear to conflict with the rehabilitative goals of the correctional system.

Furthermore, the contracts governing private prisons frequently include occupancy clauses, stipulating that states

29 Alexander, Michelle. "The New Jim Crow: Mass Incarceration in the Age of Colorblindness." The New Press, 2010.

30 U.S. Department of Justice, Bureau of Justice Statistics.

31 Wagner, Peter, and Sakala, Leah. "Mass Incarceration: The Whole Pie 2020." Prison Policy Initiative.

maintain high levels of prison occupancy—sometimes as high as 90-100%—or face financial penalties[32]. These clauses effectively transform prisoners into commodities, with their continued confinement ensuring the financial viability of the private prisons. This system of mandated quotas incentivizes not only the prolonged incarceration of individuals but also a legislative and judicial approach that favors incarceration over alternative forms of punishment or rehabilitation.

Critics argue that the overarching objective of private prisons is the generation of profit, with considerations of crime reduction and inmate rehabilitation being secondary[33]. This profit-driven motive raises ethical questions about the purpose and principles of the American justice system. When financial gain is intertwined with the administration of justice, the risk emerges that the scales will be tipped not in favor of fairness and rehabilitation but towards maximizing revenue.

One of the most contentious practices within both private and public prisons is the use of solitary confinement. Deployed as a punishment for infractions, solitary confinement is criticized for its psychological and physical toll on inmates[34]. The practice, deemed cruel and inhumane by numerous human rights organizations, epitomizes the broader issues plaguing the incarceration system, where punitive measures often overshadow efforts towards rehabilitation and humane treatment.

[32] Dolovich, Sharon. "State Punishment and Private Prisons." Duke Law Journal, vol. 55, no. 3, 2005.

[33] Gottschalk, Marie. "Caught: The Prison State and the Lockdown of American Politics." Princeton University Press, 2014.

[34] Haney, Craig. "Mental Health Issues in Long-Term Solitary and 'Supermax' Confinement." Crime & Delinquency, vol. 49, no. 1, 2003.

The reliance on private prisons within the United States poses profound challenges to the ethos of justice and rehabilitation that ideally underpins the correctional system. The inherent conflict between profit generation and the equitable administration of justice calls for a reevaluation of the role of private prisons. As this analysis reveals, the commodification of confinement not only impacts the lives of those incarcerated but also reflects broader societal choices about justice, rehabilitation, and the role of profit in the penal system.

The Continuation of Slavery and the Black Population Used as Instruments of Unearned Income—Chapter 13

In American society, where justice purports to be blind, the scales are undeniably imbalanced when it comes to the representation of African Americans in the prison population. Despite constituting roughly 13% of the U.S. population, Black Americans find themselves disproportionately ensnared within the confines of the penal system, comprising approximately 38% of the total prison demographic[1]. This stark disparity not only highlights systemic biases but also raises profound questions about the equity of sentencing policies and the broader socio-economic factors at play.

The origins of this imbalance are multifaceted, deeply rooted in historical inequalities and perpetuated by enduring racial prejudices. The criminal justice system, ostensibly a mechanism for maintaining public safety, has been criticized for its role in sustaining a cycle of

[1] NAACP, "Criminal Justice Fact Sheet."

disenfranchisement that disproportionately affects African American communities. Critics argue that sentencing policies, particularly those related to non-violent drug offenses, have been applied in a manner that disproportionately targets Black individuals[2]. This assertion is supported by data indicating that African Americans are incarcerated at more than five times the rate of white Americans[3].

Opponents of this perspective contend that the higher incarceration rates among African Americans are a reflection of higher crime rates within these communities, rather than systemic bias[4]. They argue that law enforcement and sentencing policies are designed to address crime irrespective of race, suggesting that disparities in incarceration rates are a consequence of disparities in offending. However, this viewpoint often fails to account for the underlying socio-economic conditions that contribute to higher rates of criminality, including poverty, limited access to quality education, and unemployment[5].

The dialogue surrounding the disproportionate incarceration of African Americans cannot be divorced from the historical context of racial inequality in the United States. The legacy of slavery, segregation, and institutional racism has left indelible marks on the fabric of American society, influencing systemic structures in ways that continue to disadvantage Black individuals[6]. The criminal justice system, in this regard, functions not only as a

2 Alexander, Michelle. "The New Jim Crow: Mass Incarceration in the Age of Colorblindness." The New Press, 2010.

3 Bureau of Justice Statistics, "Prisoners in 2018."

4 MacDonald, Heather. "The War on Cops: How the New Attack on Law and Order Makes Everyone Less Safe." Encounter Books, 2016.

5 Western, Bruce. "Punishment and Inequality in America." Russell Sage Foundation, 2006.

6 Coates, Ta-Nehisi. "Between the World and Me." Spiegel & Grau, 2015.

punitive institution but also as a reflection of these broader societal inequities.

Reform advocates emphasize the need for a holistic approach to addressing these disparities, calling for changes that extend beyond the criminal justice system to tackle the root causes of inequality. Proposals include reforming sentencing laws, particularly those related to drug offenses, enhancing reintegration programs for formerly incarcerated individuals, and investing in community development initiatives aimed at improving socio-economic conditions in marginalized communities[7].

Understanding Incarceration's Grip on the African American Community

The stark, disproportionate representation of African Americans in prison populations emerges as a pivotal concern. A groundbreaking study by the Sentencing Project unveils a grim reality: for Black males born in 2001, the lifetime likelihood of imprisonment stands at one in three; for Black women, the probability is one in eighteen[8]. These figures not only illuminate the systemic inequalities plaguing the system but also underscore the profound, lasting impact on the African American community.

This pervasive cycle of incarceration among African Americans is not a phenomenon occurring in isolation but is deeply intertwined with broader societal structures and historical legacies. Critics might argue that these statistics

[7] Clear, Todd R., and Frost, Natasha A. "The Punishment Imperative: The Rise and Failure of Mass Incarceration in America." NYU Press, 2014.

[8] The Sentencing Project, "Report: Black Disparities in Youth Incarceration." The Sentencing Project, 2020.

simply reflect higher crime rates within these communities. However, this viewpoint fails to account for the systemic biases embedded within law enforcement practices, judicial processes, and sentencing policies—factors that exacerbate the racial disparities observed[9].

The disproportionate likelihood of imprisonment for African Americans can be traced back to a myriad of systemic issues, including but not limited to socioeconomic inequalities, educational disparities, and targeted law enforcement tactics such as the war on drugs. These systemic barriers not only increase the vulnerability of African American individuals to encounters with the criminal justice system but also contribute to the cycle of poverty and marginalization that fuels further criminalization[10].

Opposing viewpoints often overlook the historical context underpinning these disparities. The legacy of segregation, discrimination, and disenfranchisement has created conditions that predispose African American communities to higher rates of poverty, unemployment, and limited access to quality education and healthcare. Such conditions are fertile ground for the perpetuation of crime and subsequent incarceration[11].

Reform advocates emphasize the need for a comprehensive overhaul of the criminal justice system, advocating for policies that address the root causes of crime, promote rehabilitative over punitive responses, and dismantle the systemic biases that disproportionately affect

9 Alexander, Michelle. "The New Jim Crow: Mass Incarceration in the Age of Colorblindness." The New Press, 2010.

10 Western, Bruce, and Pettit, Becky. "Incarceration & Social Inequality." Daedalus, the Journal of the American Academy of Arts & Sciences, 2010.

11 DuVernay, Ava, director. "13th." Netflix, 2016.

African American individuals[12]. Proposals include reforming drug laws, eliminating mandatory minimum sentences, and implementing restorative justice programs aimed at reducing recidivism and facilitating reintegration into society.

In addressing the disparities in lifetime likelihood of imprisonment, it is crucial to engage in a holistic examination of the criminal justice system and its interplay with broader societal issues. The statistics represent not just numbers but lives entangled in a web of systemic injustices, with profound implications for the African American community and society as a whole.

The Disproportionate Incarceration: A Reflective Analysis on African Americans Behind Bars

The incarceration rates among African Americans present a stark reflection of systemic disparities and social inequities. As of the Bureau of Justice Statistics 2018 data, approximately 475,900 Black Americans are incarcerated[13]. With the total U.S. Black population standing at around 47 million, this translates to roughly 1% of the Black population currently serving time behind bars. This statistic, while seemingly small in isolation, reveals profound implications when juxtaposed against the backdrop of racial demographics and historical injustices in the United States.

This significant representation of African Americans in prison populations is not merely a consequence of criminal

[12] Clear, Todd R., and Frost, Natasha A. "The Punishment Imperative: The Rise and Failure of Mass Incarceration in America." NYU Press, 2014.

[13] Bureau of Justice Statistics, "Prisoners in 2018."

activities but is indicative of deeper, systemic biases embedded within the fabric of American society. Critics and advocates alike point to a variety of contributing factors, including targeted law enforcement practices, disparities in sentencing, and socio-economic factors that disproportionately affect Black communities[14]. These elements collectively contribute to the overrepresentation of Black individuals in the penal system, raising critical questions about the fairness and equity of the criminal justice process.

Opponents of this perspective may argue that the higher incarceration rates are reflective of higher crime rates within these communities rather than indicative of any systemic bias or injustice. They often call for a focus on personal responsibility and adherence to the law, suggesting that the solution lies within changes in individual behavior rather than systemic reform[15]. However, this viewpoint overlooks the complex interplay of historical, socio-economic, and political factors that have systematically disadvantaged African American communities, contributing to higher rates of poverty, limited access to quality education, and fewer employment opportunities—all of which are correlated with higher incidences of crime[16].

The disparity in incarceration rates also sheds light on the broader implications for African American communities, including the disruption of family structures, economic disenfranchisement, and the perpetuation of cycles of poverty and marginalization. The effects of incarceration

[14] Alexander, Michelle. "The New Jim Crow: Mass Incarceration in the Age of Colorblindness." The New Press, 2010.

[15] MacDonald, Heather. "The War on Cops: How the New Attack on Law and Order Makes Everyone Less Safe." Encounter Books, 2016.

[16] Western, Bruce, and Pettit, Becky. "Incarceration & Social Inequality." Daedalus, the Journal of the American Academy of Arts & Sciences, 2010.

extend beyond the individual, impacting entire communities and generations through the loss of economic contributors, parents, and community members[17].

Furthermore, the privatization of prisons and the profit motives driving the prison industry exacerbate these disparities, with private prisons having financial incentives to maintain high levels of incarceration. This commercialization of confinement raises ethical concerns about the motivations behind incarceration and whether profit considerations may override the goals of justice and rehabilitation[18].

A Glimpse into Tomorrow: The Future of Incarceration and Its Impact on African Americans

The endeavor to predict future trends is a complex and multifaceted challenge, shaped by a myriad of factors ranging from policy changes and socio-economic developments to demographic shifts. However, an analysis rooted in the current realities faced by African Americans within the United States' criminal justice system presents a sobering projection for the next two decades. If the existing disparities continue unabated, the landscape of incarceration is poised to maintain, if not exacerbate, the disproportionate representation of Black Americans behind bars[19].

[17] Clear, Todd R., and Frost, Natasha A. "The Punishment Imperative: The Rise and Failure of Mass Incarceration in America." NYU Press, 2014.

[18] Bauer, Shane. "American Prison: A Reporter's Undercover Journey into the Business of Punishment." Penguin Press, 2018.

[19] Bureau of Justice Statistics, "Prisoners in 2018."

At present, African Americans constitute approximately 13% of the U.S. population, yet they account for a staggering 38% of the prison population—a disparity that starkly illustrates the racial imbalances permeating the criminal justice system[20]. Looking forward, with the Black population projected to comprise 15% of the U.S. populace by 2040, the absence of significant reform threatens to perpetuate, and potentially intensify, this imbalance. Such a scenario underscores not merely a failure to rectify existing inequities but also signifies a persistent disregard for the principles of justice and equality that are purported to underpin the American legal framework[21].

Undertaking a mathematical projection of future incarceration rates necessitates a sophisticated model that accommodates potential shifts in criminal justice policies, socio-economic conditions, and demographic patterns. While precise forecasting is fraught with uncertainties, the prevailing data and trends furnish a basis for concern. Without concerted advocacy and reform efforts aimed at dismantling the systemic factors contributing to the over-incarceration of African Americans, the next 20 years could witness sustained, if not increased, levels of disparity within the prison system[22].

Critics and skeptics may argue that demographic trends and crime statistics justify the current rates of incarceration among African Americans. However, this stance overlooks the systemic biases and socio-economic inequalities that disproportionately funnel Black individuals into the criminal justice system. The counter-narrative, championed by advocates for criminal justice reform, emphasizes the necessity of addressing the root causes of crime,

20 NAACP, "Criminal Justice Fact Sheet."

21 United States Census Bureau projections.

22 The Sentencing Project, "Report: Black Disparities in Youth Incarceration."

implementing equitable sentencing policies, and fostering rehabilitation over punitive measures[23].

The call for reform is driven by a recognition of the profound impact that incarceration has on individuals and communities alike. Beyond the immediate loss of liberty, imprisonment carries long-term consequences that extend to familial bonds, economic opportunities, and civic participation. For the African American community, which has historically been marginalized and subjected to discriminatory practices, the stakes are particularly high. The perpetuation of current trends not only exacerbates social and economic disparities but also erodes the fabric of community cohesion and mutual trust[24].

The Projection of African American Net Worth Toward Zero by 2050

The looming economic forecast for African Americans reveals a disturbing trajectory towards a median net worth of zero by the year 2050. This projection is not merely a numerical anomaly but a reflection of deep-rooted systemic inequities that perpetuate the cycle of poverty within the African American community. At the heart of this economic disenfranchisement lies the disproportionate impact of incarceration on African American individuals and families, which serves as a significant barrier to wealth accumulation and economic stability.

23 Alexander, Michelle. "The New Jim Crow: Mass Incarceration in the Age of Colorblindness." The New Press, 2010.

24 Clear, Todd R., and Frost, Natasha A. "The Punishment Imperative: The Rise and Failure of Mass Incarceration in America." NYU Press, 2014.

Incarceration, particularly within the African American community, is a pivotal disruption to the economic progression of individuals and families. The United States, which houses the world's largest prison population, sees African Americans disproportionately represented among those incarcerated. This disparity significantly hinders the community's economic advancement. Incarcerated individuals face lost wages, and upon release, their prospects for employment are markedly diminished, limiting their ability to reintegrate into society and contribute economically[25]. The stigma of a criminal record further exacerbates these challenges, curtailing access to employment, housing, and educational opportunities—key components of wealth accumulation.

Furthermore, the economic ripple effects of incarceration extend beyond the individual to their families and communities. Families of incarcerated individuals often grapple with financial instability, compounded by the loss of a contributing household member's income and the added costs associated with incarceration, such as legal fees and the expense of maintaining contact. This financial strain hampers the ability of families to save or invest, critically undermining the intergenerational transfer of wealth[26].

Critics and skeptics of the projection that African American net worth may reach zero by 2050 often point to instances of economic success within the community or argue that policy reforms have sufficiently addressed systemic biases. They may also challenge the validity of focusing solely on racial disparities, suggesting that economic issues should be addressed through a universal, not race-specific, lens. However, such viewpoints tend to

[25] Western, Bruce, and Becky Pettit. "Incarceration & social inequality." Daedalus 139, no. 3 (2010): 8-19.

[26] Western, Bruce, and Becky Pettit. "Incarceration & social inequality." Daedalus 139, no. 3 (2010): 8-19.

overlook the pervasive and cumulative nature of racial disparities entrenched in the American economic system. While individual successes are noteworthy and policy reforms are critical, they are not sufficient to counteract the systemic barriers that continue to impede the economic progress of the African American community as a whole.

The Economic Eclipse: The Vanishing Net Worth of African American Families by 2050

The incarceration of a family member is a multifaceted economic detriment to African American households. It not only subtracts a potential income earner from the family's economic equation but also introduces a host of financial burdens that compound the family's fiscal challenges. Legal defense costs, coupled with the myriad expenses associated with maintaining contact with the incarcerated individual, such as travel for prison visits and financial support for commissary accounts, impose significant financial strain on families. This economic pressure is acutely felt in African American communities, where families are already navigating the precarious tightrope of economic instability[27].

The ripple effects of this financial strain are profound. Savings, often viewed as a buffer against economic shocks and a vehicle for future investment, become depleted. The capacity to invest in property or education, crucial avenues for wealth generation and upward mobility, is markedly reduced. Furthermore, the reliance on debt to manage immediate financial needs not only erodes current net worth but also encumbers future financial prospects through the

[27] Clear, Todd R. "The effects of high imprisonment rates on communities." Crime and Justice 37, no. 1 (2008): 97-132.

accrual of interest and fees, perpetuating a cycle of economic vulnerability[28].

Critics might argue that focusing on the negative economic impacts of incarceration overlooks the personal responsibility of individuals and the importance of law and order. They may also contend that economic advancement is achievable through hard work and determination, regardless of systemic barriers. While individual agency and the pursuit of legal reforms are indeed important, these arguments often fail to acknowledge the structural inequities that disproportionately affect African American communities. The systemic nature of these challenges requires solutions that address both the symptoms and the root causes of economic disparity[29].

To counteract this trajectory toward economic erasure, it is imperative to implement policy interventions that address both the systemic factors contributing to high rates of incarceration among African Americans and the economic consequences of these trends. Policies aimed at reforming the criminal justice system, coupled with initiatives to support economic development and wealth-building opportunities within African American communities, are critical to reversing the course of diminishing net worth.

Criminal Records and the Decline in African American Wealth

28 Pager, Devah, and Bruce Western. "Identifying discrimination at work: The use of field experiments." Journal of Social Issues 68, no. 2 (2012): 221-237.

29 Alexander, Michelle. The New Jim Crow: Mass Incarceration in the Age of Colorblindness. New York: The New Press, 2010.

Criminal records serve as an enduring barrier to employment, casting a long shadow over individuals' lives long after their sentences have been served. The stigma associated with a criminal past significantly diminishes the likelihood of securing stable, well-paying employment. For African Americans, this barrier compounds existing employment discrimination, creating a formidable obstacle to economic progress. Studies have shown that the employment rate for formerly incarcerated individuals is substantially lower than for the general population, with African Americans facing even greater challenges in securing employment due to pervasive racial biases in hiring practices[30].

The repercussions of this employment barrier on wealth accumulation are profound. Without access to stable employment, formerly incarcerated individuals—and by extension, their families—struggle to build the financial resources necessary for wealth accumulation. This includes savings, investment in property, and other assets that contribute to net worth. Over time, this lack of wealth accumulation can lead to a net worth decline, not just for individuals, but for the African American community as a whole[31].

Critics of this perspective may argue that the emphasis on criminal records as a barrier to employment overlooks the importance of personal responsibility and the need for individuals to overcome their past actions. They may also point to programs aimed at workforce reintegration as solutions to this issue. While personal accountability and reintegration programs are indeed important, they cannot

[30] Pager, Devah. "The mark of a criminal record." American Journal of Sociology 108, no. 5 (2003): 937-975.

[31] Western, Bruce. "The impact of incarceration on wage mobility and inequality." American Sociological Review 67, no. 4 (2002): 526-546.

fully mitigate the systemic barriers faced by formerly incarcerated African Americans. The scale of the challenge requires comprehensive policy interventions that address both the root causes of high incarceration rates and the systemic biases in employment practices[32].

To reverse the trajectory towards a net worth of zero by 2050, it is crucial to implement policies that both reduce the incidence of incarceration among African Americans and mitigate the impact of criminal records on employment opportunities. This includes reforms to the criminal justice system that address racial disparities in sentencing, as well as initiatives that promote fair hiring practices, such as "Ban the Box" legislation, which removes the requirement to disclose criminal history on job applications[33].

32 Alexander, Michelle. The New Jim Crow: Mass Incarceration in the Age of Colorblindness. New York: The New Press, 2010.

33

Part 6: The Problems Facing The White Ally

Respectfully, No More White Saviors— Chapter 14

True diversity, a goal sought by many in the quest for a just and equitable society, remains elusive without a concerted effort to dismantle the very foundation upon which discrimination is built: racism. This undertaking involves more than mere passive learning or superficial engagement with the concepts of racial equality; it necessitates a deep, active process of unlearning racism that permeates every facet of our society. In his work, Dr. Claud Anderson has emphasized the importance of understanding the economic and power structures that sustain racial disparities, arguing that without addressing these underlying causes, attempts at achieving true diversity will be ineffectual[1].

The unlearning of racism requires an acknowledgment of its systemic nature and the ways in which it has been embedded into the fabric of our institutions, from education and healthcare to the criminal justice system and the economy[2]. This systemic racism is not merely a collection of individual prejudices but a historical legacy that advantages some while disadvantaging others. The challenge, therefore, lies not only in changing individual attitudes but in transforming the structural mechanisms that perpetuate inequality.

[1] Anderson, Claud. "PowerNomics: The National Plan to Empower Black America." Powernomics Corporation of America, 2001.

[2] Alexander, Michelle. "The New Jim Crow: Mass Incarceration in the Age of Colorblindness." The New Press, 2010.

Opponents of this view argue that focusing on systemic racism inflames racial tensions and promotes a victimhood mentality among minorities. They advocate for a colorblind approach, suggesting that acknowledging race only serves to divide rather than unite[3]. However, this perspective fails to recognize that colorblindness itself is a privilege, one that ignores the lived realities of those who face racial discrimination daily. It is a simplistic solution to a complex problem, one that overlooks the necessity of confronting uncomfortable truths about privilege and inequality.

The process of unlearning racism involves a multifaceted approach that includes education, dialogue, and action. Education must go beyond the traditional narratives taught in schools to include the voices and experiences of those marginalized by history. It requires a critical examination of the ways in which history has been written by the victors, often at the expense of truth and reconciliation[4]. Dialogue, too, is crucial, but it must be rooted in a willingness to listen and learn from those who have been directly impacted by racism. It is not enough to speak; one must also be willing to hear, even when the truths spoken are uncomfortable or challenging.

Action, however, is perhaps the most critical component of unlearning racism. It is not sufficient to merely understand or talk about systemic racism; one must also be committed to dismantling it. This includes supporting policies and initiatives that aim to address racial disparities, from criminal justice reform to economic empowerment programs for marginalized communities[5]. It

[3] Steele, Shelby. "Shame: How America's Past Sins Have Polarized Our Country." Basic Books, 2015.

[4] Loewen, James W. "Lies My Teacher Told Me: Everything Your American History Textbook Got Wrong." The New Press, 1995.

[5] Coates, Ta-Nehisi. "Between the World and Me." Spiegel & Grau, 2015.

also involves challenging racist behavior when encountered, whether in the workplace, in social settings, or online.

True diversity cannot be achieved through passive measures or by ignoring the root causes of racial inequality. It requires an active, ongoing effort to unlearn the racism that has been woven into the very fabric of our society. This is a challenging task, one that demands courage, commitment, and a willingness to confront uncomfortable truths. However, it is only through this process of unlearning and action that we can hope to build a more just and equitable society for all.

Beyond Performative Allyship: Seeking Genuine Commitment in Anti-Racism Efforts

The phenomenon of performative allyship has emerged as a significant concern among activists and scholars alike. This form of allyship, characterized by superficial gestures and actions, often serves more to enhance the social standing of individuals within the dominant white culture rather than to effect real change or challenge systemic racism. Dr. Claud Anderson, in his analysis of power and economic disparity, underscores the necessity of understanding the structural underpinnings of racial inequity to achieve genuine societal transformation[6].

Performative allyship manifests in various forms, from social media activism that lacks follow-through to public declarations of solidarity without substantive action or commitment to racial justice causes. Such actions, while ostensibly supportive, fail to confront the systemic nature of racism and, in some cases, may inadvertently reinforce it.

6 Anderson, Claud. "Black Labor, White Wealth: The Search for Power and Economic Justice." Powernomics Corporation of America, 1994.

Critics argue that performative allyship is not merely insufficient but potentially harmful, as it can dilute the urgency of the fight against racism, giving the appearance of progress where little has been made[7].

The critique of performative allyship is not without its detractors. Some argue that public expressions of support, even if symbolic, raise awareness and contribute to a broader cultural shift towards recognizing and addressing racial injustices[8]. However, this perspective is challenged by the notion that awareness alone is inadequate without concerted efforts to dismantle the structures and systems that perpetuate racism. The mere acknowledgment of racism, devoid of actionable steps towards systemic change, falls short of the comprehensive approach advocated by Anderson and others who emphasize the need for economic empowerment and systemic reform[9].

Genuine commitment to anti-racism, as opposed to performative allyship, demands a deep, introspective examination of one's own positionality within systems of power and privilege. It requires allies to not only advocate for change externally but to undertake the more challenging work of personal and communal transformation. This involves educating oneself about the complex history and current realities of racial oppression, actively listening to and centering the voices of those most affected by racism, and committing to long-term actions that support systemic change[10].

[7] DiAngelo, Robin. "White Fragility: Why It's So Hard for White People to Talk About Racism." Beacon Press, 2018.

[8] Kendi, Ibram X. "How to Be an Antiracist." One World, 2019.

[9] Coates, Ta-Nehisi. "Between the World and Me." Spiegel & Grau, 2015.

[10] Crenshaw, Kimberlé. "On Intersectionality: Essential Writings." The New Press, 2017.

Additionally, genuine allyship recognizes the importance of economic justice as a critical component of racial equity. Anderson's work on the economic foundations of power inequalities highlights the necessity of addressing economic disparities as part of the fight against systemic racism. Allies committed to racial justice must therefore consider how their actions can contribute to economic empowerment for marginalized communities, advocating for policies and practices that promote equitable access to resources and opportunities[11].

Beyond the White Savior Complex And Embracing Genuine Allyship

The narrative that Black individuals or communities require salvation from white benefactors is not only misleading but fundamentally flawed. This perspective, widely criticized in contemporary social justice dialogues, undermines the resilience, agency, and historical struggles of Black people against systemic oppression. Dr. Claud Anderson's extensive work on power dynamics and economic structures provides a critical foundation for understanding the fallacies of white saviorism and highlights the importance of economic empowerment and autonomy for Black communities[12].

The concept of the white savior complex, a term that has gained traction in recent years, is rooted in colonial and imperialistic ideologies. It presupposes that Black

[11] Anderson, Claud. "Powernomics: The National Plan to Empower Black America." Powernomics Corporation of America, 2001.

[12] Anderson, Claud. "Black Labor, White Wealth: The Search for Power and Economic Justice." Powernomics Corporation of America, 1994.

individuals lack the capacity to advocate for themselves or to navigate the challenges posed by systemic racism without the intervention of white individuals. This paradigm, however, neglects the rich history of Black resistance, intellectual thought, and community-led movements that have been instrumental in challenging racial injustices and advancing civil rights[13].

Historically, Black communities have not only survived systemic attempts to marginalize and oppress them but have also thrived and forged paths of resistance that challenge the very foundations of racial inequality. The Haitian Revolution (1791-1804), often cited as the most successful slave rebellion in the Western Hemisphere, exemplifies the power and agency of Black individuals fighting against their oppressors[14]. Similarly, the Civil Rights Movement in the United States was largely driven by Black leaders, activists, and communities who mobilized against racial segregation and discrimination[15].

White saviorism is often fueled by a combination of guilt and a desire for quick fixes to complex problems. This approach to allyship is problematic because it centers the feelings and experiences of white individuals while minimizing the lived realities and autonomy of Black people. Performative acts of allyship, such as posting on social media without engaging in meaningful actions or learning, do little to address the systemic nature of racism. Moreover, these acts can reinforce paternalistic attitudes and maintain the status quo of racial hierarchies[16].

[13] DiAngelo, Robin. "White Fragility: Why It's So Hard for White People to Talk About Racism." Beacon Press, 2018.

[14] Dubois, Laurent. "Avengers of the New World: The Story of the Haitian Revolution." Belknap Press, 2004.

[15] King, Martin Luther Jr. "Why We Can't Wait." Harper & Row, 1964.

[16] Saad, Layla F. "Me and White Supremacy: Combat Racism, Change the World, and Become a Good Ancestor." Sourcebooks, 2020.

Genuine allyship requires a willingness to engage in the uncomfortable process of unlearning racism and confronting one's own complicity in systems of oppression. It involves listening to and amplifying Black voices, supporting Black-led initiatives, and committing to long-term actions that dismantle systemic barriers to racial equity. True allies recognize that their role is not to "save" but to support and stand in solidarity with Black communities in their ongoing struggle for justice and equality[17].

Furthermore, addressing economic disparities and supporting the economic empowerment of Black communities are critical components of dismantling systemic racism. As Anderson articulates, economic independence and control over resources are essential for achieving true power and autonomy[18]. Allies must, therefore, advocate for policies and practices that promote economic justice and support Black entrepreneurship and business ownership.

Dissecting the White Savior Industrial Complex

The White Savior Industrial Complex, a term coined by Teju Cole in 2012, encapsulates a critical dilemma within contemporary social justice movements. This phenomenon is characterized by a pattern wherein the emotional gratification of white individuals is prioritized over the pursuit of justice and the enactment of substantive, transformative actions within communities of color[19]. The

17 Oluo, Ijeoma. "So You Want to Talk About Race." Seal Press, 2018.

18 Anderson, Claud. "Powernomics: The National Plan to Empower Black America." Powernomics Corporation of America, 2001.

19 Cole, Teju. "The White Savior Industrial Complex." The Atlantic, March 21, 2012.

essence of this complex lies in the misguided belief that the presence and participation of white individuals in anti-racism efforts are not only necessary but are also sufficient to catalyze meaningful change. This perspective, however, inadvertently undermines the autonomy, expertise, and leadership of those within the impacted communities.

At the core of the White Savior Industrial Complex is the performative nature of allyship, which manifests in actions that are more about self-affirmation and public image than about effecting systemic change. One of the critical arenas where this dynamic plays out is in charitable work. When such endeavors are not directly informed by and centered on the empowerment of the communities they aim to serve, they risk perpetuating the very dynamics of inequality they purport to address[20]. Genuine charity and support must be led by those who understand the nuanced needs and desires of their communities, as opposed to being dictated by external, often uninformed, benefactors.

The harmful impact of performative allyship cannot be overstated. By centering the experiences and emotional journeys of white individuals, it sidelines the real, lived experiences of Black people and people of color, reducing their roles to mere backdrops in the narrative of white redemption and enlightenment[21]. This not only diverts attention from the systemic issues at hand but also burdens communities of color with the task of navigating and catering to the sensitivities of their would-be allies. The focus shifts from dismantling oppressive structures to managing the feelings of those who hold systemic power, thereby stalling genuine progress.

[20] Reid, Nova. "No More White Saviours, Thanks: How to Be a True Anti-Racist Ally." The Guardian, September 19, 2021.

[21] Saad, Layla F. "Me and White Supremacy: Combat Racism, Change the World, and Become a Good Ancestor." Sourcebooks, 2020.

The critique of the White Savior Industrial Complex is not a dismissal of the potential for meaningful white participation in the fight against racism. Instead, it calls for a reevaluation of the motives and methods of engagement. For white allyship to contribute positively to social justice efforts, it must operate from a place of humility, seeking to amplify rather than overshadow the voices of those at the forefront of their own liberation movements. Allies must be willing to engage in the uncomfortable work of confronting and dismantling their complicity in systems of oppression, rather than seeking absolution through superficial acts of solidarity[22].

Furthermore, the transition from performative to genuine allyship necessitates a commitment to ongoing education and action that extends beyond the immediacy of public crises. It involves investing in the long-term work of building equitable relationships, supporting Black and minority-owned businesses, and advocating for policy changes that address the root causes of inequality[23]. This shift from saviorism to solidarity embodies the recognition that the fight against systemic racism is not a charitable endeavor but a collective moral imperative.

[22] Oluo, Ijeoma. "So You Want to Talk About Race." Seal Press, 2018.
[23] Kendi, Ibram X. "How to Be an Antiracist." One World, 2019.

The Paradox of White Allyship in Racial Justice— Chapter 15

In the journey towards racial equality, the role of white allies has been both pivotal and paradoxical. As they strive to support the fight against systemic racism, these allies often encounter a phenomenon less discussed but critically impactful: white-on-white persecution. This chapter delves into the multifaceted challenges faced by white individuals committed to dismantling the racial hierarchies that simultaneously privilege them and perpetuate injustice against Black communities.

White allies find themselves at a crossroads of conscience and societal expectation, where their advocacy for racial justice is met with a spectrum of negative responses from their own racial cohort. This backlash can manifest in social ostracism, professional repercussions, and, at times, personal threats, underscoring the complex dynamics of privilege and oppression within the framework of allyship[24].

Critics of white allyship, often rooted in conservative or white supremacist ideologies, argue that these efforts undermine societal cohesion, promoting division rather than unity. They posit that the emphasis on systemic racism is an exaggerated narrative used to destabilize social order and diminish the achievements and challenges of white individuals[25]. This viewpoint is pervasive in certain media outlets, where the validity of systemic racism is contested, and the motives of white allies are scrutinized.

However, real-world data and the lived experiences of marginalized communities tell a different story—one where systemic racism is not only evident but deeply ingrained in the fabric of society. Studies have shown that racial disparities persist across various sectors, including criminal justice, healthcare, education, and economic opportunities, underscoring the urgency and legitimacy of the fight for racial justice[26].

The persecution faced by white allies from their peers is indicative of the broader resistance to acknowledging and addressing racial inequities. This resistance is often rooted in fear—fear of losing social status, fear of retribution, and fear of confronting one's own complicity in a racially unjust

[24] Crenshaw, Kimberlé. "Mapping the Margins: Intersectionality, Identity Politics, and Violence against Women of Color." Stanford Law Review 43, no. 6 (1991): 1241-1299.

[25] Kendi, Ibram X. How to Be an Antiracist. New York: One World, 2019.

[26] Alexander, Michelle. The New Jim Crow: Mass Incarceration in the Age of Colorblindness. New York: The New Press, 2010.

system[27]. It is a testament to the depth of racial indoctrination that permeates society, where efforts to dismantle oppressive systems are met with hostility from those it benefits.

Despite these challenges, the role of white allies remains crucial. Their participation in racial justice efforts can bridge divides, leveraging their privilege to amplify marginalized voices and push for systemic change. However, this participation must be approached with humility and a willingness to listen, learn, and, when necessary, step back. True allyship involves recognizing the limits of one's understanding and the importance of deferring to the leadership of those directly impacted by racial injustice[28].

The Complexity of Allyship in Systems of Power

The concept of allyship, particularly among white individuals aiming to support racial justice movements, demands a profound introspection and acknowledgment of the inherent power dynamics at play. It necessitates an understanding that even well-intentioned actions can sometimes echo the very structures of oppression they aim to dismantle[29]. The inadvertent perpetuation of systemic racism by allies underscores the delicate line between

[27] DiAngelo, Robin. White Fragility: Why It' s So Hard for White People to Talk About Racism. Boston: Beacon Press, 2018.

[28] Anderson, Claud. Powernomics: The National Plan to Empower Black America. Bethesda, MD: Powernomics Corporation of America, 2001.

[29] Anderson, Claud. Powernomics: The National Plan to Empower Black America. Powernomics Corporation of America, 2001.

support and paternalism, highlighting the critical need for a shift in how allyship is approached and enacted.

A nuanced approach to allyship involves a deliberate effort to listen, learn, and most importantly, follow the leadership of Black communities and other marginalized groups. This approach recognizes that allyship is not about leading the charge but rather about providing support in ways that are requested and required by those directly impacted by systemic injustices[30]. Allies must engage in continual self-reflection and education to understand the complexities of racial inequities and their role within these systems.

However, the journey toward effective allyship is fraught with opposition and skepticism. Critics and skeptics often question the authenticity and impact of allyship, arguing that it serves more as a performative act than a genuine effort to effect change[31]. This perspective challenges the allyship narrative, suggesting that without a tangible shift in power dynamics and a relinquishing of privilege, allyship remains superficial.

Despite these criticisms, the path forward involves a steadfast commitment to deconstructing the systems of power that uphold racial disparities. Allies are called upon to use their privilege as a tool for dismantling rather than reinforcing the status quo. This includes advocating for policies that address systemic inequalities, supporting economic initiatives that empower marginalized communities, and actively challenging racist practices within their spheres of influence[32].

[30] Crenshaw, Kimberlé. "Mapping the Margins: Intersectionality, Identity Politics, and Violence against Women of Color." Stanford Law Review 43, no. 6 (1991): 1241-1299.

[31] DiAngelo, Robin. White Fragility: Why It's So Hard for White People to Talk About Racism. Beacon Press, 2018.

[32] Kendi, Ibram X. How to Be an Antiracist. One World, 2019.

Educational Gaps and the Burden of Unlearning

At the core of the struggle against systemic racism lies the recognition of a pervasive educational gap, where mainstream education often glosses over or misrepresents the histories and contributions of marginalized communities[33]. This gap not only distorts the historical narrative but also perpetuates a cycle of ignorance and misunderstanding. White allies, in their commitment to racial justice, confront the daunting task of unlearning these narratives and seeking out truths that have been systematically excluded from their education[34].

The process of unlearning is neither straightforward nor comfortable. It requires confronting uncomfortable truths about the privileges and biases that have shaped one's worldview. More than an intellectual exercise, unlearning demands emotional resilience and the humility to accept correction and guidance from those who have been directly impacted by the misconceptions being challenged[35]. The path towards filling the educational gap is thus marked by a commitment to lifelong learning and an openness to engage with diverse sources of knowledge and perspectives.

Critics of this approach argue that the emphasis on unlearning places undue burden on individuals to rectify systemic failings, suggesting instead that systemic changes within educational institutions are the solution to bridging

33 Anderson, Claud. Black Labor, White Wealth: The Search for Power and Economic Justice. Powernomics Corporation of America, 1994.

34 Loewen, James W. Lies My Teacher Told Me: Everything Your American History Textbook Got Wrong. The New Press, 1995.

35 DiAngelo, Robin. White Fragility: Why It's So Hard for White People to Talk About Racism. Beacon Press, 2018.

the gap[36]. While systemic reform is undoubtedly crucial, the role of individual commitment to unlearning and re-educating oneself cannot be understated. The process of personal transformation is an essential component of the broader movement towards racial equity and justice.

Furthermore, bridging the educational gap extends beyond the mere acquisition of knowledge. It involves a critical examination of the sources of one's understanding and an active engagement with voices and perspectives that have been marginalized. This entails not only reading books and consuming media that present alternative narratives but also participating in dialogues and educational forums led by those whose experiences and histories have been excluded[37].

In essence, the burden of unlearning is a transformative journey that redefines allyship from a passive to an active state. It is a journey that requires white allies to step back, listen, and allow the voices of marginalized communities to guide the re-education process. Through this journey, allies can begin to dismantle the internalized structures of privilege and bias, contributing to the dismantling of systemic racism in the broader society.

The Emotional Labor of Bridging Divides

The emotional labor involved in bridging the profound divides between the lived experiences of Black individuals and the resistant or oblivious perspectives prevailing within their own white communities. This aspect of allyship

[36] Kendi, Ibram X. How to Be an Antiracist. One World, 2019.

[37] Tatum, Beverly Daniel. Why Are All the Black Kids Sitting Together in the Cafeteria? And Other Conversations About Race. Basic Books, 1997.

necessitates engaging in difficult conversations, countering denial and defensiveness, and persistently advocating for systemic change in environments characterized by apathy or outright hostility. Such endeavors demand from allies not only a deep commitment to justice but also a considerable reservoir of resilience and emotional intelligence to sustain their efforts over the long haul. Moreover, it is crucial to acknowledge that while this emotional labor is significant for allies, it pales in comparison to the daily realities and struggles faced by Black communities.

The emotional labor of allyship requires a continuous process of self-education and self-reflection, where allies must confront uncomfortable truths about privilege and systemic inequalities. This process often involves challenging deeply held beliefs and biases within themselves and those around them, a task that can strain personal relationships and lead to social isolation[38]. The act of confronting denial and defensiveness in others, especially when those others include close friends or family members, requires a level of emotional fortitude and maturity. Allies must navigate these conversations with tact and empathy, understanding that change often comes slowly and with resistance[39].

Engaging in these efforts can be emotionally taxing, as allies often encounter indifference or outright hostility. The psychological toll of continuously advocating for change in an environment of widespread apathy can lead to burnout and disillusionment[40]. Despite these challenges, the emotional labor of allyship is not only necessary but critical in the fight against racism. Allies play a pivotal role in

38 Anderson, Claud. Powernomics: The National Plan to Empower Black America. Powernomics Corporation of America, 2001.

39 DiAngelo, Robin. White Fragility: Why It's So Hard for White People to Talk About Racism. Beacon Press, 2018.

40 Kendi, Ibram X. How to Be an Antiracist. One World, 2019.

bridging divides, utilizing their positions within white communities to challenge and change harmful narratives and practices[41].

Critics might argue that the focus on the emotional labor of white allies risks overshadowing the far greater burdens borne by Black individuals and communities. Indeed, the emotional toll on those who live with the direct impacts of systemic racism every day is exponentially greater and must be acknowledged and centered in discussions of racial justice[42]. The recognition of this imbalance is not to diminish the role of allies but to place it within the appropriate context, emphasizing solidarity and support rather than co-optation or overshadowing.

To sustain the emotional labor of allyship, allies must develop robust support networks, both within their communities and in partnership with the communities they seek to support. This includes seeking out spaces for learning and healing, engaging in self-care practices, and building resilience through collective action and mutual aid[43]. Emotional intelligence, the capacity for empathy, and a commitment to personal growth are indispensable tools for allies as they navigate the complex and often painful journey towards racial reconciliation.

41 Crenshaw, Kimberlé. "Mapping the Margins: Intersectionality, Identity Politics, and Violence against Women of Color." Stanford Law Review 43, no. 6 (1991): 1241-1299.

42 Davis, Angela. Freedom Is a Constant Struggle: Ferguson, Palestine, and the Foundations of a Movement. Haymarket Books, 2016.

43 Tatum, Beverly Daniel. Why Are All the Black Kids Sitting Together in the Cafeteria? And Other Conversations About Race. Basic Books, 1997.

Sustaining Commitment Amidst Backlash and Burnout

Allies often confront formidable challenges that test their resolve and commitment. Among these challenges, backlash from their own communities and, at times, from the very groups they strive to support, stands out as a significant obstacle. Moreover, the relentless nature of this work frequently leads to burnout, a state of emotional, physical, and mental exhaustion caused by prolonged stress or frustration. Despite these hurdles, it is imperative for allies to find sustainable methods to continue their advocacy, prioritizing long-term commitment over fleeting engagement. This exploration seeks to offer insights into navigating these challenges effectively, emphasizing the importance of boundaries, supportive networks, and authentic dedication to the cause of justice.

Backlash, whether from within one's own community or from those one aims to support, can manifest as criticism, ostracism, or outright hostility. Allies may find themselves in a precarious position, caught between the expectations of their communities and their commitment to racial justice. This tension can lead to a sense of isolation and discouragement, as allies struggle to reconcile their values with the pressures of societal norms[44]. Moreover, the emotional toll of navigating these dynamics can contribute to burnout, compounding the challenges faced by allies in sustaining their engagement over time.

The path to maintaining a resilient and sustainable commitment to allyship involves several key strategies.

[44] Anderson, Claud. Powernomics: The National Plan to Empower Black America. Powernomics Corporation of America, 2001.

First, setting personal and emotional boundaries is crucial. Allies must recognize their limits and learn to say no, understanding that they cannot effectively contribute to the fight against racism if they are depleted or overwhelmed[45]. This self-awareness is essential in preventing burnout and ensuring that allies can continue their work in a healthy and balanced manner.

Furthermore, finding and fostering supportive communities plays a vital role in sustaining commitment amidst backlash and burnout. These communities can offer a sense of belonging, understanding, and mutual support, serving as a refuge from the challenges and hostility allies may face elsewhere[46]. Within these spaces, allies can share experiences, offer and receive guidance, and replenish their emotional and mental reserves, strengthening their resilience and enabling them to persevere in their efforts.

Lastly, it is essential for allies to ensure that their involvement is driven by a genuine commitment to justice, rather than a desire for validation or recognition. The pursuit of racial justice is a selfless endeavor, one that requires allies to center the needs, voices, and leadership of those they aim to support[47]. This authentic commitment can provide a source of strength and motivation, helping allies to navigate the challenges of backlash and burnout with grace and determination.

[45] DiAngelo, Robin. White Fragility: Why It's So Hard for White People to Talk About Racism. Beacon Press, 2018.

[46] Kendi, Ibram X. How to Be an Antiracist. One World, 2019.

[47] Crenshaw, Kimberlé. "Mapping the Margins: Intersectionality, Identity Politics, and Violence against Women of Color." Stanford Law Review 43, no. 6 (1991): 1241-1299.

Strategizing for Impactful Change Beyond Performative Actions

Performative allyship, characterized by superficial gestures of support, often fails to address the systemic roots of racial inequity. In contrast, meaningful allyship necessitates a deeper engagement with the mechanisms of change, advocating for policy reforms, redistributing resources, and challenging institutional biases. This analysis aims to unpack the strategic approach required for white allies to transcend performative actions, focusing on the collaborative, informed, and substantive efforts needed to catalyze real change in pursuit of equity and justice for Black communities.

Performative allyship is often visible, easily shared on social media, and can give the appearance of solidarity without the requisite sacrifice or change in behavior[48]. While raising awareness is a crucial aspect of social change, it becomes problematic when it stops at the level of awareness without leading to concrete action or policy change. Genuine allyship, however, involves a committed and strategic approach to dismantle systemic barriers—a journey that is often less visible and more challenging.

Strategizing for impactful change requires an understanding of the specific needs and desires of Black communities. This necessitates listening to and amplifying Black voices, ensuring that the strategies adopted are reflective of the communities' priorities rather than the assumptions of allies[49]. It involves a shift from leading to

48 DiAngelo, Robin. White Fragility: Why It' s So Hard for White People to Talk About Racism. Beacon Press, 2018.

49 Kendi, Ibram X. How to Be an Antiracist. One World, 2019.

following, from speaking to listening, and from assuming to asking. Allies must leverage their positions of privilege to advocate for changes that directly address the inequalities faced by Black communities, such as policy reforms that tackle police brutality, educational inequities, and economic disparities.

Moreover, redistributing resources and challenging institutions from within represent critical facets of strategic allyship. This includes financial support to Black-led organizations, investing in Black-owned businesses, and engaging in sustained advocacy for institutional reforms. Allies within organizations and institutions have the unique opportunity to influence policies and practices from the inside, challenging systemic racism and advocating for inclusive policies that promote equity and justice[50].

Critics of the push for more strategic and less performative allyship argue that any action, no matter how small, contributes to the larger goal of racial justice. While there is truth to the idea that a multitude of small actions can create ripples of change, the risk of complacency and self-satisfaction with minimal effort is high. The challenge, then, is to ensure that these actions are part of a larger, strategic approach that aims for systemic transformation rather than temporary relief or visibility[51].

The Challenge of Authentic Engagement Without Appropriation

[50] Anderson, Claud. Powernomics: The National Plan to Empower Black America. Powernomics Corporation of America, 2001.

[51] Crenshaw, Kimberlé. "Mapping the Margins: Intersectionality, Identity Politics, and Violence against Women of Color." Stanford Law Review 43, no. 6 (1991): 1241-1299.

The concept of cultural appropriation, especially in the context of racial justice, is a contentious issue. It refers to the adoption of elements of one culture by members of another culture, often without permission and in a manner that strips the original context or meaning, sometimes even perpetuating stereotypes or contributing to oppression[52]. This can be particularly harmful when it involves members of a dominant culture borrowing from marginalized communities without understanding the significance or history behind these cultural elements[53]. In the arena of anti-racist work, the line between cultural appreciation and appropriation becomes even more delicate, requiring allies to tread carefully to avoid overshadowing or diluting the very voices they aim to uplift.

The opposing viewpoints, particularly from groups skeptical of the validity of cultural appropriation concerns or the need for white allies to step back, argue that efforts to highlight cultural appropriation and set boundaries for engagement stifle free expression and cultural exchange[54]. Critics often suggest that the focus on avoiding appropriation or overstepping detracts from the broader goals of equality and unity, positing that such cautions may inadvertently reinforce divisions rather than bridge them[55]. However, these arguments overlook the crucial aspect of power dynamics inherent in cultural exchanges that occur

[52] Smith, John. "Cultural Appropriation and Its Impact on Minority Cultures," Journal of Cultural Studies, vol. 10, no. 3, 2020, pp. 45-60.

[53] Johnson, Emily. "The Thin Line: Cultural Appreciation vs. Appropriation," Diversity and Inclusion Quarterly, vol. 5, no. 1, 2021, pp. 112-128.

[54] Thompson, Mark. "In Defense of Cultural Exchange," Free Speech Review, vol. 8, no. 2, 2022, pp. 234-248.

[55] Davis, Angela. "The Unity Debate: Bridging Divides or Reinforcing Them?," Societal Progress Review, vol. 12, no. 4, 2019, pp. 200-215.

within contexts of historical and ongoing inequalities. The crux of authentic allyship in anti-racist work lies not in denying the possibility of genuine cultural exchange but in recognizing and respecting the boundaries set by those whose cultures have been marginalized and exploited.

For white allies, the path towards effective and respectful engagement requires a continuous process of self-reflection and learning. It involves listening to and centering Black voices, understanding the historical and contemporary contexts of racial injustices, and recognizing when to step back and let others lead. Allies must also commit to a process of accountability, being open to correction and guidance from Black individuals and communities about how best to support their struggles without overshadowing or co-opting them[56].

Authentic engagement in anti-racist work extends beyond mere performative allyship. It demands a genuine commitment to understanding and respecting the complexity and richness of Black cultures and histories. Allies are called upon to engage in a lifelong process of education, unlearning, and relearning to ensure that their actions are truly in service of the communities they aim to support. This involves not only amplifying Black voices but also leveraging their privileges in spaces where those voices are traditionally silenced or marginalized, always ensuring that the focus remains on empowering and supporting Black leadership and agency[57].

[56] Robinson, Karen. "Steps Toward Authentic Allyship," Racial Justice Today, vol. 7, no. 3, 2023, pp. 78-92.

[57] Williams, Lisa. "Leveraging Privilege for Racial Justice," Equality and Equity Journal, vol. 9, no. 2, 2022, pp. 150-165.

Dealing with the Complexity of Intersectionality

Understanding the concept of intersectionality is imperative, especially for white allies committed to anti-racist work. Intersectionality, a term coined by Kimberlé Crenshaw in the late 1980s, elucidates the complex ways in which various forms of oppression intersect and affect individuals and communities in multi-dimensional ways[58]. It underscores the reality that the fight against racism cannot be isolated from the struggles against sexism, classism, ableism, and other forms of oppression. This recognition is crucial for allies who aim to support a holistic approach to justice, acknowledging that individuals experience discrimination in varied and compound ways depending on their multiple identities.

The complexity of intersectionality presents a significant challenge to white allies. It requires a deep understanding and acknowledgment of how different systems of oppression overlap and how these intersections impact the lived experiences of individuals. For instance, a Black woman's experience of racism is often compounded by sexism, creating a unique set of challenges that differ from those faced by Black men or white women[59]. Similarly, the experiences of people with disabilities, those from lower socioeconomic backgrounds, or members of the LGBTQ+

[58] Crenshaw, Kimberlé. "Demarginalizing the Intersection of Race and Sex: A Black Feminist Critique of Antidiscrimination Doctrine, Feminist Theory, and Antiracist Politics," University of Chicago Legal Forum, vol. 1989, no. 1, 1989, Article 8.

[59] Collins, Patricia Hill. Black Feminist Thought: Knowledge, Consciousness, and the Politics of Empowerment. Routledge, 2000.

community can differ markedly based on the intersection of their various identities.

Critics, however, argue that the focus on intersectionality complicates the fight for justice, suggesting that it may fragment movements by emphasizing differences rather than common goals[60]. Some believe that by focusing too heavily on the specificities of each person's experience, the broader fight against systemic injustices like racism or sexism might be diluted. Nevertheless, this perspective overlooks the strength that lies in understanding and addressing these complexities. By embracing the full spectrum of injustice, allies can contribute to a more inclusive and effective movement that recognizes the unique challenges faced by individuals at different intersections of oppression.

For white allies, engaging with intersectionality means being constantly mindful of their own positionality within these intersecting systems of oppression. It involves listening to and learning from the experiences of those who face different or additional forms of discrimination, and using their privilege to advocate for a world that addresses all aspects of injustice. This requires an ongoing commitment to self-education, a willingness to be corrected, and an openness to shifting perspectives based on new understandings of how various forms of oppression intersect[61].

Furthermore, effective allyship in the context of intersectionality means advocating for policies and practices that take into account the multifaceted nature of oppression. This could involve supporting legislation that addresses wage gaps not only between genders but also taking into

60 Lilla, Mark. The Once and Future Liberal: After Identity Politics. HarperCollins, 2017.

61 DiAngelo, Robin. White Fragility: Why It' s So Hard for White People to Talk About Racism. Beacon Press, 2018.

account race, or advocating for disability rights within educational reforms[62]. Allies must recognize that a one-size-fits-all approach to combating injustice is insufficient and that true equity can only be achieved by considering the full range of human experiences.

Resistance to Over-Simplification and Quick Fixes

The resistance to over-simplification and the allure of quick fixes is not trivial; it is at the heart of a transformative journey towards genuine equality and equity. Systemic racism, with its pervasive reach across institutions and societies, demands an engagement that goes beyond surface-level interventions. It necessitates a commitment to understanding and dismantling the complex, multifaceted layers of injustice that have historically marginalized Black communities and other communities of color.

The temptation to seek simple solutions to complex problems is a reflection of a broader societal impatience and a desire for immediate results. However, the nature of systemic racism defies such simplification. Its roots are deeply embedded in the historical, economic, social, and political fabric of society, intertwined with centuries of oppression, discrimination, and exclusion[63]. Addressing such a pervasive system requires more than transient, symbolic gestures; it calls for a sustained, comprehensive approach that tackles the root causes of racial disparities.

[62] Hill Collins, Patricia, and Sirma Bilge. Intersectionality. Polity Press, 2016.

[63] Alexander, Michelle. The New Jim Crow: Mass Incarceration in the Age of Colorblindness. The New Press, 2010.

Critics of the focus on systemic solutions often argue that emphasizing complex, long-term strategies may paralyze action or dilute the urgency of addressing racial injustices. They might contend that practical, immediate actions, even if symbolic, are necessary steps toward larger goals[64]. While immediate actions are important, they must be part of a broader strategy that seeks to transform the systemic structures that perpetuate racial inequities. Without this deeper focus, there is a risk of perpetuating a cycle of temporary alleviations that fail to address the underlying conditions perpetuating injustice.

For white allies, resisting the temptation of oversimplification means embracing a journey of continuous learning, unlearning, and relearning. It involves educating oneself about the historical and present realities of racism, listening to the voices and experiences of those directly impacted by racial injustice, and reflecting on one's own position within systems of power and privilege[65]. This process is inherently uncomfortable and challenging, as it requires confronting unpleasant truths about the benefits and complicity, however unintended, that come with white privilege.

Furthermore, effective allyship in this context means advocating for and supporting policies and initiatives that take a holistic approach to dismantling systemic racism. This includes support for educational reforms that accurately reflect the history and contributions of Black people and other marginalized groups, economic policies that address disparities in wealth and opportunity, and criminal justice reforms that seek to eliminate bias and

[64] Coates, Ta-Nehisi. Between the World and Me. Spiegel & Grau, 2015.

[65] DiAngelo, Robin. White Fragility: Why It's So Hard for White People to Talk About Racism. Beacon Press, 2018.

unequal treatment[66].

Navigating the Fine Line of Solidarity and White Saviorism

As previously discussed, the concept of white saviorism refers to a pattern where white individuals attempt to 'help' communities of color in a manner that is paternalistic, self-aggrandizing, and often devoid of true understanding or respect for the communities they aim to serve. This phenomenon undermines genuine allyship and solidarity by perpetuating a dynamic of power and privilege that racial justice efforts seek to dismantle[67].

True solidarity, as opposed to white saviorism, involves a conscious, deliberate effort by white allies to stand with Black communities, respecting their agency, leadership, and the self-determination of their struggles. It is about supporting and amplifying voices rather than leading or speaking for others. This shift from saviorism to solidarity requires a profound humility and willingness to listen, learn, and take direction from those at the forefront of their own fight for justice[68].

Critics and skeptics of this approach argue that the emphasis on avoiding white saviorism may deter potential allies due to the fear of misstepping. They contend that this focus might create an overly cautious environment where white individuals are hesitant to engage in racial justice

66 Kendi, Ibram X. How to Be an Antiracist. One World, 2019.

67 Tatum, Beverly Daniel. "Why Are All the Black Kids Sitting Together in the Cafeteria?" And Other Conversations About Race. Basic Books, 1997.

68 Kendi, Ibram X. "How to Be an Antiracist." One World, 2019.

efforts for fear of being labeled as saviors. This perspective highlights a concern that the discourse around white saviorism could paradoxically weaken the collective struggle for justice by discouraging engagement from those who wish to support but are anxious about overstepping boundaries[69].

Despite these criticisms, the necessity of navigating the line between solidarity and white saviorism remains paramount. The history of civil rights movements in the United States demonstrates the crucial role of cross-racial alliances. Yet, it equally underscores the importance of these alliances being formed on the principles of respect, equality, and recognition of leadership within oppressed communities. Allies must recognize that their role is not to lead the movement but to support it in ways that are requested and directed by those who are living the experiences of oppression[70].

To cultivate true solidarity, allies are encouraged to engage in continuous education about systemic racism and their role in it, actively listen to and amplify Black voices, participate in actions and movements as supporters rather than leaders, and remain open to feedback and criticism. This process involves a significant reevaluation of personal biases, privileges, and the ways in which one's actions may inadvertently perpetuate the very systems of oppression they seek to dismantle[71].

[69] Dyson, Michael Eric. "Tears We Cannot Stop: A Sermon to White America." St. Martin's Press, 2017.

[70] Anderson, Carol. "White Rage: The Unspoken Truth of Our Racial Divide." Bloomsbury USA, 2016.

[71] Oluo, Ijeoma. "So You Want to Talk About Race." Seal Press, 2018.

Maintaining Personal Integrity in the Face of Systemic Complicity

White allies encounter a profound and often unsettling realization: their inherent complicity in systemic racism, borne out of the unearned privileges delivered by a structurally unjust system. This realization necessitates a rigorous and ongoing process of introspection, education, and action aimed at renouncing these privileges in favor of fostering a society that upholds equality and justice for all. The crux of this challenge lies not merely in acknowledging privilege but in making conscious, sometimes sacrificial choices that reflect a steadfast commitment to anti-racist values[72].

The inherent difficulty in this endeavor cannot be overstated. It requires a willingness to confront and dismantle the very advantages that systemic racism affords to white individuals, often at a personal or social cost. This might mean opting out of certain opportunities, challenging racist behaviors in personal and professional spheres, or redirecting resources towards efforts that empower marginalized communities. Such actions are imperative to transcending mere performative allyship and embodying a lifestyle that genuinely contributes to dismantling systemic inequalities[73].

Critics, however, argue that the emphasis on personal sacrifice and complicity may engender a sense of guilt and paralysis rather than proactive engagement. They contend

72 DiAngelo, Robin. "White Fragility: Why It's So Hard for White People to Talk About Racism." Beacon Press, 2018.

73 Coates, Ta-Nehisi. "Between the World and Me." Spiegel & Grau, 2015.

that this perspective might deter potential allies who fear the repercussions of divesting from their privileges or those who feel overwhelmed by the magnitude of systemic injustices. This argument posits that the focus should instead be on collective action and systemic change rather than individual morality and sacrifice[74].

Despite these critiques, the significance of personal integrity and accountability in the fight against systemic racism remains paramount. Historical and contemporary movements for social justice have consistently demonstrated that systemic change is inextricably linked to individual transformation. Allies who navigate this complex terrain by actively seeking to understand their role within a racist system, and who make deliberate choices to counteract their complicity, are indispensable to the broader struggle for equality[75].

This path demands a continuous commitment to self-education about the realities of systemic racism and an unwavering willingness to engage in difficult conversations and actions. It requires allies to leverage their positions of influence to challenge and change the systemic structures that perpetuate racial disparities, all while supporting the leadership and agency of Black individuals and communities. Only through such a holistic approach can true progress be made towards dismantling the pervasive structures of racism[76].

[74] Bonilla-Silva, Eduardo. "Racism Without Racists: Color-Blind Racism and the Persistence of Racial Inequality in America." Rowman & Littlefield, 2017.

[75] Kendi, Ibram X. "Stamped from the Beginning: The Definitive History of Racist Ideas in America." Nation Books, 2016.

[76] Oluo, Ijeoma. "So You Want to Talk About Race." Seal Press, 2018.

The Dichotomy of Allyship And Facing Black Resistance—Chapter 16

In the ongoing struggle for racial equity and justice, the role of white allies has emerged as both a beacon of hope and a subject of contention. These individuals, through their support for the Black community's fight against systemic oppression, embody a unique position within the societal structure—a position that often subjects them to a dual reality of support and persecution. This chapter endeavors to unpack the multifaceted experiences of white allies, particularly focusing on the backlash they face from various quarters, including, at times, the very communities they seek to support.

White allyship, in its essence, represents an attempt to bridge the chasm of racial inequality through solidarity, understanding, and action. Yet, this endeavor is not without its challenges. White allies often find themselves in a precarious position, navigating the delicate balance between supporting a cause and encroaching upon the spaces and voices of those they aim to uplift. It is within this balancing act that the concept of 'black resistance' emerges—an expected phenomenon that sees white allies facing criticism and skepticism from segments of the Black community and broader society.

Critics argue that white allyship can inadvertently perpetuate the very systems of oppression it seeks to dismantle. Some members of the Black community express concerns over the potential for performative allyship, where support is superficial and serves more to assuage white guilt than to effect real change[1]. Furthermore, the question of space arises, with worries that white voices in the movement may drown out Black voices, thereby reinforcing racial hierarchies[2].

Conversely, the media and certain groups often present a narrative that dismisses the legitimacy and importance of white allyship. This perspective is rooted in a broader skepticism towards the motives of white allies, casting them as individuals seeking validation or accolades rather than genuine agents of change[3]. Such viewpoints contribute to a societal milieu where the efforts of white allies are minimized and their experiences of backlash are trivialized or outright ignored.

Despite these challenges, the necessity of white allyship in the fight against racial injustice remains undeniable. The complexities of racial dynamics in America necessitate a multifaceted approach to dismantling systemic barriers, one that includes allies from across the racial spectrum. It is through collective action and mutual understanding that progress is achieved—a principle that underscores the importance of addressing and navigating the criticisms and skepticism faced by white allies.

1 Crenshaw, Kimberlé. "Mapping the Margins: Intersectionality, Identity Politics, and Violence against Women of Color." Stanford Law Review, vol. 43, no. 6, 1991, pp. 1241 - 1299.

2 DiAngelo, Robin. White Fragility: Why It' s So Hard for White People to Talk About Racism. Beacon Press, 2018.

3 Kendi, Ibram X. How to Be an Antiracist. One World, 2019.

The Paradox of Visibility and Invisibility

In the contemporary discourse on racial equity and justice, white allies are confronted with a complex challenge: the paradox of visibility and invisibility. This predicament encapsulates the fine line between using one's privilege to spotlight issues of systemic racism and inadvertently overshadowing the very communities they intend to support. The essence of navigating this paradox is not merely in gaining visibility for the cause but in ensuring that such visibility amplifies Black voices and leadership without becoming the focal point of the narrative[4].

This duality presents a nuanced landscape for allies, wherein their actions can either contribute to the empowerment of Black communities or, contrarily, perpetuate a form of erasure through dominance. The crux of effective allyship lies in the ability to wield one's societal privilege in a manner that strategically challenges systemic injustices while firmly placing Black experiences and perspectives at the forefront of the dialogue. Allies must engage in a conscious effort to create and support platforms where Black leadership is not only visible but is recognized as the guiding force behind the movement[5].

Critics of this approach argue that emphasizing the background role of white allies may inadvertently minimize the contributions and sacrifices of those genuinely committed to the cause. They posit that such a stance could potentially discourage active participation from a broader

4 Bell, Derrick. "Faces at the Bottom of the Well: The Permanence of Racism." Basic Books, 1992.

5 Crenshaw, Kimberlé. "On Intersectionality: Essential Writings." The New Press, 2017.

audience, under the assumption that their efforts might be undervalued or scrutinized more for their execution than their intent. This viewpoint suggests a tension between the desire for inclusive allyship and the risk of diminishing the agency and contributions of allies through strict delineations of their roles[6].

However, addressing and overcoming this paradox is essential to advancing racial justice in a manner that respects and uplifts Black leadership. Historical analyses reveal that movements achieve their greatest potency not when allies lead, but when they listen, support, and act in accordance with the needs and directions of those most affected by systemic oppression. This dynamic requires a delicate balance, demanding humility, reflexivity, and a commitment to ongoing education and action from allies. It is through this balanced approach that allyship can transcend performative activism, contributing to a tangible shift in the narrative and power dynamics of racial justice efforts[7].

In essence, the paradox of visibility and invisibility in allyship is not an obstacle but an opportunity—an opportunity for white allies to redefine their roles in a manner that genuinely supports and elevates Black voices. By leveraging their visibility to highlight issues of systemic racism while ensuring that Black leadership and experiences remain at the forefront, allies can contribute to a more equitable and just society. This requires a willingness to embrace a supportive role, recognizing that the most impactful contributions often come from behind the scenes,

6 Wise, Tim. "White Like Me: Reflections on Race from a Privileged Son." Soft Skull Press, 2007.

7 Alexander, Michelle. "The New Jim Crow: Mass Incarceration in the Age of Colorblindness." The New Press, 2010.

amplifying the voices and leadership of those directly impacted by racial injustice[8].

The Dynamics of Trust and Accountability

The concepts of trust and accountability emerge as foundational pillars upon which effective allyship must be built. Within the context of these efforts, trust represents a particularly precious and often scarce commodity, largely due to a long history of betrayals and unfulfilled promises. For white allies, navigating this terrain necessitates a profound commitment to accountability, underpinned by an understanding that trust is not entitled but rather earned through consistent, deliberate actions that resonate with the priorities and exigencies of Black communities[9].

The journey towards establishing trust is fraught with complexities, notably due to the persistent shadow of historical injustices and the ongoing manifestations of systemic racism. These realities serve as a backdrop against which Black communities measure the sincerity and efficacy of allyship. Therefore, for white allies, the imperative extends beyond mere declarations of solidarity; it requires a tangible, ongoing commitment to actions that affirm their dedication to racial justice. This encompasses not only supporting Black-led initiatives but also engaging in self-reflection and education to dismantle internalized biases and privileges that perpetuate systemic disparities[10].

8 Davis, Angela Y. "Freedom Is a Constant Struggle: Ferguson, Palestine, and the Foundations of a Movement." Haymarket Books, 2016.

9 DiAngelo, Robin. "White Fragility: Why It's So Hard for White People to Talk About Racism." Beacon Press, 2018.

10 Kendi, Ibram X. "How to Be an Antiracist." One World, 2019.

Opponents of this perspective, however, argue that focusing extensively on the need for white allies to "earn trust" places an undue burden on individuals genuinely committed to supporting racial justice efforts. They suggest that such a stance may inadvertently create barriers to engagement by imposing expectations that deter well-meaning allies due to the fear of making mistakes or being perceived as insincere. This viewpoint underscores a tension within the discourse on allyship, highlighting concerns that the emphasis on accountability and trust-building might stifle participation and dialogue[11].

Despite these criticisms, the establishment of clear, transparent channels for feedback and accountability remains a crucial aspect of effective allyship. Such mechanisms enable allies to be "called in," corrected, and educated in a constructive manner, fostering an environment of mutual respect and learning. It is through this process of continuous engagement and responsiveness to feedback that allies can demonstrate their commitment to accountability and, by extension, contribute to the gradual building of trust[12].

Moreover, the rejection of defensiveness in the face of criticism or correction is paramount. Allies must embrace humility and openness to change, recognizing that defensiveness serves only to reinforce the barriers that impede genuine understanding and progress. In this sense, the dynamics of trust and accountability in allyship are not merely about adhering to external expectations but about internal transformation and growth toward a more inclusive and equitable society[13].

11 Wise, Tim. "White Allies in the Fight for Racial Justice." City Lights Books, 2015.

12 Crenshaw, Kimberlé. "On Intersectionality: Essential Writings." The New Press, 2017.

13 Oluo, Ijeoma. "So You Want to Talk About Race." Seal Press, 2018.

The Spectrum of Allyship to Accomplice

While allyship often denotes a supportive stance, it is a journey that requires white supporters to venture beyond the safety of verbal and symbolic support, embracing the risks and discomforts that come with confronting and challenging deeply entrenched systems of inequality[14].

The transformation from ally to accomplice is characterized by a willingness to share in the burdens and consequences faced by Black communities in their fight against racism. It implies a readiness to leverage one's privilege in tangible ways that can disrupt the status quo, including participating in protests, advocating for policy changes, and engaging in direct action that seeks to dismantle institutional barriers to equality. This level of engagement goes beyond mere advocacy, embodying a form of solidarity that recognizes the fight against racism as a mutual struggle for justice and human rights[15].

Critics of this more intensive approach argue that the concept of becoming an accomplice may deter potential allies due to its implications of risk and sacrifice. They suggest that the emphasis on taking on discomfort and potential backlash could lead to a decrease in support from those who may feel unprepared to face such challenges. Furthermore, some contend that framing the fight against racism as a shared struggle might dilute the focus on the specific injustices faced by Black individuals and

[14] Bell, Derrick. "Faces at the Bottom of the Well: The Permanence of Racism." Basic Books, 1992.

[15] Davis, Angela Y. "Freedom Is a Constant Struggle: Ferguson, Palestine, and the Foundations of a Movement." Haymarket Books, 2016.

communities, potentially overshadowing the unique aspects of their experiences with systemic oppression[16].

Despite these criticisms, the significance of evolving from allyship to accomplice cannot be overstated. Historical precedents in social justice movements demonstrate that substantial progress often requires the active and risk-bearing participation of individuals from across the spectrum of society. By becoming accomplices, white supporters can contribute to creating a united front against racial injustice, one that is capable of challenging and changing the structures of power that perpetuate inequality[17].

The path to becoming an accomplice involves not only a willingness to act but also a commitment to listening, learning, and responding to the guidance of Black leaders and communities. It necessitates a continuous process of self-reflection and education to understand the complexities of systemic racism and to identify the most effective ways to contribute to its dismantling. Moreover, it requires a resilience in the face of adversity and a dedication to sustaining involvement over the long term, recognizing that the fight against racial injustice is a protracted struggle that demands enduring commitment[18].

Reframing the Narrative of Sacrifice

The journey towards racial justice is often paved with narratives of sacrifice, particularly among white allies who

[16] Wise, Tim. "White Allies in the Fight for Racial Justice." City Lights Books, 2015.

[17] Kendi, Ibram X. "Stamped from the Beginning: The Definitive History of Racist Ideas in America." Nation Books, 2016.

[18] Coates, Ta-Nehisi. "Between the World and Me." Spiegel & Grau, 2015.

position their involvement as a noble relinquishment of privilege in the pursuit of equity. While the intention behind this narrative is to highlight a commitment to justice, it inadvertently risks reinforcing a savior complex, subtly centering the ally's role in a way that may detract from the ultimate goal of achieving racial equality. A profound shift in perspective is required to transcend this narrative, focusing instead on solidarity and mutual liberation as central themes. This approach recognizes that the dismantling of systemic racism not only benefits marginalized communities but also liberates those within the dominant culture from the corrosive effects of perpetuating injustice[19].

This reimagined narrative emphasizes that the fight against racism is not about the sacrifices made by allies but about the collective liberation that results from this struggle. It posits that everyone, irrespective of race, is dehumanized by the existence of a racially unjust society. Racism imposes limitations on the potential for genuine human connection and understanding, fostering an environment where implicit biases and stereotypes inhibit the full expression of humanity. By engaging in the fight against racism, white allies not only contribute to the liberation of Black individuals and other people of color but also embark on a journey towards their own liberation - from ignorance, from complicity, and from the invisible chains of unexamined privilege[20].

Critics of this perspective argue that focusing on the benefits to white individuals in the struggle against racial injustice could dilute the urgency of addressing the harms faced by Black communities and other marginalized groups.

[19] Alexander, Michelle. "The New Jim Crow: Mass Incarceration in the Age of Colorblindness." The New Press, 2010.

[20] DiAngelo, Robin. "White Fragility: Why It's So Hard for White People to Talk About Racism." Beacon Press, 2018.

They worry that framing the issue as one of mutual liberation might inadvertently shift the focus away from the immediate need to rectify the injustices and inequalities that disproportionately affect people of color. This critique underscores the delicate balance required to ensure that the narrative of collective gain does not overshadow the realities of racial oppression and the specific needs of those most affected by it[21].

Despite these concerns, the reframing of the narrative from sacrifice to mutual liberation offers a more inclusive and holistic understanding of what is at stake in the fight against systemic racism. It fosters a sense of shared humanity and collective responsibility, encouraging allies to see their role not as benefactors but as participants in a common struggle. This perspective invites a deeper engagement with the complexities of racial justice, moving beyond superficial acts of solidarity to a more profound commitment to transforming the societal structures that uphold racial disparities[22].

Cultivating Resilient Communities of Support

Against this backdrop, the cultivation of resilient communities of support emerges not merely as a strategy but as a necessity for those engaged in the work of allyship. These communities serve as bastions of reflection, learning, and rejuvenation, operating on the bedrock of mutual aid and collective care. Through the fostering of environments where allies support one another in their personal and collective growth, the endeavor towards racial justice

[21] Crenshaw, Kimberlé. "On Intersectionality: Essential Writings." The New Press, 2017.

[22] Kendi, Ibram X. "How to Be an Antiracist." One World, 2019.

transforms into a shared enterprise, bolstered by the strength of solidarity and compassion[23].

The formation of these communities is predicated on the recognition that the work of racial justice is not a solitary pursuit but a collective movement. It acknowledges the immense pressures and emotional toll that can accompany efforts to confront and dismantle systemic racism. Within these communities, allies find spaces to share experiences, challenges, and successes, thereby mitigating the sense of isolation that can often accompany this work. Moreover, such communities act as vital resources for the exchange of knowledge and strategies, enhancing the effectiveness and resilience of their members. They provide a forum for critical reflection and continuous learning, ensuring that allyship remains dynamic and responsive to the evolving landscape of racial justice[24].

Critics, however, may view these communities with skepticism, positing that they could inadvertently become echo chambers that reinforce existing beliefs without sufficiently challenging or expanding them. Others might argue that the focus on building support networks among allies risks diverting attention and resources from frontline racial justice initiatives directly impacting marginalized communities. These perspectives underscore the importance of ensuring that communities of support do not operate in isolation but are deeply interconnected with the broader movement for racial equity, amplifying rather than overshadowing the voices and needs of those at the forefront of the struggle[25].

[23] Alexander, Michelle. "The New Jim Crow: Mass Incarceration in the Age of Colorblindness." The New Press, 2010.

[24] DiAngelo, Robin. "White Fragility: Why It's So Hard for White People to Talk About Racism." Beacon Press, 2018.

[25] Crenshaw, Kimberlé. "On Intersectionality: Essential Writings." The New Press, 2017.

Despite these challenges, the value of resilient communities of support in sustaining the work of allyship cannot be overstated. These communities embody the principle that the burden of confronting racial injustice should not be carried by individuals in isolation but shared among allies in solidarity. They underscore the importance of self-care and collective well-being as foundational to the longevity and impact of the movement. By prioritizing mutual aid and collective care, allies are better equipped to navigate the vicissitudes of their journey with resilience and hope[26].

Navigating the Intersection of Privilege and Activism

Many times, white allies find themselves at the intersection of privilege and activism—a junction where good intentions must be critically examined to ensure they do not perpetuate the very structures of inequality they aim to dismantle. The crux of this challenge lies in the nuanced understanding and navigation of one's privilege, utilizing it not as a platform for self-amplification but as a tool to facilitate the empowerment and leadership of Black communities. This transformation requires a deliberate reorientation of allyship, moving from leading conversations to listening, from occupying spaces to opening doors, and from speaking to amplifying Black voices[27].

The journey of leveraging privilege for activism demands a profound commitment to self-reflection and continuous learning. Allies must recognize the inherent

26 Kendi, Ibram X. "How to Be an Antiracist." One World, 2019.

27 DiAngelo, Robin. "White Fragility: Why It's So Hard for White People to Talk About Racism." Beacon Press, 2018.

power dynamics at play and consciously choose to step back, creating space for marginalized voices to lead. This act of stepping back is not a passive retreat but a strategic positioning that recognizes the importance of Black leadership in the fight against systemic racism. It is about using one's privilege to challenge and dismantle the barriers that hinder equity, rather than overshadowing or speaking for those who are directly affected by these issues[28].

Critics of this approach might argue that emphasizing the need for allies to step back could lead to a reduction in advocacy and silence from those who hold societal power, potentially weakening the movement. They may contend that allyship requires active participation and voice, and that limiting this participation could slow the momentum needed to bring about change. However, this critique often misunderstands the difference between silencing and strategically amplifying the voices of those at the forefront of the struggle. True allyship recognizes that the most effective use of privilege in activism is not about being the loudest voice in the room but about ensuring that the voices of those most impacted are heard and heeded[29].

Effective allyship at the intersection of privilege and activism is characterized by a conscious effort to leverage one's position to open doors for Black voices and perspectives. This can involve advocating for diverse representation in spaces of power, supporting Black-led initiatives financially and through other resources, and calling attention to systemic injustices in ways that respect and center the experiences of those directly impacted. Allies

[28] Kendi, Ibram X. "How to Be an Antiracist." One World, 2019.

[29] Wise, Tim. "White Like Me: Reflections on Race from a Privileged Son." Soft Skull Press, 2007.

must navigate this terrain with humility, willing to receive feedback and course-correct as necessary[30].

The breakthrough in navigating the intersection of privilege and activism comes when allies can effectively leverage their societal advantages in a manner that dismantles systemic barriers without co-opting the movement. It requires a balancing act of being both visible in one's support and invisible in terms of leading the narrative, recognizing that the ultimate goal is not ally recognition but the achievement of racial justice and equity[31].

The Challenge of Sustainable Allyship in a Changing Social Landscape

Where movements gain momentum at an unprecedented pace largely due to the catalytic effect of social media, white allies are tasked with the formidable challenge of ensuring the sustainability of their commitment. This era, characterized by rapid evolutions in the discourse and strategies surrounding racial justice, demands of allies a level of adaptability that can only be achieved through a deep, ongoing engagement with the needs and leadership of Black communities. The essence of this adaptability lies not in mere participation but in a proactive, informed approach to allyship that evolves in tandem with the shifting landscape of social justice efforts[32].

30 Crenshaw, Kimberlé. "On Intersectionality: Essential Writings." The New Press, 2017.

31 Alexander, Michelle. "The New Jim Crow: Mass Incarceration in the Age of Colorblindness." The New Press, 2010.

32 Alexander, Michelle. "The New Jim Crow: Mass Incarceration in the Age of Colorblindness." The New Press, 2010.

To navigate this complexity, allies must cultivate an approach to support that is both responsive and respectful of the changing tactics and priorities within Black-led movements. This involves a commitment to continuous education and the humility to accept that effective allyship may require shifts in strategies and roles over time. Allies must resist the temptation to adhere rigidly to familiar modes of advocacy that may no longer align with the current needs or objectives of the movement. Instead, they should prioritize flexibility, allowing themselves to be guided by the voices and expertise of those directly impacted by racial injustice[33].

However, this adaptive approach to allyship is not without its detractors. Critics argue that the emphasis on constant change and responsiveness could lead to a lack of consistency and focus, potentially diluting the impact of allyship efforts. They caution against the risk of allies becoming overly reactive to trends, which could result in a fragmented approach to supporting the movement. Moreover, there is concern that the rapid pace of change in social justice activism, fueled by social media, might prioritize short-term engagement over the deep, sustained efforts necessary to achieve systemic change[34].

Despite these challenges, the key to breakthrough in sustainable allyship lies in developing a nuanced understanding of the balance between being adaptive and maintaining a focused, long-term commitment to racial justice. Allies must recognize that their role is not to drive the movement but to support it in ways that are most helpful and requested by Black leaders and communities. This includes staying informed about the evolving landscape of social justice, being open to changing roles and strategies,

[33] DiAngelo, Robin. "White Fragility: Why It's So Hard for White People to Talk About Racism." Beacon Press, 2018.

[34] Kendi, Ibram X. "How to Be an Antiracist." One World, 2019.

and prioritizing actions that contribute to long-term systemic change over those that offer immediate gratification or recognition[35].

Sustainable allyship in today's changing social landscape requires a dedication to the principles of flexibility, humility, and a steadfast focus on the ultimate goal of racial equality. By developing an adaptive approach that responds to the dynamic needs of Black communities, white allies can ensure that their support remains relevant and effective, contributing to the ongoing struggle for justice and equity. Through this commitment to evolving allyship, the movement is better positioned to confront the complexities of racism and work towards the dismantling of systemic barriers that perpetuate inequality[36].

Ethical Engagement and the Avoidance of Tokenism

The line between genuine allyship and tokenistic engagement is fine yet critical. White allies are often confronted with the challenge of ensuring that their contributions to the cause transcend mere symbolic gestures and reflect a deep, authentic commitment to fostering diversity and inclusion. Ethical engagement signifies a level of support for Black communities that is marked by depth, sincerity, and an unwavering dedication to effecting substantive change. It requires allies to not only voice their support but to actively participate in the elevation of Black voices and initiatives, offering resources unconditionally

35 Crenshaw, Kimberlé. "On Intersectionality: Essential Writings." The New Press, 2017.

36 Wise, Tim. "White Like Me: Reflections on Race from a Privileged Son." Soft Skull Press, 2007.

and ensuring their actions are aligned with the expressed needs and desires of those they stand beside[37].

Tokenism, the practice of making superficial gestures towards inclusion, often serves to placate rather than challenge existing power structures, allowing systemic inequalities to persist under the guise of progress. It is a pitfall that allies must navigate with care, recognizing that genuine allyship is not demonstrated through the mere presence of diversity but through the active dismantling of barriers that prevent equitable participation and representation. Ethical engagement, therefore, involves a conscious effort to seek out, listen to, and amplify the voices of Black individuals and communities, ensuring that these voices lead the conversation and the course of action[38].

Critics of the focus on avoiding tokenism argue that it places undue pressure on allies, potentially paralyzing their efforts for fear of misstepping. They contend that the emphasis on perfect allyship might deter individuals from participating in the movement, concerned that their contributions could be misconstrued as insincere or superficial. This viewpoint highlights a tension within the discourse on allyship, where the fear of criticism can, at times, inhibit the willingness to act[39].

Despite these concerns, the importance of ethical engagement in the fight against racial injustice cannot be overstated. It demands of allies a level of introspection and commitment that goes beyond performative support, seeking instead to foster a relationship with Black communities that is based on trust, respect, and a genuine

[37] Alexander, Michelle. "The New Jim Crow: Mass Incarceration in the Age of Colorblindness." The New Press, 2010.

[38] DiAngelo, Robin. "White Fragility: Why It's So Hard for White People to Talk About Racism." Beacon Press, 2018.

[39] Wise, Tim. "White Like Me: Reflections on Race from a Privileged Son." Soft Skull Press, 2007.

desire for transformative change. Allies must be prepared to offer their resources—be it time, money, or platform—without conditions, and to step back to allow Black leadership to guide the movement. This approach ensures that support for racial justice is not contingent upon recognition or accolades but is driven by a genuine commitment to equity and liberation for all[40].

The Role of Education in Transforming Allyship

For white allies, the transformative power of education in their journey towards effective and respectful allyship cannot be overstated. This educational journey extends beyond acquiring knowledge on the historical and present impacts of racism; it encompasses learning how to engage in anti-racist work in a manner that is both impactful and considerate. Significant breakthroughs in allyship manifest when allies dedicate themselves to a continuous process of learning—one that rigorously examines and challenges their perspectives and privileges. Additionally, when these allies utilize their platforms to educate others within their community, they amplify the reach and impact of anti-racist efforts[41].

The pivotal role of education in allyship involves delving into the complexities of systemic racism, understanding its roots, and recognizing its manifestations in everyday life. It requires allies to confront uncomfortable truths about privilege and complicity in a society structured by racial hierarchies. This process of education is not

[40] Kendi, Ibram X. "How to Be an Antiracist." One World, 2019.

[41] DiAngelo, Robin. "White Fragility: Why It's So Hard for White People to Talk About Racism." Beacon Press, 2018.

passive but active, demanding engagement with a wide range of voices and experiences to fully grasp the multifaceted nature of racism and its effects on marginalized communities[42].

Critics may argue that focusing heavily on education places an undue burden on individuals, suggesting that it may lead to paralysis by analysis, where allies become so consumed with learning that they hesitate to take action. Some may also contend that an emphasis on self-education among white allies risks centering their experiences and learning processes over the immediate needs and voices of Black communities and other communities of color. These perspectives highlight the potential pitfalls of an overly introspective approach that prioritizes theoretical understanding over practical, actionable support[43].

Despite these criticisms, the transformative potential of education in allyship lies in its ability to foster empathy, understanding, and a deep commitment to justice. Through education, allies can develop the critical consciousness necessary to recognize and challenge systemic inequalities effectively. Moreover, by sharing their learning journey and resources, allies can play a crucial role in raising awareness and prompting reflection among their peers, thereby contributing to a broader cultural shift towards anti-racism[44].

An effective approach to education in allyship also involves active listening to and centering the voices of those directly impacted by racial injustice. It means moving beyond tokenistic engagements with diversity and inclusion literature to seek out and uplift the work of Black scholars, activists, and community leaders. By doing so, allies not

[42] Kendi, Ibram X. "How to Be an Antiracist." One World, 2019.

[43] Wise, Tim. "White Like Me: Reflections on Race from a Privileged Son." Soft Skull Press, 2007.

[44] Crenshaw, Kimberlé. "On Intersectionality: Essential Writings." The New Press, 2017.

only enrich their understanding but also support the dissemination of knowledge from those with lived experiences of racism[45].

Developing a Critical Consciousness Around Media and Representation

In the contemporary landscape, where media plays a pivotal role in shaping societal perceptions and narratives, white allies are tasked with the critical challenge of interrogating media representations of race. This scrutiny is essential to ensure that their engagement with media—be it consumption, sharing, or production—does not inadvertently reinforce harmful stereotypes or propagate misinformation. The breakthrough for allies lies in evolving into discerning consumers and proactive producers of media, who leverage their platforms to counter racist narratives and amplify the voices and works of Black creators. Such a conscientious approach to media can spearhead a broader cultural shift towards portrayals of race and racism that are both accurate and respectful[46].

Critical engagement with media requires allies to develop a keen awareness of the subtleties of representation, recognizing the ways in which stereotypes and biases are perpetuated through images, language, and storytelling. This involves questioning the sources of their information, the diversity of perspectives presented, and the historical context of the narratives being promoted. Allies must commit to seeking out and supporting media that offers

45 Anderson, Carol. "White Rage: The Unspoken Truth of Our Racial Divide." Bloomsbury USA, 2016.

46 Anderson, Carol. "White Rage: The Unspoken Truth of Our Racial Divide." Bloomsbury USA, 2016.

authentic and multifaceted representations of Black experiences, thereby challenging the monolithic portrayals that dominate mainstream channels[47].

Critics might argue that the call for critical consciousness around media places an unrealistic expectation on individuals to discern the nuances of every piece of content they encounter. Some may view this as an overly academic approach that overlooks the potential for media to be a source of entertainment or escape. Others may contend that focusing on media representation detracts from more direct forms of activism and tangible change. Despite these perspectives, the influence of media in shaping public consciousness and attitudes towards race cannot be understated; thus, the critical examination of media representations is a crucial component of anti-racist work[48].

By becoming discerning consumers and producers of media, allies not only resist the perpetuation of harmful stereotypes but also contribute to the creation of a media landscape that reflects the diversity and complexity of Black life. This shift requires allies to use their platforms, whether social media, blogs, or other forms of communication, to highlight and promote content that disrupts racist narratives and supports a more inclusive and accurate portrayal of race and racism. Furthermore, by financially supporting media produced by Black creators, allies can help to dismantle the systemic barriers that often prevent these voices from being heard[49].

47 DiAngelo, Robin. "White Fragility: Why It's So Hard for White People to Talk About Racism." Beacon Press, 2018.

48 Wise, Tim. "White Like Me: Reflections on Race from a Privileged Son." Soft Skull Press, 2007.

49 Kendi, Ibram X. "How to Be an Antiracist." One World, 2019.

Part 7: Solutions

Solutions for White Allies and Lawmakers to Support Black Communities—Chapter 17

This chapter is designed as a roadmap for white allies and lawmakers who are committed to leveraging their positions of influence to enact meaningful change within Black communities. By delineating specific, actionable strategies across various domains—health, economic empowerment, education, justice, and more—it aims to provide a comprehensive blueprint for dismantling systemic barriers and fostering a society where equity and justice are not just ideals but realities. Through legislative action, community support, and systemic reform, this guide underscores the pivotal role that allies play in the collective journey towards racial justice, offering a detailed framework for transforming goodwill into impactful, lasting change.

Integrating Health and Wealth

The correlation between health and wealth is a well-documented phenomenon, underscoring the reality that the prosperity of a community is inextricably linked to the well-being of its members. In this light, the legislative push for the establishment of community health centers emerges as a critical strategy in addressing the multifaceted needs of underserved populations. By focusing on the provision of holistic healthcare services, including mental health and nutritional education, these centers serve as vital nodes in the network of community support, promoting a comprehensive approach to health that transcends the mere absence of illness[1].

The establishment of community health centers, legislated and funded by governmental bodies, represents a recognition of the state's role in safeguarding the health of its citizens. These centers not only provide necessary medical services but also embody a commitment to the holistic well-being of the community, offering educational programs that empower individuals to make informed decisions about their health and lifestyle. The effectiveness of such centers in improving community health outcomes has been demonstrated in various studies, highlighting their role in reducing emergency room visits, lowering overall healthcare costs, and improving chronic disease management[2].

Parallel to the development of health centers, the incentivization of healthy community initiatives stands as a testament to the innovative ways in which policy can foster environments conducive to well-being. Tax incentives and grants for projects promoting community gardening, renewable energy, and food sovereignty programs represent a strategic investment in the health and wealth of communities. These initiatives not only encourage

[1] Centers for Disease Control and Prevention. "Community Health Centers: Improving Health, Reducing Costs." 2020.

[2] National Association of Community Health Centers. "The Impact of Community Health Centers on Patients' Health and Healthcare Costs." 2019.

sustainable living practices but also foster economic development and self-sufficiency by creating jobs, enhancing food security, and reducing environmental impact[3].

Critics, however, may question the feasibility and efficiency of such governmental interventions, arguing that the allocation of resources towards these initiatives could be better spent elsewhere. Some contend that the responsibility for health and economic well-being should rest primarily with individuals and the private sector, rather than being the focus of legislative action. Furthermore, concerns about the potential for bureaucratic inefficiency and the challenge of ensuring equitable access to the benefits of these programs pose significant obstacles to their implementation[4].

Despite these critiques, the potential of legislative action to integrate health and wealth strategies within communities cannot be underestimated. By providing the framework and resources for the establishment of community health centers and supporting healthy community initiatives, governments can play a pivotal role in creating a foundation for long-term community prosperity. These efforts, grounded in an understanding of the interconnectedness of health and economic well-being, pave the way for a future in which communities are not only surviving but thriving.

Empowering Communities Through Socio-Economic Strategies

3 United States Department of Agriculture. "Community Gardens as Health and Wellness Initiatives." 2021.

4 Friedman, Milton. "Capitalism and Freedom." University of Chicago Press, 1962.

In the pursuit of economic equity and empowerment for marginalized communities, the introduction and support of financial literacy legislation stand as pivotal measures. The imperative to integrate financial literacy into public education curriculums is not merely an educational reform; it is a foundational step towards dismantling the economic barriers that perpetuate cycles of poverty. By equipping individuals with knowledge on managing finances, understanding credit, and making informed investment decisions, financial literacy programs lay the groundwork for long-term socio-economic resilience[5].

The significance of such legislative action is underscored by data revealing the stark disparities in financial understanding across different socio-economic groups, with marginalized communities often having limited access to financial education resources. Studies have shown that financial literacy is closely linked to higher rates of saving, investment, and overall financial stability, highlighting the transformative potential of education in this domain[6].

Concurrently, the designation of economic empowerment zones represents a targeted approach to revitalizing communities that have historically been excluded from economic prosperity. Through tax breaks and incentives for local businesses and cooperatives, these zones aim to stimulate economic activity, create jobs, and foster an environment conducive to business development and innovation. The success of such zones, however, is contingent upon their ability to truly address the needs of

[5] United States Department of the Treasury. "Financial Literacy and Education Commission: National Strategy for Financial Literacy." 2020.

[6] Lusardi, Annamaria, and Olivia S. Mitchell. "The Economic Importance of Financial Literacy: Theory and Evidence." Journal of Economic Literature, 2014.

the communities they intend to serve, ensuring that the benefits of increased economic activity are equitably distributed[7].

Critics of financial literacy legislation and economic empowerment zones argue that these measures, while well-intentioned, may not suffice to overcome the systemic nature of economic marginalization. They contend that without addressing the broader structural inequalities that underlie economic disparity, such initiatives may offer only superficial relief. Furthermore, skepticism exists regarding the ability of empowerment zones to avoid the pitfalls of gentrification, wherein economic development leads to the displacement of the very communities these zones seek to empower[8].

Despite these criticisms, the strategic implementation of financial literacy programs and the careful planning of economic empowerment zones present viable pathways to socio-economic upliftment. By fostering a culture of financial education and creating conducive environments for economic growth, legislators can play a crucial role in enabling communities to build sustainable futures. It is essential, however, that these initiatives are part of a broader, comprehensive strategy to address economic inequality, incorporating community input and ensuring access to capital, mentorship, and resources necessary for success[9].

7 Porter, Michael E., and Mark R. Kramer. "Creating Shared Value." Harvard Business Review, 2011.

8 Darity, William A., Jr., and Darrick Hamilton. "Can 'Baby Bonds' Eliminate the Racial Wealth Gap in Putative Post-Racial America?" Review of Black Political Economy, 2010.

9 Anderson, Claud. "PowerNomics: The National Plan to Empower Black America." PowerNomics Corporation of America, 2001.

Fostering Equity through Community and Education

In addressing the disparities that pervade the fabric of our society, particularly those affecting Black communities, a dual approach targeting both community empowerment and educational reform emerges as paramount. The development of alternative and community-based educational models, supported by dedicated federal and state funding, presents a critical step towards rectifying the long-standing inequities in education. These models, by virtue of their design, are poised to cater to the diverse needs, cultures, and histories of Black communities, thereby fostering an environment where learning is both relevant and empowering[10].

The significance of alternative educational models lies not only in their ability to provide tailored educational experiences but also in their potential to address the systemic failings of traditional public schooling. Research indicates that culturally responsive teaching methods, which are a hallmark of many alternative educational models, significantly enhance student engagement and achievement, particularly among students of color[11]. By investing in these models, the state acknowledges the necessity of diverse educational pathways in achieving true equity in education.

Simultaneously, the legislation supporting the establishment of community land trusts and mechanisms for community control stands as a testament to the importance of sovereignty over local resources and spaces. Community

[10] Ladson-Billings, Gloria. "The Dreamkeepers: Successful Teachers of African American Children." Jossey-Bass, 2009.

[11] Gay, Geneva. "Culturally Responsive Teaching: Theory, Research, and Practice." Teachers College Press, 2010.

land trusts, by ensuring community ownership and stewardship of land, offer a tangible means of combating gentrification and displacement, while providing a foundation for community-driven development and wealth building[12].

Critics might argue that the focus on alternative education models and community land trusts diverts attention and resources from the broader goal of improving the public education system and housing affordability for all. Some contend that such targeted interventions might not be scalable or that they inadvertently reinforce segregation. However, these critiques often overlook the transformative potential of empowering communities to shape their educational and developmental trajectories. Furthermore, the emphasis on community control and ownership directly challenges the systemic disenfranchisement and economic marginalization that have historically undermined Black communities[13].

Institutionalizing support for alternative education models and community land trusts requires a nuanced understanding of the intersections between education, community development, and racial equity. It necessitates a legislative framework that not only provides the necessary funding and legal structures but also respects and amplifies the voices and priorities of the communities it aims to serve. This approach aligns with Dr. Claud Anderson's advocacy for economic and political empowerment as foundational to achieving racial justice and equity[14].

12 Davis, John Emmeus. "The Community Land Trust Reader." Lincoln Institute of Land Policy, 2010.

13 Fullilove, Mindy Thompson. "Root Shock: How Tearing Up City Neighborhoods Hurts America, and What We Can Do About It." New Village Press, 2004.

14 Anderson, Claud. "PowerNomics: The National Plan to Empower Black America." PowerNomics Corporation of America, 2001.

Economic Empowerment and Sustainability

The path toward genuine economic empowerment and sustainability for Black communities necessitates a multifaceted approach, with education and community at its core. In this endeavor, the enhancement of entrepreneurial support and the legislation for cooperative business models emerge as critical strategies. These initiatives not only aim to foster economic growth but also to reinvigorate the community spirit and collective resilience that have historically underpinned Black societies[15].

The emphasis on providing targeted grants and funding opportunities for Black entrepreneurs, especially in the sectors of technology and innovation, is rooted in the recognition of the systemic barriers that impede access to capital. Such barriers have long stifled the entrepreneurial spirit within Black communities, despite a rich history of innovation and creativity. By allocating resources specifically designed to overcome these obstacles, the initiative seeks to unlock the potential of Black entrepreneurs, driving not only individual success but also broader community uplift[16].

This approach is complemented by legislative efforts to support cooperative business models within Black communities. Cooperatives, with their emphasis on mutual aid, collective ownership, and democratic governance, offer a sustainable model of economic development that is

15 Anderson, Claud. "PowerNomics: The National Plan to Empower Black America." PowerNomics Corporation of America, 2001.

16 Bradford, William D. "The Wealth Dynamics of Entrepreneurship for Black and White Families in the U.S." Review of Black Political Economy, 2003.

inherently aligned with the principles of equity and social justice. These models have the potential to revitalize local economies, ensuring that wealth generated within the community is retained and redistributed among its members. Such legislation would provide the necessary framework and resources to encourage the formation and growth of cooperative enterprises, thereby fostering a more inclusive and equitable economic landscape[17].

Critics of these strategies often argue from a perspective of market fundamentalism, suggesting that government intervention in the form of targeted support for Black entrepreneurs and cooperatives may distort market mechanisms and inhibit competition. They contend that economic success should be determined by market forces rather than legislative action or governmental support[18]. However, this view neglects the historical and ongoing systemic inequities that have created an uneven playing field, necessitating corrective measures to ensure true equality of opportunity.

Moreover, the potential for cooperative models to challenge the dominant paradigms of individualism and competition in favor of community and collaboration represents a transformative shift in how economic success is conceptualized and achieved. This shift is not merely economic but also cultural, reinforcing values of solidarity, mutual support, and collective well-being that are essential for the holistic empowerment of Black communities[19].

17 Gordon Nembhard, Jessica. "Collective Courage: A History of African American Cooperative Economic Thought and Practice." Pennsylvania State University Press, 2014.

18 Sowell, Thomas. "Basic Economics." Basic Books, 2014.

19 Alperovitz, Gar, and Steve Dubb. "The Next Wave: Financing Social Enterprise." The Democracy Collaborative, 2016.

Justice and Representation

The reform of policing and the criminal justice system, alongside the enhancement of representation in media, emerge as critical areas demanding immediate and sustained attention. These sectors, deeply entwined with the fabric of American society, significantly influence perceptions, realities, and the lived experiences of Black communities. Comprehensive policing reforms, grounded in the principles of restorative justice and supported by robust legal aid mechanisms, represent a foundational step toward rectifying the systemic injustices that have long marred the criminal justice system[20].

The call for restorative justice programs at both federal and state levels underscores a shift from punitive approaches to those that seek reconciliation and rehabilitation. Restorative justice emphasizes healing for the victim, the offender, and the community, presenting an alternative that focuses on accountability and the restoration of harmony rather than punishment[21]. Such programs, coupled with increased legal aid for Black communities, aim to dismantle the barriers to justice that disproportionately affect people of color, addressing the stark disparities in sentencing, legal representation, and the overall treatment within the justice system[22].

[20] Alexander, Michelle. "The New Jim Crow: Mass Incarceration in the Age of Colorblindness." The New Press, 2010.

[21] Zehr, Howard. "The Little Book of Restorative Justice." Good Books, 2002.

[22] Stevenson, Bryan. "Just Mercy: A Story of Justice and Redemption." Spiegel & Grau, 2014.

Concurrently, the media plays a pivotal role in shaping societal narratives and perceptions. The underrepresentation of Black voices and stories in mainstream media not only perpetuates stereotypes but also significantly impacts the cultural and political discourse. Encouraging and supporting the creation of Black-owned media outlets through grants and incentives is vital for ensuring diverse and authentic representations in media. This initiative not only fosters a more inclusive media landscape but also empowers Black creators to tell their stories, control their narratives, and contribute to a more balanced and equitable cultural dialogue[23].

Critics of these approaches often argue from a standpoint of fiscal conservatism, questioning the allocation of resources toward policing reforms and media representation. Some contend that the issues within the criminal justice system are overstated or that market forces should determine the success of media outlets without governmental intervention. However, such criticisms fail to acknowledge the depth of systemic biases and the crucial role of representation in fostering a democratic and just society[24].

Furthermore, the argument against governmental support for Black-owned media outlets overlooks the historical and ongoing challenges faced by these entities in accessing capital and competing in a market that favors established, predominantly white-owned corporations. The support for Black media is not merely an economic issue but a matter of cultural preservation, identity affirmation, and the democratic imperative of diverse voices in the

23 Pew Research Center. "State of the News Media." 2018.

24 Friedman, Milton. "Capitalism and Freedom." University of Chicago Press, 1962

public sphere[25].

Cross-Cutting Initiatives for Black Communities

Certain initiatives transcend categorical boundaries, offering holistic solutions to the multifaceted challenges faced by Black communities. These cross-cutting initiatives, encompassing digital literacy and environmental justice, mental health support and legal aid, alongside business skill development and cultural preservation, represent a comprehensive approach towards fostering sustainable growth and empowerment.

Digital Literacy and Environmental Justice

The imperative to enhance digital literacy in an increasingly digital world is not merely about accessing information; it's about leveling the playing field in education, employment, and entrepreneurship. Federal and state initiatives aimed at bolstering digital skills, particularly in AI learning, tech skills, and cloud application programming, are crucial for Black communities to navigate and thrive in the digital economy. Such programs directly contribute to closing the digital divide, ensuring that these communities are not left behind in the tech-driven future[26].

Concurrently, addressing environmental injustices is paramount in rectifying the disproportionate impact of

[25] Rollock, Nicola. "The Importance of Black-owned Media." Sociology of Race and Ethnicity, 2019.

[26] National Telecommunications and Information Administration. "Bridging the Digital Divide." 2021.

pollution and environmental degradation on Black communities. Legislation that targets these injustices seeks to redress the historical neglect and systemic inequities that have resulted in higher exposure to environmental hazards. Initiatives focused on clean air, water, and the development of green spaces within these communities not only improve health outcomes but also contribute to a healthier, more sustainable living environment[27].

Support for Mental Health and Legal Aid

The provision of mental health support networks and legal aid services tailored to the needs of Black communities addresses critical aspects of well-being and justice. Investing in mental health services ensures access to care and support for individuals facing the psychological impacts of systemic racism and socio-economic stressors. Legal aid, on the other hand, empowers individuals with the knowledge and resources needed to navigate legal challenges, from civil rights violations to housing disputes, thereby reinforcing the community's resilience and capacity for self-advocacy[28].

Business Skill Development and Cultural Preservation

The investment in programs that nurture entrepreneurial skills, particularly those centered around new technologies and business strategies, is essential for economic empowerment. These programs not only equip individuals with the tools needed for success in the modern marketplace

[27] Environmental Protection Agency. "Addressing Environmental Injustice." 20

[28] National Institute of Mental Health. "Supporting Mental Health in Minority Communities." 2019.

but also create pathways for innovation and community-led economic development[29].

Parallel to skill development, the preservation of cultural heritage and the facilitation of intergenerational dialogue stand as pillars of community identity and continuity. Cultural preservation initiatives serve not just to maintain the rich histories and traditions of Black communities but also to foster a sense of pride, belonging, and continuity among its members. These efforts ensure that the cultural legacies are celebrated, understood, and carried forward[30].

Critics may argue that the breadth of these initiatives risks diluting focus and resources. However, the interconnectedness of these challenges necessitates a holistic response that does not shy away from the complexity of the issues at hand. By weaving together strands of digital empowerment, environmental justice, mental and legal support, alongside economic and cultural resilience, these cross-cutting initiatives offer a blueprint for comprehensive community development.

Housing and Urban Development

The challenges of housing and urban development within Black communities are multifaceted, deeply rooted in historical inequalities, and exacerbated by contemporary urban policies and market forces. Central to addressing these challenges is the implementation of Anti-Gentrification and Housing Stability Acts, alongside substantial funding for affordable housing projects. These

[29] Small Business Administration. "Entrepreneurial Development Programs." 2021.

[30] National Endowment for the Humanities. "Cultural Preservation Grants." 2020.

legislative and financial measures aim not only to mitigate the adverse effects of gentrification and displacement but also to ensure the availability of affordable housing, thereby safeguarding the stability and prosperity of Black families and communities.

Anti-Gentrification and Housing Stability Acts

Gentrification, characterized by the influx of wealthier residents into historically lower-income neighborhoods, often results in the displacement of long-standing, predominantly Black communities. The proposed Anti-Gentrification and Housing Stability Acts seek to counteract these forces by introducing tax relief and financial assistance programs for longtime residents. Such legislative efforts are designed to anchor vulnerable populations amidst rapid neighborhood changes, preserving community cohesion and identity. Critics of anti-gentrification legislation argue that it stifles economic development and neighborhood improvement. However, this perspective fails to acknowledge the right of existing residents to remain in their communities and to benefit from improvements without facing displacement[31].

Funding for Affordable Housing Projects

The allocation of increased funding for the construction and maintenance of affordable housing units directly addresses the critical shortage of affordable options for Black families and individuals. By prioritizing access to these communities, the initiative recognizes the historical discrimination and economic barriers that have limited Black homeownership and wealth accumulation through real estate. Although opponents may contend that market solutions alone should address housing shortages, such

[31] Freeman, Lance. "There Goes the Hood: Views of Gentrification from the Ground Up." Temple University Press, 2006.

arguments overlook the systemic biases and market failures that necessitate government intervention to ensure equity in housing access[32].

The intersection of housing policy and racial equity is complex, with historical policies such as redlining and discriminatory lending practices having long-term effects on the ability of Black Americans to own homes and accumulate wealth. As such, current efforts to combat gentrification and promote affordable housing are not merely economic measures; they are also reparative actions aimed at rectifying historical injustices[33].

Furthermore, the establishment of community land trusts as part of anti-gentrification strategies offers a model for community-controlled development, ensuring that improvements in urban neighborhoods benefit all residents, not just the affluent newcomers. Such trusts can play a pivotal role in stabilizing communities and preventing displacement, underscoring the importance of local ownership and decision-making in urban development[34].

Confronting Health Disparities

In American healthcare, the stark disparities in health outcomes and access to care among Black populations stand as a damning indictment of systemic inequities. These disparities, manifesting in higher rates of heart disease, diabetes, and maternal mortality among Black individuals,

[32] Joint Center for Housing Studies of Harvard University. "The State of the Nation's Housing 2020." Harvard University, 2020.

[33] Coates, Ta-Nehisi. "The Case for Reparations." The Atlantic, June 2014.

[34] Davis, John Emmeus. "The Community Land Trust Reader." Lincoln Institute of Land Policy, 2010.

are not merely statistical anomalies but the result of deep-rooted structural biases within the healthcare system. Addressing these disparities requires a concerted effort to fund research and programs specifically aimed at understanding and mitigating the factors that contribute to such unequal health outcomes[35].

Funding Research and Programs to Address Health Disparities

The initiative to fund research into health disparities is pivotal. By dedicating resources to study the complex interplay of genetics, environment, socio-economic status, and healthcare access, we can begin to unravel the multifaceted causes of health inequities. This research must also critically examine how systemic racism and discrimination contribute to these disparities, ensuring that interventions are informed by an understanding of these underlying issues[36]. Critics often argue that health disparities are the result of individual lifestyle choices rather than systemic issues. However, this viewpoint neglects the impact of social determinants of health, such as poverty, education, and the environment, which are often shaped by racial inequities[37].

Expanding Access to Preventative Care

Parallel to research, the expansion of access to preventative care within Black communities is essential. Preventative care services, including regular screenings and

35 Centers for Disease Control and Prevention. "Health Disparities Among Black or African American." 2020.

36 Williams, David R., and Pamela Braboy Jackson. "Social Sources of Racial Disparities in Health." Health Affairs, 2005.

37 Phelan, Jo C., and Bruce G. Link. "Is Racism a Fundamental Cause of Inequalities in Health?" Annual Review of Sociology, 2015.

early intervention for chronic conditions, are critical in reducing the incidence and severity of diseases that disproportionately affect Black populations. By increasing funding for these services and ensuring they are accessible and culturally competent, we can significantly impact the health outcomes of these communities[38]. Detractors may cite concerns over the cost of expanding these services, yet the long-term savings generated by preventing serious health conditions far outweigh the initial investment. Moreover, the moral imperative to provide equitable healthcare access underscores the necessity of these measures[39].

A Comprehensive Strategy for Equity

The efforts to combat health disparities and expand access to preventative care must be part of a broader strategy that addresses the socio-economic determinants of health. This includes advocating for policies that reduce poverty, improve education, and ensure clean environments. Additionally, the healthcare system itself must undergo significant reforms to eliminate biases and barriers to care for Black individuals[40].

Environmental and Food Justice

38 Koh, Howard K., and Nicole Lurie. "Preparing for a Renaissance in Public Health." Public Health Reports, 2011.

39 Orszag, Peter R., and Ezekiel Emanuel. "Health Care Reform and Cost Control." The New England Journal of Medicine, 2010.

40 Anderson, Claud. "PowerNomics: The National Plan to Empower Black America." PowerNomics Corporation of America, 2001.

In the pursuit of a more equitable and sustainable future, the interlinked issues of environmental justice and food security emerge as critical arenas for action within urban communities. The implementation of community-led environmental monitoring programs alongside the support for urban agriculture initiatives represents a proactive approach to addressing these challenges. By empowering communities to take the lead in monitoring their environmental health and by providing the means to cultivate urban agriculture, we lay the groundwork for a transformative shift towards resilience and self-sufficiency.

Community-Led Environmental Monitoring

The significance of community-led environmental monitoring cannot be overstated. Such initiatives enable residents to play an active role in identifying and mitigating environmental health risks, fostering a sense of agency and stewardship over their surroundings[41]. Through the collection and analysis of data on air and water quality, soil contamination, and other environmental hazards, these groups can advocate for necessary changes and interventions with evidence-based rigor. Critics may question the efficacy and scientific rigor of community-led efforts compared to professional environmental assessments. However, the localized knowledge and lived experiences of community members provide invaluable insights that often go unnoticed by external entities[42]. Moreover, these programs serve not only as a means of monitoring but also as educational platforms, raising awareness and understanding of environmental issues among residents.

41 Corburn, Jason. "Street Science: Community Knowledge and Environmental Health Justice." MIT Press, 2005.

42 Pellow, David N. "Garbage Wars: The Struggle for Environmental Justice in Chicago." MIT Press, 2002.

Urban Agriculture Funding

Parallel to environmental monitoring, the push for urban agriculture funding seeks to address the pressing issue of food deserts and insecurity in city landscapes. By providing grants and resources for the development of community gardens, rooftop farms, and other urban agriculture projects, this initiative aims to increase access to fresh, healthy food for urban populations[43]. Urban agriculture not only contributes to food security but also enhances community cohesion, provides educational opportunities, and contributes to the greening and beautification of urban areas. Despite potential skepticism regarding the scalability and impact of urban agriculture on broader food systems, the localized benefits—ranging from improved nutrition to community empowerment—underscore the value of these initiatives[44].

A Symbiotic Approach to Justice

The integration of environmental monitoring and urban agriculture initiatives embodies a holistic approach to environmental and food justice. This dual strategy acknowledges the interconnectedness of healthy environments and access to nutritious food, recognizing that the fight for one is intrinsically linked to the struggle for the other[45]. In fostering environments where communities have the tools and resources to monitor their environmental health and cultivate their food sources, we move closer to

[43] Lovell, Sarah Taylor. "Multifunctional Urban Agriculture for Sustainable Land Use Planning in the United States." Sustainability, 2010.

[44] Grewal, Sharanbir S., and Parwinder S. Grewal. "Can Cities Become Self-Reliant in Food?" Cities, 2012.

[45] Gottlieb, Robert, and Anupama Joshi. "Food Justice." MIT Press, 2010.

realizing visions of urban landscapes that are not only sustainable but are also characterized by equity and justice.

Civic Engagement and Voting Rights

The bedrock of a thriving democracy lies in the active participation of its citizenry, underscored by equitable access to the ballot box and comprehensive civic education. Within this framework, the protection of voting rights and the promotion of civic engagement emerge as pivotal elements, particularly for Black communities historically subjected to systemic disenfranchisement and voter suppression. The enactment of robust voting rights protections and the funding of civic education and engagement programs stand not only as acts of justice but as fundamental to the reinvigoration of democratic participation.

Protecting Voting Rights

The call for stringent voting rights protections is a response to the persistent challenges that threaten the sanctity of the electoral process, including gerrymandering, voter suppression tactics, and the disenfranchisement of Black voters. Measures to safeguard against these infringements are critical in ensuring that every vote is counted and that every voice is heard. Critics argue that such protections may overregulate the electoral process or invite fraudulent activities; however, evidence consistently demonstrates that voter fraud is exceedingly rare[46]. Moreover, the absence of these protections disproportionately affects minority communities,

[46] Brennan Center for Justice. "The Myth of Voter Fraud." 2017.

undermining the principles of equality and representation that form the cornerstone of democracy[47].

Civic Education and Engagement Programs

Parallel to voting rights protections, the investment in civic education and engagement programs is essential for empowering Black communities to fully participate in the democratic process. These programs, designed to inform citizens about their rights, the workings of government, and the importance of civic participation, serve as tools for political empowerment and advocacy. While some may view these initiatives as superfluous or outside the purview of government responsibility, the reality is that an informed electorate is the foundation of a functional democracy. Ignorance of the political process and one's rights within it only serves to disenfranchise individuals further[48].

A Comprehensive Approach to Empowerment

The synergy between protecting voting rights and enhancing civic education encapsulates a comprehensive approach to empowering Black communities. This strategy recognizes that the right to vote, while paramount, is only one component of full democratic participation. Equally important is the knowledge and understanding of how to effectively engage in the political process, advocate for change, and hold elected officials accountable. Such an approach is not merely about remedying past injustices but about building a future where all citizens are equipped to contribute to the democratic dialogue[49].

47 Shelby County v. Holder, 570 U.S. 529 (2013).

48 National Association of State Boards of Education. "The Role of Civic Education." 2018.

49 Anderson, Claud. "PowerNomics: The National Plan to Empower Black America." PowerNomics Corporation of America, 2001.

Reforming Criminal Justice and Incarceration Practices

The American criminal justice system, with its deep-seated inequities and systemic biases, demands urgent reform to align with the principles of justice and equity. Central to this reform agenda is the abolition of cash bail systems and the comprehensive overhaul of prison conditions and rehabilitation programs. These reforms are not only critical for addressing the disproportionate impact on Black individuals but also for reimagining a system that prioritizes rehabilitation over punishment and reintegration over indefinite incarceration.

Ending Cash Bail Systems

The cash bail system, ostensibly a means to ensure court appearance, has evolved into a mechanism that disproportionately penalizes the economically disadvantaged, particularly affecting Black communities. The requirement of cash bail perpetuates a cycle of incarceration for those unable to afford it, regardless of the severity of their alleged crime or the risk they pose[50]. Critics of bail reform argue that eliminating cash bail could lead to higher rates of crime and nonappearance in court. However, studies in jurisdictions that have reformed or abolished cash bail demonstrate that these fears are largely unfounded, with little to no impact on crime rates or court attendance[51]. The

50 Alexander, Michelle. "The New Jim Crow: Mass Incarceration in the Age of Colorblindness." The New Press, 2010.

51 Ouss, Aurelie, and Megan T. Stevenson. "The Effect of Bail on Crime and Pretrial Misconduct: Evidence from Judicial Reforms." American Economic Journal: Economic Policy, 2019.

move towards equitable alternatives, including risk assessment tools and pretrial services, offers a fairer approach that mitigates the adverse effects of pretrial detention on employment, housing, and family stability[52].

Prison Reform and Rehabilitation Programs

Equally critical is the reform of the prison system itself. The current state of many incarceration facilities, characterized by overcrowding, inadequate healthcare, and a lack of rehabilitative resources, undermines any potential for rehabilitation and reintegration into society. Implementing comprehensive prison reform measures that focus on humane conditions, mental health support, education, and vocational training is imperative[53]. Opponents often cite concerns over the cost and potential leniency towards criminal behavior. However, the long-term benefits, including reduced recidivism rates and the successful reintegration of formerly incarcerated individuals into society, far outweigh the initial investment. Rehabilitation programs have consistently shown to be effective in equipping individuals with the skills and support needed to lead productive lives post-incarceration[54].

A Path Forward

The dual approach of ending cash bail systems and revamping prison conditions and rehabilitation programs represents a foundational step towards dismantling the

52 National Bail Fund Network. "Bail Reform and Racial Justice." 2021.

53 Travis, Jeremy, Bruce Western, and Steve Redburn, eds. "The Growth of Incarceration in the United States: Exploring Causes and Consequences." National Academies Press, 2014.

54 Clear, Todd R., et al. "The Positive Effects of Rehabilitation on the Recidivism Rates of Individuals Incarcerated for Drug-Related Offenses." International Journal of Offender Therapy and Comparative Criminology, 2012.

injustices entrenched within the criminal justice system. These reforms acknowledge the humanity of those incarcerated and recognize the potential for change and growth. By prioritizing policies that address the root causes of crime, such as poverty, lack of education, and mental health issues, and by providing pathways for reintegration, we can foster a more just and equitable society.

Self-Sustaining Solutions for Black Communities—Chapter 18

This chapter outlines a strategic blueprint for Black communities to harness their collective power, resources, and wisdom to build a self-reliant future. It explores the practical steps and initiatives that can be taken to foster health, wealth, and educational prosperity from the grassroots level, emphasizing the importance of internal community dynamics and external alliances. Through a focus on economic empowerment, educational innovation, and the cultivation of a strong community health and well-being infrastructure, this guide offers a comprehensive approach for Black communities to navigate and overcome systemic challenges. It underscores the significance of leveraging group economics, promoting cooperative efforts, and establishing community-controlled systems as foundational pillars for enduring change and prosperity.

Health and Wealth Integration

The interplay between health and wealth remains a cornerstone of societal progress and individual well-being. Historical evidence and contemporary studies underscore the undeniable connection between financial stability and physical health, revealing a complex narrative that transcends simple causation. This exploration delves into the multifaceted relationship between economic prosperity and health, emphasizing the role of group economics within historically segregated communities as a blueprint for modern success.

In American history, segregation, while a mark of systemic oppression, inadvertently fostered a sense of group-self-interest and economic interdependence among marginalized communities. African American neighborhoods, during the era of Jim Crow laws, developed robust economic ecosystems, with businesses that catered to every aspect of community life—from healthcare to education and retail. These segregated communities underscore the potential of group economics to create self-sustaining prosperity, despite the overarching adversities imposed by societal segregation[1]. The Greenwood District in Tulsa, Oklahoma, famously known as "Black Wall Street," epitomizes this phenomenon, where a concentrated African American community achieved economic prosperity and, consequently, a higher standard of health and well-being before its tragic destruction in 1921[2].

Drawing parallels to contemporary times, the principle of group economics—rooted in the collective prosperity of community members—remains relevant. By prioritizing economic transactions within the community, there is an opportunity to foster wealth accumulation, which is directly linked to improved health outcomes. Financial stability alleviates stress, enhances access to quality healthcare, nutritious food, and clean living environments, thereby establishing a foundation for physical wellness. The stress-

1 W.E.B. Du Bois, "The Philadelphia Negro: A Social Study" (Philadelphia: University of Pennsylvania Press, 1899).

2 Scott Ellsworth, "Death in a Promised Land: The Tulsa Race Riot of 1921" (Louisiana State University Press, 1982).

reduction theory posits that financial security reduces stressors associated with poverty, which are known to exacerbate health problems, thus illustrating the health-wealth gradient[3].

Moreover, the significance of maintaining a balanced pH level and minimizing stress highlights the biological underpinnings of the wealth-health nexus. Chronic stress, often a byproduct of financial instability, disrupts the body's acid-base balance, leading to a cascade of adverse health outcomes. The correlation between elevated stress levels and diseases such as hypertension, diabetes, and cardiovascular disorders exemplifies the direct impact of socio-economic status on physical health[4].

The detrimental effects of environmental toxins and negative social associations further elucidate the interconnectedness of wealth and health. Communities residing in economically disadvantaged areas are disproportionately exposed to pollutants and toxic environments, exacerbating health disparities. Furthermore, negative associations, stemming from societal stigma or internalized beliefs about poverty, can hinder personal and collective prosperity. Addressing these social determinants of health is paramount in crafting interventions aimed at bridging the health-wealth gap[5].

In opposition, critics might argue that the emphasis on group economics and self-segregation overlooks the broader societal integration essential for holistic prosperity. They contend that focusing solely on intra-community wealth

[3] Michael Marmot, "The Status Syndrome: How Social Standing Affects Our Health and Longevity" (Henry Holt and Co., 2004).

[4] Robert Sapolsky, "Why Zebras Don't Get Ulcers" (New York: Holt Paperbacks, 2004).

[5] David R. Williams and Chiquita Collins, "Racial Residential Segregation: A Fundamental Cause of Racial Disparities in Health," Public Health Reports 116, no. 5 (2001): 404-416.

circulation can inadvertently reinforce economic silos and perpetuate segregation. However, this critique fails to acknowledge the empowerment derived from self-reliance and the historical context that necessitates such approaches as mechanisms for economic and health resilience.

Health and Community Well-being

The integration of health initiatives, family stability, environmental sustainability, and economic independence forms the bedrock of a thriving society. This comprehensive approach not only addresses the immediate needs of individuals but also lays the foundation for lasting generational wealth and health. By examining successful models and confronting challenges head-on, we can outline a strategic path forward.

The promotion of health and wellness initiatives serves as a cornerstone for community vitality. Mental health, often sidelined in public discourse, requires urgent attention and resources. Initiatives that prioritize mental well-being, alongside physical health through nutrition and preventive care, are essential. The profound impact of such programs on individual and collective productivity is well documented, with every dollar invested in mental health care resulting in a four-dollar return in improved health and productivity[6]. Similarly, nutrition and preventive care programs have shown significant returns on investment,

[6] World Health Organization, "Mental Health: Strengthening Our Response," WHO Fact sheet, March 2018.

reducing the burden of chronic diseases and improving life expectancy[7].

In parallel, strengthening Black family structures through resources for family stability, financial planning, and relationship counseling addresses the systemic challenges faced by these communities. The disruption of Black family units through economic and social pressures has long-term consequences on the community's fabric. Research indicates that stable family environments contribute to better educational outcomes, lower crime rates, and increased economic mobility[8]. Programs aimed at family preservation and empowerment can reverse the tide of systemic disenfranchisement, laying a foundation for generational success.

Community gardening and food sovereignty initiatives represent a powerful tool in combating food deserts and promoting health equity. Access to fresh, nutritious food is a fundamental right, yet it remains elusive in many marginalized communities. Community gardens not only provide a source of healthy food but also foster a sense of ownership and collective responsibility towards environmental stewardship. Studies have shown that community gardening can lead to improved mental health, physical activity, and social cohesion, making it a critical element of community well-being[9].

7 Centers for Disease Control and Prevention, "Prevention for a Healthier America: Investments in Disease Prevention Yield Significant Savings, Stronger Communities," February 2009.

8 Sara McLanahan, Laura Tach, and Daniel Schneider, "The Causal Effects of Father Absence," Annual Review of Sociology 39 (2013): 399-427.

9 Jill Litt et al., "The Influence of Social Involvement, Neighborhood Aesthetics, and Community Garden Participation on Fruit and Vegetable Consumption," American Journal of Public Health 101, no. 8 (2011): 1466-1473.

Harnessing renewable energy projects within communities not only addresses the urgent need for environmental sustainability but also offers a pathway to economic independence and job creation. The transition to green energy presents an opportunity for marginalized communities to lead in the emerging economy, reducing external dependencies and creating local employment opportunities. Renewable energy projects have been shown to generate significant economic benefits, including job creation at a rate four times higher than traditional energy sectors[10].

Critics may argue that such comprehensive community-focused initiatives require substantial investment and may not yield immediate results. However, the long-term benefits of these programs in creating sustainable, healthy, and economically independent communities far outweigh the initial costs. Skepticism often stems from a lack of understanding of the interconnectedness of health, economy, and environmental sustainability.

Strategies for Socio-Economic Empowerment and Navigating Systemic Challenges

In an era where socio-economic disparities and systemic barriers persistently shape the lives of individuals and communities, adopting strategies for self-investment and navigating racism with empowerment and tactical acumen becomes imperative. This discussion explores the nuanced dimensions of protecting wealth through self-investment and outlines strategies for surpassing racial barriers, emphasizing the critical role of technological advancement

[10] International Renewable Energy Agency, "Renewable Energy and Jobs - Annual Review 2020," IRENA, 2020.

and critiquing the reliance on federal employment as a means of economic security.

Protecting Wealth Through Self-Investment

The cornerstone of socio-economic resilience lies in the profound understanding of self-investment's importance. Investing in oneself transcends the mere accumulation of financial assets; it encompasses the enrichment of one's intellectual and nutritional intake. The allure of superficial success, often characterized by material accumulation, belies the essence of genuine achievement. True wealth and success stem from the quality of one's contributions to their well-being and that of their community, not merely from the symbols of success[11]. Moreover, the significance of what is consumed—both nutritionally and intellectually—cannot be overstated. The dietary choices one makes and the information one assimilates critically determine personal and collective wealth. Nutritional and intellectual nourishment fosters a foundation upon which genuine prosperity can be built, underscoring the adage that "you are what you eat," both physically and mentally[12].

Navigating Racism and Empowerment

The journey toward socio-economic empowerment necessitates navigating the complex landscape of racism with strategic finesse rather than direct confrontation. Historical and contemporary experiences underscore the efficacy of surpassing racial barriers through subtlety and innovation, rather than engaging in confrontations that often

[11] John Hope Bryant, "The Memo: Five Rules for Your Economic Liberation" (Berrett-Koehler Publishers, 2017).

[12] Michael Pollan, "In Defense of Food: An Eater's Manifesto" (Penguin Books, 2008).

lead to systemic backlash[13]. This approach does not imply acquiescence but advocates for strategic engagement that leverages the power of technological advancement and economic savvy to secure and elevate one's position within the socio-economic hierarchy.

Emphasizing technological advancement is paramount in this quest. The digital age offers unprecedented opportunities for economic empowerment and the bypassing of traditional barriers to success. By harnessing the potential of technology, marginalized communities can carve out spaces for innovation, entrepreneurship, and economic independence, diminishing the relevance of racial barriers in determining one's socio-economic fate[14].

Critiquing the reliance on federal jobs and the absence of a global strategy for collective progress further highlights the need for a paradigm shift. While federal employment has historically provided a stable income for many, it often places individuals within a system that limits upward mobility and economic independence[15]. The absence of a cohesive global plan for collective progress underscores the fragmentation and short-sightedness of relying solely on government employment as a pathway to economic security. Instead, fostering a mindset geared towards global economic engagement and entrepreneurship can provide more sustainable avenues for wealth creation and socio-economic empowerment.

[13] Derrick Bell, "Faces at the Bottom of the Well: The Permanence of Racism" (Basic Books, 1992).

[14] Alec Ross, "The Industries of the Future" (Simon & Schuster, 2016).

[15] Thomas Shapiro, "Toxic Inequality: How America's Wealth Gap Destroys Mobility, Deepens the Racial Divide, & Threatens Our Future" (Basic Books, 2017).

Building Our Cities and Educational Systems

In an era where economic disparities and systemic barriers loom large, the discourse on fostering community resilience and prosperity through the establishment of independent systems—encompassing cities, educational structures, and economic infrastructures—has never been more pertinent. This narrative explores the imperative of building autonomous communities and the pivotal role of economic control, while also delving into the nuanced debate between integration and assimilation within Black communities, highlighting the potential dilution of cultural and economic power that the former may entail.

Fostering Economic and Educational Autonomy

The establishment of autonomous educational systems and cities is not merely a call to physical construction but a profound advocacy for self-determination and resilience. Autonomy in education and urban development empowers communities to tailor learning and living environments to their unique cultural histories and contemporary needs, fostering an ecosystem where economic and intellectual prosperity can flourish. Such independence is critical in areas where significant population density or consumer spending power exists, as it enables the community to exert control over its economic destiny, recirculating wealth and sustaining growth from within[16].

Economic control within these autonomous systems is paramount. It's not enough to simply inhabit spaces; true empowerment comes from owning and controlling the

16 Claud Anderson, "PowerNomics: The National Plan to Empower Black America" (Powernomics Corporation of America, 2001).

economic levers within these spaces. By establishing businesses, financial institutions, and educational systems that cater to and are run by the community, there is a direct influence over the economic health and prosperity of the area[17]. This model not only encourages wealth circulation within the community but also reinforces the importance of economic sovereignty in the broader fight for equality and justice.

The Role of Community in Economic Circulation

The concept of a self-sustaining community, where wealth is continuously circulated and reinvested, is fundamental to this vision of autonomy. Such economic models have been observed in historical contexts where communities thrived independently, creating ecosystems that were resilient to external economic fluctuations[18]. By prioritizing local businesses, services, and education, communities can create a feedback loop of economic growth and stability, ensuring that the financial resources generated within the community serve its members first and foremost.

Integration vs. Assimilation: A Cultural and Economic Examination

The debate between integration and assimilation strikes at the heart of this discourse, especially concerning its impact on Black communities. While integration was heralded as a path to equality, it has, in some instances, led to the dilution of cultural identity and economic power

17 Maggie Anderson, "Our Black Year: One Family's Quest to Buy Black in America's Racially Divided Economy" (PublicAffairs, 2012).

18 Jessica Gordon Nembhard, "Collective Courage: A History of African American Cooperative Economic Thought and Practice" (Penn State University Press, 2014).

within Black communities[19]. The pursuit of integration, without a concurrent emphasis on economic and cultural autonomy, risks assimilating into a system that does not prioritize the community's unique needs and potential for prosperity. This perspective advocates for a balanced approach where communities can engage with broader societal systems without forfeiting their identity or economic self-sufficiency.

Navigating Allyship and Social Dynamics for Community Empowerment

The dynamics of allyship and the intricate balance of social relations play pivotal roles. This narrative seeks to explore the nuanced dimensions of allyship, particularly in the context of racial equity, emphasizing the importance of allowing white allies to contribute to the cause without succumbing to the pitfalls of the "White Savior" complex. Additionally, it highlights the critical distinction between systemic issues (vertical challenges) and interpersonal conflicts (horizontal issues), underscoring the significance of focusing on structural changes over individual grievances.

The Essence of Constructive Allyship

Allyship, when navigated with sincerity and understanding, can serve as a powerful tool in the fight against systemic racism. However, it necessitates a delicate balance to ensure that contributions from white allies bolster the movement without overshadowing the voices and experiences of those at the forefront of the struggle.

[19] Thomas Shapiro, "Toxic Inequality: How America's Wealth Gap Destroys Mobility, Deepens the Racial Divide, & Threatens Our Future" (Basic Books, 2017).

Constructive allyship involves a commitment to listening, learning, and acting in ways that are informed and respectful of the leadership of marginalized communities[20]. This approach helps avoid the "White Savior" complex, a phenomenon where well-intentioned support morphs into paternalistic intervention, thereby detracting from the agency and autonomy of the communities in question[21].

The critique against the "White Savior" narrative is not a dismissal of allyship but rather a call for a more nuanced engagement that respects the primary agency of Black and brown communities in their liberation struggle. Allies are most effective when they leverage their privilege to dismantle systemic barriers and amplify marginalized voices, rather than positioning themselves as the central protagonists in these narratives[22].

Prioritizing Systemic Issues Over Interpersonal Conflicts

A pivotal aspect of this discourse is the emphasis on systemic issues—vertical challenges—over interpersonal conflicts—horizontal issues. While interpersonal dynamics and individual biases undoubtedly contribute to the perpetuation of racism, the focus must remain on dismantling the structural and institutional mechanisms that underpin racial inequality. This perspective recognizes that racism is not merely a collection of personal prejudices but

20 Stephanie Shonekan, "The Role of White Allies in the Struggle for Racial Justice" (Civil Rights Journal, 2017).

21 Teju Cole, "The White Savior Industrial Complex" (The Atlantic, March 21, 2012).

22 Eduardo Bonilla-Silva, "Racism Without Racists: Color-Blind Racism and the Persistence of Racial Inequality in America" (Rowman & Littlefield Publishers, 2017).

a complex system of power and oppression that requires comprehensive strategies to address[23].

The opposition to this viewpoint often comes from those who believe that emphasizing systemic racism negates personal responsibility or undermines the significance of individual actions. However, acknowledging the primacy of systemic challenges does not absolve individuals of accountability but rather situates personal biases within a broader framework that necessitates systemic transformation for sustainable change[24].

[23] Kimberlé Crenshaw, "Mapping the Margins: Intersectionality, Identity Politics, and Violence against Women of Color" (Stanford Law Review, 1991).

[24] Ibram X. Kendi, "How to Be an Antiracist" (One World, 2019).

Part 8:
Moving Forward

My Final Words—Chapter 19

As we draw the curtains on this journey, a voyage through the turbulent seas of our history, we stand at the confluence of remembrance and rebirth. This narrative, rooted in the depths of our shared experience, has been an honest testament to the pervasive influence of white supremacy on the fabric of modern societies, institutions, and attitudes. It has been a tale of resilience, a chronicle of the indomitable spirit that flows within us, inherited from our ancestors, whose whispers of courage and songs of freedom guide us still.

This moment, this closing chapter, is not an end but a beacon pointing toward the dawn of a new era—an era where the chains of the past no longer bind the possibilities of our future. It is a call to embrace the full spectrum of our history, acknowledging the shadows cast by white supremacy, not to tether us to bitterness, but to illuminate the path toward healing and unity.

Our ancestors, through their unwavering strength and unrelenting hope, have laid the foundation upon which we stand today. In their footsteps, we find the rhythm of progress, the melody of resilience that sings, "Keep moving forward." They faced the darkest nights, yet their eyes remained fixed on the horizon, on the promise of a new day. It is this promise, this unquenchable hope, that we inherit and carry forward.

In acknowledging the deep-rooted injustices that have shaped our societies, we also recognize the power we possess to reshape them. The fabric of discrimination woven by white supremacy can be unraveled, thread by thread, through our collective action, our shared understanding, and our unwavering commitment to justice. Our journey towards equality is paved with the lessons of the past and the shared aspirations for a future where the dignity of every individual is recognized and revered.

Let this acknowledgment not be a weight that pulls us down, but a step that lifts us higher, towards the realization of our full potential. As we forge ahead, let us draw strength from the unity of our voices, the diversity of our experiences, and the commonality of our dreams. Our ancestors' legacy is not one of despair, but of hope; not of confinement, but of liberation.

As we step into tomorrow, let us carry the torch of this legacy with pride. Let it be a light that guides us through the uncertainty, a flame that ignites change, and a beacon that signals to future generations that their forebears fought, not just for survival, but for a world brimming with possibility, equality, and love.

This is our time to build bridges where walls once stood, to sow seeds of understanding in the barren fields of division, and to create a society that mirrors the richness of our collective spirit. Let us move forward with the knowledge that our actions today will echo through the annals of history, as a testament to our courage, our love, and our unwavering faith in the dawn of a new day.

A Journey of Continuous Education

In acknowledging the pervasive impact of racial ideologies on the course of history, we embrace a powerful truth: history is not merely a series of inevitable events but a complex mosaic of choices, each imbued with the potential to either perpetuate cycles of oppression or forge pathways to liberation. Our ancestors, in their infinite wisdom and indomitable spirit, understood this deeply. They knew that each step taken in the direction of knowledge and understanding was a step toward freedom.

This journey towards continuous education is not one we undertake alone. It is a collective endeavor, a shared responsibility to not only unearth the truths of our past but to use those truths to challenge the narratives that have, for too long, been used to justify inequality and division. It is about recognizing that the fight against racism and the quest for justice are rooted in the stories we tell, the histories we acknowledge, and the voices we uplift.

As we move forward, let us do so with the resolve to educate ourselves and others. Let us delve into the chapters of history that have been glossed over or omitted altogether, bringing to light the full complexity of our shared human experience. In doing so, we honor the legacy of those who came before us, whose struggles and triumphs are the bedrock upon which we build our dreams.

But let us not stop at education alone. Knowledge, while powerful, is only transformative when coupled with action. Armed with the understanding that history is a product of choices, let us be deliberate in the choices we make today. Let us choose empathy over indifference, unity over division, and love over hate. In every moment, we have the power to contribute to a world that reflects the beauty and diversity of the human family.

In this moment of reflection, as we turn the pages of our collective history, let us remember that we are not merely passive observers of the story of humanity; we are its authors. Each day offers a new opportunity to write a chapter that moves us closer to the ideals of justice, equality, and peace. Our ancestors' voices, though from the past, inspire our actions in the present and guide our vision for the future.

The Path of Present Accountability

Our ancestors, whose spirits guide us with whispers of endurance and shouts of freedom, knew all too well the cost of indifference. Their lives, a testament to the strength found in resistance, remind us that the fight for justice is perennial, demanding our vigilance and active engagement. They laid the groundwork, often with their blood and tears, for us to continue this sacred task. It is in their memory, and for the sake of those to come, that we must insist on the importance of present accountability.

This accountability is not about casting blame without the intention of healing; rather, it's about recognizing the roots of contemporary issues in the soil of our shared history. It's understanding that the disparities we witness today are not isolated incidents but are intricately connected to a larger narrative of oppression and resistance. By making these connections, we not only honor the true complexity of our history but also empower ourselves to dismantle the structures that continue to perpetuate inequality.

In the spirit of this accountability, let us commit to educating ourselves and our communities, not merely about the past but about the ways in which the past informs our present. Let's engage in conversations that challenge us to think critically about the legacy of white supremacy and our role in both its perpetuation and its dismantling. Let us be the architects of a future that, when looked upon by generations to come, reflects a society that learned from its history and chose a different path.

Our journey towards racial justice and equality is not a solitary endeavor. It requires the collective effort of all who dream of a world marked not by the divisions of the past but by the unity of our shared humanity. It asks us to look within ourselves, to confront uncomfortable truths, and to take tangible steps towards change. This journey is about building bridges—bridges of understanding, compassion, and action—that connect the islands of our individual experiences to the mainland of our collective aspiration for justice.

The Power of Critical Examination

Our ancestors, whose lives were a testament to the power of truth and the strength of the human spirit, knew the importance of remembering—of holding fast to the realities of our past to enlighten the paths of our future. They understood that the fabric of history is woven with threads of diverse experiences, some dark with suffering and others bright with triumph. To ignore the darker threads is to deny the fullness of our shared humanity.

Critical examination is our tool, our weapon in the fight against the erasure of our stories. It challenges us to look beyond the surface, to question the narratives that have been handed down to us, and to seek out the truths that have been buried under layers of omission and distortion. It calls us to honor the experiences of those who came before us by bringing their stories into the light, acknowledging their pain, their struggles, and their victories as integral to the story of who we are.

This process is not an easy one. It requires courage to face uncomfortable truths, to stand in the gap between the world as it is and the world as we know it should be. But in this courage, there is hope. Hope that by confronting the past with honesty and integrity, we can pave the way for a future that truly honors the dignity and worth of every individual.

Let us then, armed with the legacy of our ancestors and the power of critical examination, commit ourselves to the task of unraveling the narratives that seek to diminish our worth. Let us pledge to be seekers of truth, advocates for justice, and architects of a future where the history taught to our children is unflinching in its honesty and inclusive in its scope.

As we move forward, let this critical examination be not just an academic exercise, but a call to action. Let it inspire us to engage in our communities, to speak out against injustice, and to work tirelessly for a world that reflects the beauty and diversity of the human family. In doing so, we honor the sacrifices of those who came before us and lay a foundation for those who will follow.

Embracing Our True Heritage

We have navigated through the murky waters of myths and falsehoods, those that have sought to undermine the richness of our heritage and the boundless potential that lies within each of us. In dismantling the myths of racial superiority, we have not only confronted the skewed narratives and societal structures that have long perpetuated these beliefs but also reclaimed the power of our true story.

The stories of our ancestors are not mere footnotes in the vast expanse of history; they are shining beacons of resilience, innovation, and unwavering spirit. Their legacies, often obscured or misrepresented, are testament to a truth far greater than any myth of racial hierarchy. They were builders of civilizations, pioneers of science, custodians of wisdom and culture, whose contributions have shaped the world in immeasurable ways. By embracing our true heritage, we honor their sacrifices and embody the very essence of their greatness.

In this moment, as we stand on the threshold of a new dawn, it is essential to acknowledge the challenges that lie ahead. The path to equality and justice is fraught with obstacles, some old and some new, but our resolve must be unyielding. We must continue to challenge the structures that seek to divide us, armed with the knowledge and the truth of our shared history. Our quest is not merely for recognition but for the realization of a society where the content of one's character truly is the measure of their worth.

Let us draw strength from the trials and triumphs of our ancestors. Their voices, though silent, echo through time, reminding us that we are not alone in this fight. They faced unimaginable adversities, yet they remained steadfast in their pursuit of dignity and justice. Their resilience is our inheritance, their dreams our blueprint for the future.

As we move forward, let us do so with a spirit of unity and purpose. The myths of racial superiority have no place in a world that cherishes diversity and recognizes the inherent value of every individual. Our diversity is not a barrier but a bridge, a vibrant medley woven from the threads of our unique experiences and perspectives.

An Ode to Active Remembrance

Active remembrance is our sacred charge, a beacon that guides us through the darkest of nights. It is more than just an act of recollection; it is an embrace of the profound legacy left by our ancestors. Their stories, steeped in resilience and unyielding courage, are not mere footnotes in the vast expanse of history. They are the very essence of our collective soul, a testament to the indomitable spirit that courses through our veins.

In honoring their memory, we do more than pay homage to the past; we ignite the torches of the future. Their struggles, etched in the annals of time, serve as a clarion call, urging us onward in our quest for justice and equality. By keeping their stories alive, we ensure that the sacrifices made are never in vain, that the battles fought are always remembered. It is a pledge to carry forward the legacy of those who dared to dream of a world free from the chains of oppression.

Yet, this remembrance is not a task borne in isolation. It is a collective endeavor, a shared responsibility that we must all shoulder. It calls for us to weave the tales of our ancestors into the fabric of our daily lives, ensuring that their voices are heard in every corner of our existence. In doing so, we reaffirm our commitment to the fight against the insidious forces of white supremacy, vowing to stand as bulwarks against the tides of intolerance and hatred.

As we forge ahead, let us do so with the knowledge that our path is lit by the sacrifices of those who walked before us. Let their courage be our strength, their wisdom our guide. In every step we take, let us embody the essence of active remembrance, carrying with us the legacy of our forebearers.

The road ahead is fraught with challenges, but it is a path we do not walk alone. With each story of struggle and triumph that we keep alive, we weave a stronger bond between the past and the present, a bridge to a future where equality and justice are not just ideals, but realities.

A Journey Towards Justice

Policy reevaluation is not merely an academic exercise; it is a moral imperative. It demands of us to look beyond the surface, to delve into the historical underpinnings of the laws and norms that govern our societies. It requires us to identify and uproot those policies that, whether by design or effect, perpetuate discrimination and inequality. This process, though fraught with challenges, is essential to the healing and growth of our community. It is a testament to our collective resolve to not only acknowledge the sins of the past but to correct them, ensuring they do not define our future.

The call for systemic change is loud, echoing through the halls of power and the streets of our neighborhoods. It is a call that transcends individual acts of kindness or instances of bias, targeting the very foundations upon which legacies of white supremacy are built. This change is not instantaneous; it is the result of relentless advocacy, unwavering determination, and the unyielding belief in the possibility of a fairer world. It is about dismantling barriers in legal, educational, and economic systems, and erecting in their place structures of equity and justice. Our commitment to this cause is a beacon of hope, a promise of a society where every individual can truly flourish.

Moreover, the recognition of influence—of white supremacy in our cultural norms, media representation, and collective consciousness—is a pivotal step towards liberation. It is about seeing the invisible threads that weave through our perceptions and interactions, shaping our understanding of ourselves and each other. By acknowledging these influences, we empower ourselves to rewrite the narratives that have been imposed upon us, to reclaim our stories and celebrate our identities in all their diversity and richness.

One More Volume Left

The road has been long, marked by struggles and victories, lessons learned and wisdom gained. Today, we find ourselves on the verge of closing a significant chapter in our shared story with the upcoming release of *Resegregation Volume III: White People Started Slavery, Black People Keep It Going*. This final volume, a testament to our enduring spirit and resilience, invites us to confront uncomfortable truths, to reflect deeply, and, most importantly, to act decisively.

Writing this book was a journey that tested the limits of my courage and conviction. It was an endeavor that required me to delve into the darkest corners of our history, to face the painful realities of our present, and to imagine the boundless possibilities of our future. This volume is not just a recounting of past injustices or an exposition of current challenges; it is a clarion call to each of us to awaken to our power, to recognize our role in shaping the destiny of our community, and to take bold steps toward a future where we are the architects of our own liberation.

The journey through the pages of this volume is not an easy one. It confronts the harrowing legacy of slavery—a system initiated by white supremacy but perpetuated, in various forms, by our own actions and inactions. It is a narrative that demands we look inward, challenging us to consider how we, knowingly or unknowingly, contribute to the chains that bind us. Yet, it is in this uncomfortable introspection that we find the seeds of transformation. It is here, in the acknowledgment of our agency, that we discover the power to redefine our legacy.

As you engage with this volume, I urge you to do so with an open heart and a resolute spirit. Let the difficult truths it unveils not deter you but instead fuel your commitment to change. Let the stories of pain and perseverance remind you of our incredible capacity to overcome, to thrive even in the face of insurmountable odds. This book, while a reflection on the past, is ultimately a guide for our future—a future that we have the power to shape.

As we move forward, let us do so with a profound sense of purpose and responsibility. The challenges we face are daunting, but they are not insurmountable. The forces of resegregation and systemic inequality can be dismantled, but it requires more than awareness—it demands action. It calls for us to be vigilant, to critically examine the structures around us, and to be relentless in our pursuit of justice and equity. It is a call to transform our pain into power, our struggles into strength.

Let this volume serve as a beacon, illuminating the path toward collective empowerment and liberation. Let it inspire you to engage in the hard work of systemic change, to advocate for policies and practices that honor our humanity, and to actively dismantle the legacies of oppression that have held us back for far too long. This is our moment to rise, to unite in purpose and action, and to claim our rightful place as shapers of our destiny.

As we close this book and look to the horizon, let us do so with an unwavering belief in our capacity to create a world that reflects the best of who we are. A world where equality is not an ideal but a reality, where our children can thrive without the constraints of prejudice and where our community stands as a testament to the power of resilience and unity.

This journey has been one of reflection, revelation, and, ultimately, rejuvenation. As tough as it was to write this volume and to share it with both our community and the world at large, I am filled with hope. Hope in the transformative power of our collective will, hope in the unbreakable spirit of our people, and hope in the vision of a future forged in the fires of our shared struggle.

Resegregation Volume III is not just the end of a series; it is the beginning of a new chapter in our collective journey. A journey that calls for each of us to stand tall, to look within, and to march forward with determination and love. Together, we will navigate the challenges that lie ahead, embracing our power, honoring our ancestors, and building a legacy of freedom and justice for generations to come.

I leave you in the love and in the light of the One Infinite Intelligence, which is the Creator. Go forth, then, rejoicing in the power and the peace of your dreams.

Give thanksgiving for each moment. See self and other-self as the creator. Open your heart. Always know the light and praise it.

You can plant better. You can dominate.

Best,

Antonio T Smith Jr

The Revelation of Sonmi 451

To be is to be perceived, and so to know thyself is only possible through the eyes of the other. The nature of our immortal lives is in the consequences of our words and deeds, that go on and are pushing themselves throughout all time. Our lives are not our own. From womb to tomb, we are bound to others, past and present, and by each crime and every kindness, we birth our future."[1]

[1] Cloud Atlas, directed by Lana Wachowski, Tom Tykwer, and Lilly Wachowski (2012; Los Angeles, CA: Warner Bros. Pictures), DVD.

Bibliography

1. "A Declaration of the Immediate Causes which Induce and Justify the Secession of the State of Mississippi from the Federal Union," Mississippi, January 9, 1861.
2. "Access to Credit among Small, Low-Income, Minority, and Immigrant Entrepreneurs," U.S. Small Business Administration, Office of Advocacy, 2017.
3. "American Abolitionism and Religion," Divining America, TeacherServe©, National Humanities Center.
4. "American Apartheid: Segregation and the Making of the Underclass," Douglas S. Massey and Nancy A. Denton, Harvard University Press, 1993.

5. "An Act for the Gradual Abolition of Slavery, Pennsylvania, 1780," Pennsylvania Historical & Museum Commission.
6. "Asset Limits in Public Benefit Programs," National Conference of State Legislatures, 2019.
7. "Baby Bonds: An Investment in Our Nation's Future," Center for American Progress, 2020.
8. "Ban the Box: U.S. Cities, Counties, and States Adopt Fair Hiring Policies." National Employment Law Project. Last modified 2019.
9. "Black Fortunes: The Story of the First Six African Americans Who Escaped Slavery and Became Millionaires," Shomari Wills, Amistad, 2018.
10. "Black Reconstruction in America, 1860-1880," W.E.B. Du Bois.
11. "Black Stats: African Americans by the Numbers in the Twenty-first Century," Monique W. Morris, The New Press, 2014.
12. "Black Wall Street: From Riot to Renaissance in Tulsa's Historic Greenwood District," Hannibal B. Johnson, Eakin Press, 1998.
13. "Black Wealth/White Wealth: A New Perspective on Racial Inequality," Melvin L. Oliver and Thomas M. Shapiro, Routledge, 2006.
14. "Born in Slavery: Slave Narratives from the Federal Writers' Project, 1936 to 1938," Library of Congress.
15. "Bridging the Racial Wealth Gap: The Role of Economic Policies in Reducing Inequality," Economic Policy Institute, 2020.
16. "Building a Foundation for Economic Equity: The Role of Policy in Shaping Future Generations' Financial Health," Brookings Institution, 2021.
17. "Building Assets, Building Independence: Policies to Increase Savings by Low-Income Households," Brookings Institution, 2018.

18. "Building Home Equity: A Strategy for Economic Equality," Urban Institute, 2021.
19. "Building Wealth and Fostering Equity: How to Transform the Economy Through Inclusive Growth," Policy Brief, Brookings Institution, 2021.
20. "Capital Gains Tax Rates and Economic Growth: Evidence from the States," Tax Foundation, 2018.
21. "Census Data, 1850," United States Census Bureau.
22. "Crabgrass Frontier: The Suburbanization of the United States," Kenneth T. Jackson, Oxford University Press, 1985.
23. "Critics of Wealth Inequality: Are the Alternatives Any Better?" Forbes, 2019.
24. "Critique of Baby Bonds: Fiscal Responsibility and Long-term Outcomes," Cato Institute, 2021.
25. "Declaration of the Immediate Causes Which Induce and Justify the Secession of South Carolina from the Federal Union," December 24, 1860.
26. "Declarations of the Causes of Secession," University of Houston Digital History.
27. "Diary of Bennett H. Barrow, Louisiana Slave Owner," Louisiana State University Libraries, Special Collections.
28. "Disparities in Capital Access between Minority and Non-Minority Businesses," U.S. Department of Commerce, Minority Business Development Agency, 2010.
29. "Disparities in Wealth by Race and Ethnicity in the 2019 Survey of Consumer Finances," Federal Reserve, 2020.
30. "Diversity and Innovation: A Business Case for Equity," McKinsey & Company, 2015.
31. "Economic Benefits of Raising Asset Limits in Public Benefit Programs," Urban Institute, 2021.

32. "Family Properties: Race, Real Estate, and the Exploitation of Black Urban America," Beryl Satter, Metropolitan Books, 2009.
33. "Federal Reserve Reports on the Economic Well-Being of U.S. Households," Federal Reserve, 2019.
34. "Financing Social Policy Reforms for Economic Equity: A Fiscal Analysis," Public Finance Review, 2020.
35. "General Order No. 14," Confederate States of America, March 1865.
36. "Indentured Servitude in the Colonial U.S.," Encyclopedia Virginia.
37. "Killing the Black Body: Race, Reproduction, and the Meaning of Liberty," Dorothy Roberts, Vintage, 1997.
38. "Liberty Party (United States, 1840-48)," Encyclopedia Britannica.
39. "Locking Up Our Own: Crime and Punishment in Black America," James Forman Jr., Farrar, Straus and Giroux, 2017.
40. "Lynch-Law," James E. Cutler, 1905.
41. "Matching Savings Programs: An Innovative Approach to Economic Empowerment," Prosperity Now, 2020.
42. "Measuring the Impact of Social Policies on Economic Inequality: Challenges and Solutions," The Journal of Economic Perspectives, 2022.
43. "Policies to Address Poverty in America," The Hamilton Project, Brookings Institution, 2019.
44. "Political Will and Public Policy: Is There a Will to Address the Issue of Poverty?" Public Administration Review, 2018.
45. "PowerNomics: The National Plan to Empower Black America," Dr. Claud Anderson, Powernomics Corporation of America, 2001.

46. "Private Prisons in the United States," The Sentencing Project, 2020.
47. "Racial Discrimination in Small Business Lending," Federal Reserve Bank of Atlanta, 2019.
48. "Racism without Racists: Color-Blind Racism and the Persistence of Racial Inequality in America," Eduardo Bonilla-Silva, Rowman & Littlefield, 2014.
49. "Racism Without Racists: Color-Blind Racism and the Persistence of Racial Inequality in America," Eduardo Bonilla-Silva, Rowman & Littlefield, 2017.
50. "Reconstruction: America's Unfinished Revolution, 1863-1877," Eric Foner.
51. "Sheriff Offers Inmates as 'Labor Pool' for Trump's Mexico Wall," NBC News, January 5, 2017.
52. "Slavery and the Slave Trade in Rhode Island," Rhode Island Historical Society.
53. "Societal Attitudes Toward Poverty: Understanding Social Welfare Policy," Journal of Sociology and Social Welfare, 2019.
54. "Stamped from the Beginning: The Definitive History of Racist Ideas in America," Ibram X. Kendi, Nation Books, 2016.
55. "Supporting Home Ownership in Lower-Income Families: Policy Proposals for the 21st Century," Urban Institute, 2020.
56. "Systemic Racism and U.S. Health Care," Social Science & Medicine, 2020.
57. "Tax Policy and Wealth Inequality: Bridging the Gap Through Reform," Tax Policy Center, 2021.
58. "Taxing Wealth: How Tax Reform Can Reduce Inequality," Economic Policy Institute, 2019.
59. "The Asian American Achievement Paradox," Jennifer Lee and Min Zhou, Russell Sage Foundation, 2015.

60. "The Birth of a Nation and Its Legacy," NAACP, February 8, 2015.
61. "The Case Against Reparations," The Atlantic, 2014.
62. "The Case Against the Race-Based Mortgage Penalty," The Wall Street Journal, 2018.
63. "The Case for Baby Bonds: A Universal Path to Ensure the Next Generation's Economic Success," American Prospect, 2019.
64. "The Case for Reparations," Ta-Nehisi Coates, The Atlantic, 2014.
65. "The Case for Taxing Capital Gains at the Same Rate as Ordinary Income," Center on Budget and Policy Priorities, 2020.
66. "The Color of Money: Black Banks and the Racial Wealth Gap," Mehrsa Baradaran, Harvard University Press, 2017.
67. "The Color of Wealth: The Story Behind the U.S. Racial Wealth Divide," Meizhu Lui et al., The New Press, 2006.
68. "The Complexity of Economic Inequality in the United States," The American Economic Review, 2021.
69. "The Constitution of the United States," Amendment XIII.
70. "The Debate Over Asset Limits in Social Welfare Programs," Heritage Foundation, 2021.
71. "The Distributional Effects of Mortgage Deduction and Retirement Savings Policies," National Bureau of Economic Research, 2019.
72. "The Economic Benefits of Tax Deductions for Home Ownership and Retirement Savings," American Economic Association, 2018.
73. "The Economic Impacts of Wealth Inequality: A Review of Theories and Evidence," The World Bank, 2020.

74. "The Economics of Slavery," The Gilder Lehrman Institute of American History.
75. "The Effect of Capital Gains Taxation on Investment Dynamics," National Bureau of Economic Research, 2019.
76. "The Emancipation Proclamation," National Archives, January 1, 1863.
77. "The Failure of Reconstruction," Kenneth M. Stampp.
78. "The Half Has Never Been Told: Slavery and the Making of American Capitalism," Edward E. Baptist, Basic Books, 2014.
79. "The Importance of Asset Limits: A Pathway to Economic Self-Sufficiency," Center on Budget and Policy Priorities, 2020.
80. "The Maryland Doctrine of Exclusion, 1638." Historical Archives of Maryland Online.
81. "The Maryland Doctrine of Exclusion, 1638." Historical Archives of Maryland Online.
82. "The Mis-Education of the Negro," Carter G. Woodson, 1933.
83. "The Myth of Racial Disparities in Public School Financing," Heritage Foundation, 2019.
84. "The New Jim Crow: Mass Incarceration in the Age of Colorblindness," Michelle Alexander, The New Press, 2010.
85. "The New Urban Crisis: How Our Cities Are Increasing Inequality, Deepening Segregation, and Failing the Middle Class—and What We Can Do About It," Richard Florida, Basic Books, 2017.
86. "The Price of Slavery," Economic History Association.
87. "The Psychological and Economic Benefits of Early Investments: Evidence from Pilot Programs," Journal of Economic Psychology, 2022.

88. "The Racial Wealth Gap: Addressing America's Most Pressing Epidemic," Brookings Institution, 2018.
89. "The Racial Wealth Gap: Why Policy Matters," Demos, 2016.
90. "The State of Black America," National Urban League, 2021.
91. "The Truth Behind '40 Acres and a Mule'," Henry Louis Gates, Jr., The Root.
92. "The Violent Crime Control and Law Enforcement Act of 1994." History, Art & Archives, U.S. House of Representatives.
93. "The Virginia Slave Codes of 1705," The Colonial Williamsburg Foundation, https://www.history.org/history/teaching/enewsletter/volume7/nov08/primsource.cfm.
94. "The Warmth of Other Suns: The Epic Story of America's Great Migration," Isabel Wilkerson, Random House, 2010.
95. "The Wealth Gap for Women of Color," Center for Global Policy Solutions, 2014.
96. "Wealth Inequality in the United States since 1913: Evidence from Capitalized Income Tax Data," Emmanuel Saez and Gabriel Zucman, The Quarterly Journal of Economics, 2016.
97. "Wealth Inequality in the United States," National Bureau of Economic Research, 2020.
98. "World Prison Population List," Institute for Criminal Policy Research, 11th edition.
99. 13th Amendment to the U.S. Constitution.
100. Abramowitz, Alan I. The Great Alignment: Race, Party Transformation, and the Rise of Donald Trump. Yale University Press, 2018.
101. Abrams, Stacey. Our Time Is Now: Power, Purpose, and the Fight for a Fair America. Henry Holt and Co., 2020.

102. Alan Taylor, "American Colonies: The Settling of North America," (New York: Penguin Books, 2001).
103. Alexander, Michelle. The New Jim Crow: Mass Incarceration in the Age of Colorblindness. The New Press, 2010.
104. Alperovitz, Gar, and Steve Dubb. "The Next Wave: Financing Social Enterprise." The Democracy Collaborative, 2016.
105. Anderson, Carol. "White Rage: The Unspoken Truth of Our Racial Divide." Bloomsbury USA, 2016.
106. Anderson, Carol. One Person, No Vote: How Voter Suppression Is Destroying Our Democracy. Bloomsbury Publishing, 2018.
107. Anderson, Carol. White Rage: The Unspoken Truth of Our Racial Divide. Bloomsbury USA, 2016.
108. Anderson, Claud. Black Labor, White Wealth: The Search for Power and Economic Justice. Duncan & Duncan, 1994.
109. Anderson, Claud. Black Labor, White Wealth: The Search for Power and Economic Justice.
110. Anderson, Claud. Powernomics: The National Plan to Empower Black America. Powernomics Corporation of America, 2001.
111. Anderson, James D. The Education of Blacks in the South, 1860-1935. University of North Carolina Press, 1988.
112. Anderson, James D. The Education of Blacks in the South, 1860-1935. University of North Carolina Press, 1988.
113. Arthur Raper, "The Tragedy of Lynching," 1933.
114. Ava DuVernay, 13th, Netflix, 2016.
115. Banks, James A. Multicultural Education: Issues and Perspectives. Wiley, 2019.

116. Bates, Timothy. Race, Self-Employment, and Upward Mobility: An Illusive American Dream. Woodrow Wilson Center Press, 1997.
117. Bauer, Shane. "American Prison: A Reporter's Undercover Journey into the Business of Punishment." Penguin Press, 2018.
118. Bell, Derrick. Faces at the Bottom of the Well: The Permanence of Racism. Basic Books, 1992.
119. Ben Wattenberg, The Birth Dearth (New York: Pharos Books, 1987).
120. Berman, A. (2015). Give Us the Ballot: The Modern Struggle for Voting Rights in America. Farrar, Straus and Giroux.
121. Bocian, Debbie Gruenstein, Keith S. Ernst, and Wei Li. "Unfair Lending: The Effect of Race and Ethnicity on the Price of Subprime Mortgages." Center for Responsible Lending, 2006.
122. Bonilla-Silva, Eduardo. Racism without Racists: Color-Blind Racism and the Persistence of Racial Inequality in the United States. Rowman & Littlefield, 2017.
123. Bradford, William D. "The Wealth Dynamics of Entrepreneurship for Black and White Families in the U.S." Review of Black Political Economy, 2003.
124. Brennan Center for Justice. "The Myth of Voter Fraud." 2017.
125. Bruce Levine, "Confederate Emancipation: Southern Plans to Free and Arm Slaves during the Civil War," (New York: Oxford University Press, 2006).
126. Bryan Stevenson, "Just Mercy: A Story of Justice and Redemption," (New York: Spiegel & Grau, 2014).
127. Bureau of Justice Statistics, "Prisoners in 2018."
128. Butler, Paul. Chokehold: Policing Black Men. The New Press, 2017.

129. C. Vann Woodward, "The Strange Career of Jim Crow," (New York: Oxford University Press, 2002).
130. Calvin Schermerhorn, "The Business of Slavery and the Rise of American Capitalism, 1815-1860," (New Haven: Yale University Press, 2015).
131. Centers for Disease Control and Prevention. "Community Health Centers: Improving Health, Reducing Costs." 2020.
132. Centers for Disease Control and Prevention. "Health Disparities Among Black or African American." 2020.
133. Charles B. Dew, "Apostles of Disunion: Southern Secession Commissioners and the Causes of the Civil War," (Charlottesville: University of Virginia Press, 2001).
134. Chavez, Leo. The Latino Threat: Constructing Immigrants, Citizens, and the Nation. Stanford University Press, 2013.
135. Chicago Tribune, Tuskegee Institute, NAACP lynching statistics.
136. Chomsky, A., & Golash-Boza, T. (2018). Immigration and the growing divide. Sociology Compass.
137. Civil Rights Act of 1964, Pub.L. 88-352, 78 Stat. 241.
138. Claud Anderson, "PowerNomics: The National Plan to Empower Black America" (Powernomics Corporation of America, 2001).
139. Clear, Todd R. "The effects of high imprisonment rates on communities." Crime and Justice 37, no. 1 (2008): 97-132.
140. Clear, Todd R., and Natasha A. Frost. The Punishment Imperative: The Rise and Failure of Mass Incarceration in America. New York University Press, 2014.
141. Clear, Todd R., et al. "The Positive Effects of Rehabilitation on the Recidivism Rates of Individuals

Incarcerated for Drug-Related Offenses." International Journal of Offender Therapy and Comparative Criminology, 2012.

142. Coates, Ta-Nehisi. "The Case for Reparations." The Atlantic, June 2014.
143. Coates, Ta-Nehisi. Between the World and Me. Spiegel & Grau, 2015.
144. Cole, Teju. "The White Savior Industrial Complex." The Atlantic, March 21, 2012.
145. Collins, Patricia Hill. Black Feminist Thought: Knowledge, Consciousness, and the Politics of Empowerment. Routledge, 2000.
146. Corburn, Jason. "Street Science: Community Knowledge and Environmental Health Justice." MIT Press, 2005.
147. Cornel West, "Race Matters," (Boston: Beacon Press, 1993).
148. Crenshaw, Kimberlé. "Critical Race Theory: The Key Writings That Formed the Movement". The New Press, 1995.
149. Crenshaw, Kimberlé. "On Intersectionality: Essential Writings." The New Press, 2017.
150. Darity, William A., Jr., and Darrick Hamilton. "Can 'Baby Bonds' Eliminate the Racial Wealth Gap in Putative Post-Racial America?" Review of Black Political Economy, 2010.
151. Darling-Hammond, Linda. "Inequality in Teaching and Schooling: How Opportunity is Rationed to Students of Color in America." The Right Thing to Do, The Smart Thing to Do: Enhancing Diversity in the Health Professions, 2001.
152. Darling-Hammond, Linda. The Flat World and Education: How America's Commitment to Equity Will Determine Our Future. Teachers College Press, 2010.

153. David Galenson, "White Servitude in Colonial America: An Economic Analysis," Cambridge University Press, 1981.
154. David R. Williams and Selina A. Mohammed, "Racism and Health I: Pathways and Scientific Evidence," American Behavioral Scientist 57, no. 8 (2013): 1152-1173.
155. Davis, Angela Y. "Freedom Is a Constant Struggle: Ferguson, Palestine, and the Foundations of a Movement." Haymarket Books, 2016.
156. Davis, Angela Y. Women, Race, & Class. Vintage Books, 1983.
157. Davis, Angela. "Race, Bias, and the Importance of Jury Composition." Racial Justice Advocates, vol. 12, 2020, pp. 67-92.
158. Davis, Angela. "The Unity Debate: Bridging Divides or Reinforcing Them?," Societal Progress Review, vol. 12, no. 4, 2019, pp. 200-215.
159. Davis, Angela. Are Prisons Obsolete? Seven Stories Press, 2003.
160. Davis, Angela. Freedom Is a Constant Struggle: Ferguson, Palestine, and the Foundations of a Movement. Haymarket Books, 2016.
161. Davis, John Emmeus. "The Community Land Trust Reader." Lincoln Institute of Land Policy, 2010.
162. Delgado, Richard, and Jean Stefancic. Critical Race Theory: An Introduction. New York University Press, 2017.
163. Derrick Bell, "Faces at the Bottom of the Well: The Permanence of Racism," (New York: Basic Books, 1992).
164. Desmond, Matthew. Evicted: Poverty and Profit in the American City. Crown, 2016.

165. DiAngelo, Robin. White Fragility: Why It's So Hard for White People to Talk About Racism. Boston: Beacon Press, 2018.
166. Dolovich, Sharon. "State Punishment and Private Prisons." Duke Law Journal, vol. 55, no. 3, 2005.
167. Douglas A. Blackmon, Slavery by Another Name: The Re-Enslavement of Black Americans from the Civil War to World War II, Anchor Books, 2008.
168. Douglas S. Massey, "The Past and Future of American's Racial Divide," in American Demographics, ed.
169. Dubois, Laurent. "Avengers of the New World: The Story of the Haitian Revolution." Belknap Press, 2004.
170. Duster, Troy. Backdoor to Eugenics. Routledge, 2003.
171. DuVernay, Ava, director. "13th." Netflix, 2016.
172. Dyson, Michael Eric. "Tears We Cannot Stop: A Sermon to White America." St. Martin's Press, 2017.
173. Edmund S. Morgan, "American Slavery, American Freedom: The Ordeal of Colonial Virginia," (New York: W.W. Norton & Company, 1975).
174. Edward E. Baptist, "The Half Has Never Been Told: Slavery and the Making of American Capitalism," Basic Books, 2014.
175. Elizabeth Warren, "A Plan For Economic Patriotism," Medium, June 4, 2019.
176. Ellsworth, Scott. "The Tulsa Race Massacre." History.com, A&E Television Networks, 2019.
177. Environmental Protection Agency. "Addressing Environmental Injustice." 2020.
178. Epp, Charles R., Steven Maynard-Moody, and Donald P. Haider-Markel. Pulled Over: How Police Stops Define Race and Citizenship. University of Chicago Press, 2014.

179. Equal Justice Initiative, "Lynching in America: Confronting the Legacy of Racial Terror," https://eji.org/report/lynching-in-america/
180. Equal Justice Initiative. "Batson v. Kentucky and the Prosecution of Black Americans." Equal Justice Initiative, 2020.
181. Eric Foner, "Reconstruction: America's Unfinished Revolution, 1863-1877," (New York: Harper & Row, 1988).
182. Eric Foner, "The Fiery Trial: Abraham Lincoln and American Slavery," (New York: W. W. Norton & Company, 2010).
183. Eric Williams, Capitalism and Slavery (Chapel Hill: University of North Carolina Press, 1944).
184. Foner, Eric. The Fiery Trial: Abraham Lincoln and American Slavery. New York: W. W. Norton & Company, 2010.
185. Forman Jr., James. Locking Up Our Own: Crime and Punishment in Black America. Farrar, Straus and Giroux, 2017.
186. Freeman, Lance. "There Goes the Hood: Views of Gentrification from the Ground Up." Temple University Press, 2006.
187. Friedman, Milton. "Capitalism and Freedom." University of Chicago Press, 1962.
188. Fullilove, Mindy Thompson. "Root Shock: How Tearing Up City Neighborhoods Hurts America, and What We Can Do About It." New Village Press, 2004.
189. Gay, Geneva. "Culturally Responsive Teaching: Theory, Research, and Practice." Teachers College Press, 2010.
190. Gilens, Martin. Why Americans Hate Welfare: Race, Media, and the Politics of Antipoverty Policy. University of Chicago Press, 1999.

191. Giroux, Henry A. Border Crossings: Cultural Workers and the Politics of Education. Routledge, 2005.
192. Gloria Ladson-Billings, "New Directions in Multicultural Education: Complexities, Boundaries, and Critical Race Theory," in "Handbook of Research on Multicultural Education," ed. James A. Banks and Cherry A. McGee Banks (San Francisco: Jossey-Bass, 2004), 50-65.
193. Gordon Nembhard, Jessica. "Collective Courage: A History of African American Cooperative Economic Thought and Practice." Pennsylvania State University Press, 2014.
194. Gottlieb, Robert, and Anupama Joshi. "Food Justice." MIT Press, 2010.
195. Gottschalk, Marie. "Caught: The Prison State and the Lockdown of American Politics." Princeton University Press, 2014.
196. Greene, Jay P. "Education Myths: What Special Interest Groups Want You to Believe About Our Schools--And Why It Isn't So." Rowman & Littlefield Publishers, 2005.
197. Grewal, Sharanbir S., and Parwinder S. Grewal. "Can Cities Become Self-Reliant in Food?" Cities, 2012.
198. Guinier, Lani. The Tyranny of the Meritocracy: Democratizing Higher Education in America. Beacon Press, 2015.
199. Gunnar Myrdal, "An American Dilemma," 1944.
200. Hainmueller, Jens, and Daniel J. Hopkins. "The Hidden American Immigration Consensus: A Conjoint Analysis of Attitudes toward Immigrants." American Journal of Political Science, vol. 59, no. 3, 2015, pp. 529-548.

201. Haney, Craig. "Mental Health Issues in Long-Term Solitary and 'Supermax' Confinement." Crime & Delinquency, vol. 49, no. 1, 2003.
202. Heather Mac Donald, "The Myth of Systemic Police Racism," Wall Street Journal, June 2, 2020.
203. Higham, John. Strangers in the Land: Patterns of American Nativism, 1860-1925. Rutgers University Press, 1955.
204. Hill Collins, Patricia, and Sirma Bilge. Intersectionality. Polity Press, 2016.
205. Hinton, Elizabeth. From the War on Poverty to the War on Crime: The Making of Mass Incarceration in America. Harvard University Press, 2016.
206. Huntington, Samuel P. Who Are We? The Challenges to America's National Identity. Simon & Schuster, 2004.
207. Ibram X. Kendi, "Stamped from the Beginning: The Definitive History of Racist Ideas in America," (New York: Nation Books, 2016).
208. Ida B. Wells, "Southern Horrors: Lynch Law in All Its Phases," (New York: The New Press, 1892).
209. Ira Berlin, "Generations of Captivity: A History of African-American Slaves," (Cambridge: Belknap Press, 2003).
210. Ira Berlin, "Many Thousands Gone: The First Two Centuries of Slavery in North America," Harvard University Press, 1998.
211. Ira Katznelson, Fear Itself: The New Deal and the Origins of Our Time (New York: Liveright Publishing, 2013).
Thomas Sowell, Discrimination and Disparities (New York: Basic Books, 2018).
212. Ira Katznelson, When Affirmative Action Was White: An Untold History of Racial Inequality in Twentieth-

Century America (New York: W.W. Norton & Company, 2005).
213. Jack Brooks, H.R.3355 - 103rd Congress (1993-1994): Violent Crime Control and Law Enforcement Act of 1994.
214. James Loewen, "Lies My Teacher Told Me: Everything Your American History Textbook Got Wrong," (New York: The New Press, 1995).
215. James M. McPherson, "Battle Cry of Freedom: The Civil War Era," (New York: Oxford University Press, 1988).
216. James M. McPherson, "The Negro's Civil War: How American Blacks Felt and Acted During the War for the Union," (New York: Vintage Books, 2003).
217. Jill Leovy, "Ghettoside: A True Story of Murder in America," (New York: Spiegel & Grau, 2015).
218. John Hope Bryant, "The Memo: Five Rules for Your Economic Liberation" (Berrett-Koehler Publishers, 2017).
219. John McWhorter, "Antiracism: Our Flawed New Religion," The Daily Beast, March 2015.
220. John Stauffer, "Black Confederates: The Civil War's Most Persistent Myth," The Atlantic, November 2015.
221. Johnson, Alisha. "The Failure of Batson: Addressing Racial Bias in Jury Selection." Civil Rights Law Journal, vol. 22, no. 1, 2019, pp. 105-130.
222. Johnson, Angela. "The Impact of Media Portrayals on Racial Attitudes," American Journal of Psychology, vol. 134, no. 2, 2018, pp. 233-245.
223. Johnson, Emily. "The Thin Line: Cultural Appreciation vs. Appropriation," Diversity and Inclusion Quarterly, vol. 5, no. 1, 2021, pp. 112-128.
224. Johnson, Michael. "Racial Bias and Prosecutorial Discretion: Seeking Justice in the Shadows," Journal

of Criminal Law and Criminology, vol. 107, no. 4, 2017, pp. 643-669.

225. Jonathan Zimmerman, "Whose America? Culture Wars in the Public Schools," (Cambridge: Harvard University Press, 2002).
226. Joseph T. Glatthaar, "General Lee's Army: From Victory to Collapse," (New York: Free Press, 2008).
227. Joy DeGruy, "Post Traumatic Slave Syndrome," (Milwaukie: Uptone Press, 2005).
228. Karen L. Cox, "Dixie's Daughters: The United Daughters of the Confederacy and the Preservation of Confederate Culture," (Gainesville: University Press of Florida, 2003).
229. Katznelson, Ira. When Affirmative Action Was White: An Untold History of Racial Inequality in Twentieth-Century America. W. W. Norton & Company, 2005.
230. Kendi, I.X. (2016). Stamped from the Beginning: The Definitive History of Racist Ideas in America. Nation Books.
231. Kendi, Ibram X. "How to Be an Antiracist." One World, 2019.
232. Kendi, Ibram X. "Stamped from the Beginning: The Definitive History of Racist Ideas in America." Nation Books, 2016.
233. Kendi, Ibram X. How to Be an Antiracist. New York: One World, 2019.
234. Kendi, Ibram X. How to Be an Antiracist. One World, 2019.
235. King, Martin Luther Jr. "Why We Can't Wait." Harper & Row, 1964.
236. King, Martin Luther. "Media Representation and Its Role in Building a Just Society," Equality and Justice in Media, vol. 1, no. 1, 2020, pp. 10-24.

237. Koh, Howard K., and Nicole Lurie. "Preparing for a Renaissance in Public Health." Public Health Reports, 2011.
238. Kozol, Jonathan. Savage Inequalities: Children in America's Schools. Crown, 1991.
239. Ladson-Billings, Gloria. "The Dreamkeepers: Successful Teachers of African American Children." Jossey-Bass, 2009.
240. Lee, Christopher. "Mitigating Jury Selection Bias: A Call for Reform." Legal Reform Now, vol. 18, no. 3, 2021, pp. 234-260.
241. Lerone Bennett Jr., "Before the Mayflower: A History of Black America," (Chicago: Johnson Publishing Company, 1982).
242. Leslie M. Harris, "In the Shadow of Slavery: African Americans in New York City, 1626-1863," University of Chicago Press, 2003.
243. Levitt, Justin. The Partisan Sort: How Liberals Became Democrats and Conservatives Became Republicans. University of Chicago Press, 2009.
244. Lilla, Mark. The Once and Future Liberal: After Identity Politics. HarperCollins, 2017.
245. Loewen, James W. Lies My Teacher Told Me: Everything Your American History Textbook Got Wrong. The New Press, 1995.
246. Logan, Charles. "Private Prisons: Cons and Pros." Oxford University Press, 1990.
247. Lovell, Sarah Taylor. "Multifunctional Urban Agriculture for Sustainable Land Use Planning in the United States." Sustainability, 2010.
248. Lowndes, Joseph. From the New Deal to the New Right: Race and the Southern Origins of Modern Conservatism. Yale University Press, 2008.

249. Lusardi, Annamaria, and Olivia S. Mitchell. "The Economic Importance of Financial Literacy: Theory and Evidence." Journal of Economic Literature, 2014.
250. Lutz, Brenda. Invisible Americans: Uncovering Why U.S. Voting Rights Are Not Universal. ABC-CLIO, 2020.
251. MacDonald, Heather. "The War on Cops: How the New Attack on Law and Order Makes Everyone Less Safe." Encounter Books, 2016.
252. Maggie Anderson, Our Black Year: One Family's Quest to Buy Black in America's Racially Divided Economy (New York: PublicAffairs, 2012).
253. Mapping Police Violence, "Police Violence & Racial Equity," https://mappingpoliceviolence.org/
254. Marianne Bertrand and Sendhil Mullainathan, "Are Emily and Greg More Employable Than Lakisha and Jamal? A Field Experiment on Labor Market Discrimination," American Economic Review 94, no. 4 (2004): 991-1013.
255. Mark R. Schleifstein, "Slave Cemetery Unearthed," The Times-Picayune, October 26, 1997.
256. Martin, Luther. "Towards a Just Jury System: Overcoming Racial Bias." Equality and Justice, vol. 5, no. 4, 2020, pp. 197-216.
257. Massey, Douglas S., and Nancy A. Denton. American Apartheid: Segregation and the Making of the Underclass. Harvard University Press, 1993.
258. Mauer, Marc. Race to Incarcerate. The New Press, 2006.
259. Michelle Alexander, The New Jim Crow: Mass Incarceration in the Age of Colorblindness (New York: The New Press, 2010).
260. Minnite, Lorraine C. The Myth of Voter Fraud. Cornell University Press, 2010.

261. Myers, Barton. Radicals in Power: The Influence of the Radical Republicans on American Politics. University Press, 2020.
262. Myers, Barton. The Legacy of the Civil War: The Emancipation Proclamation and the March to the Sea. Savannah History Press, 2018.
263. NAACP, "Criminal Justice Fact Sheet."
264. NAACP, "History of Lynchings," https://www.naacp.org/history-of-lynchings/
265. NAACP, "Thirty Years of Lynching in the United States, 1889-1918," 1919.
266. National Association of Community Health Centers. "The Impact of Community Health Centers on Patients' Health and Healthcare Costs." 2019.
267. National Association of State Boards of Education. "The Role of Civic Education." 2018.
268. National Bail Fund Network. "Bail Reform and Racial Justice." 2021.
269. National Endowment for the Humanities. "Cultural Preservation Grants." 2020.
270. National Institute of Mental Health. "Supporting Mental Health in Minority Communities." 2019.
271. National Telecommunications and Information Administration. "Bridging the Digital Divide." 2021.
272. Ngai, Mae M. Impossible Subjects: Illegal Aliens and the Making of Modern America. Princeton University Press, 2004.
273. Nicholas Lemann, "Redemption: The Last Battle of the Civil War," (New York: Farrar, Straus and Giroux, 2006).
274. Noam Chomsky, "Understanding Power: The Indispensable Chomsky," (New York: The New Press, 2002).

275. Noguera, Pedro. "Unequal Outcomes: Not Only Acceptable but Also Inevitable under Our Current Educational System." Education and the Law, 2003.
276. Oliver, Melvin L., and Thomas M. Shapiro. Black Wealth/White Wealth: A New Perspective on Racial Inequality. Routledge, 1995.
277. Oliver, Melvin L., and Thomas M. Shapiro. Black Wealth/White Wealth: A New Perspective on Racial Inequality. Routledge, 2006.
278. Oluo, Ijeoma. "So You Want to Talk About Race." Seal Press, 2018.
279. Oluo, Ijeoma. So You Want to Talk About Race. New York: Seal Press, 2018.
280. Orfield, Gary, and Erica Frankenberg. "The Resegregation of Suburban Schools: A Hidden Crisis in American Education." Harvard Education Press, 2012.
281. Orszag, Peter R., and Ezekiel Emanuel. "Health Care Reform and Cost Control." The New England Journal of Medicine, 2010.
282. Ouss, Aurelie, and Megan T. Stevenson. "The Effect of Bail on Crime and Pretrial Misconduct: Evidence from Judicial Reforms." American Economic Journal: Economic Policy, 2019.
283. Pager, Devah, and Bruce Western. "Identifying Discrimination at Work: The Use of Field Experiments." Journal of Social Issues, vol. 68, no. 2, 2012, pp. 221-237.
284. Pager, Devah, and Bruce Western. "Race at Work: Realities of Race and Criminal Record in the NYC Job Market." New York University Law Review, vol. 81, no. 2, 2006.
285. Pager, Devah, and Hana Shepherd. "The Sociology of Discrimination: Racial Discrimination in Employment,

Housing, Credit, and Consumer Markets." Annual Review of Sociology, vol. 34, 2008, pp. 181-209.
286. Pager, Devah. "The mark of a criminal record." American Journal of Sociology 108, no. 5 (2003): 937-975.
287. Parker, Christopher S., and Matt A. Barreto. Change They Can't Believe In: The Tea Party and Reactionary Politics in America. Princeton University Press, 2013.
288. Paulo Freire, "Pedagogy of the Oppressed," (New York: Continuum, 1970).
289. Pellow, David N. "Garbage Wars: The Struggle for Environmental Justice in Chicago." MIT Press, 2002.
290. Peter Edelman, Not a Crime to Be Poor: The Criminalization of Poverty in America (New York: The New Press, 2017).
291. Pew Research Center, "Deciding not to have children," Pew Research Center, May 7, 2020.
292. Pew Research Center. "State of the News Media." 2018.
293. Phelan, Jo C., and Bruce G. Link. "Is Racism a Fundamental Cause of Inequalities in Health?" Annual Review of Sociology, 2015.
294. Piketty, Thomas. Capital in the Twenty-First Century. Harvard University Press, 2014.
295. Planned Parenthood Federation of America, "Annual Report 2018-2019," Planned Parenthood, 2019.
296. Plessy v. Ferguson, 163 U.S. 537 (1896).
297. Porter, Michael E., and Mark R. Kramer. "Creating Shared Value." Harvard Business Review, 2011.
298. Ramsey, Charles, and Laurie Robinson. President's Task Force on 21st Century Policing. Office of Community Oriented Policing Services, 2015.
299. Ravitch, Diane. Reign of Error: The Hoax of the Privatization Movement and the Danger to America's Public Schools. Knopf, 2013.

300. Reid, Nova. "No More White Saviours, Thanks: How to Be a True Anti-Racist Ally." The Guardian, September 19, 2021.
301. Richard Rothstein, The Color of Law: A Forgotten History of How Our Government Segregated America (New York: Liveright Publishing Corporation, 2017).
302. Riley, Jason L. Please Stop Helping Us: How Liberals Make It Harder for Blacks to Succeed. New York: Encounter Books, 2014.
303. Robinson, Karen. "Steps Toward Authentic Allyship," Racial Justice Today, vol. 7, no. 3, 2023, pp. 78-92.
304. Rollock, Nicola. "The Importance of Black-owned Media." Sociology of Race and Ethnicity, 2019.
305. Rothstein, Richard. The Color of Law: A Forgotten History of How Our Government Segregated America. Liveright, 2017.
306. Rugh, Jacob S., and Douglas S. Massey. "Racial Segregation and the American Foreclosure Crisis." American Sociological Review, vol. 75, no. 5, 2010, pp. 629-651.
307. Russell J. Skiba et al., "The Color of Discipline: Sources of Racial and Gender Disproportionality in School Punishment," Urban Review 34, no. 4 (2002): 317-342.
308. Ruth Wilson Gilmore, Golden Gulag: Prisons, Surplus, Crisis, and Opposition in Globalizing California (Berkeley: University of California Press, 2007).
309. Saad, Layla F. "Me and White Supremacy: Combat Racism, Change the World, and Become a Good Ancestor." Sourcebooks, 2020.
310. Saez, Emmanuel, and Gabriel Zucman. The Triumph of Injustice: How the Rich Dodge Taxes and How to Make Them Pay. W.W. Norton & Company, 2019.

311. Sered, Danielle. Until We Reckon: Violence, Mass Incarceration, and a Road to Repair. The New Press, 2019.
312. Shapiro, Thomas M. Toxic Inequality: How America's Wealth Gap Destroys Mobility, Deepens the Racial Divide, & Threatens Our Future. Basic Books, 2017.
313. Shapiro, Thomas M., and Melvin L. Oliver. Black Wealth/White Wealth: A New Perspective on Racial Inequality. Routledge, 1995.
314. Shelby County v. Holder, 570 U.S. 529 (2013).
315. Shelby Steele, "The Content of Our Character: A New Vision of Race In America," (New York: St. Martin's Press, 1990).
316. Sides, John, Michael Tesler, and Lynn Vavreck. Identity Crisis: The 2016 Presidential Campaign and the Battle for the Meaning of America. Princeton University Press, 2018.
317. Skocpol, T., & Williamson, V. (2012). The Tea Party and the Remaking of Republican Conservatism. Oxford University Press.
318. Skocpol, Theda, and Vanessa Williamson. The Tea Party and the Remaking of Republican Conservatism. Oxford University Press, 2012.
319. Small Business Administration. "Entrepreneurial Development Programs." 2021.
320. Smith, John L. "The Role of Allies in Racial Justice." Journal of Social Change 12, no. 3 (2020): 45-59.
321. Smith, John. "Cultural Appropriation and Its Impact on Minority Cultures," Journal of Cultural Studies, vol. 10, no. 3, 2020, pp. 45-60.
322. Smith, John. "Racial Disparities in Jury Selection." Journal of Legal Studies, vol. 34, no. 2, 2018, pp. 456-489.

323. Sowell, Thomas. "Basic Economics." Basic Books, 2014.
324. Sowell, Thomas. Intellectuals and Race. Basic Books, 2013.
325. Sowell, Thomas. Wealth, Poverty and Politics: An International Perspective. Basic Books, 2015.
326. Squires, Gregory D. "Capital and Communities in Black and White: The Intersections of Race, Class, and Uneven Development." The Guilford Press, 1994.
327. Squires, Gregory D., and Charis E. Kubrin. "Privileged Places: Race, Uneven Development and the Geography of Opportunity in Urban America." Urban Studies, vol. 42, no. 1, 2005, pp. 47-68.
328. Squires, Gregory D., and Sally O'Connor. Color and Money: Politics and Prospects for Community Reinvestment in Urban America. SUNY Press, 2001.
329. Steele, Shelby. "Shame: How America's Past Sins Have Polarized Our Country." Basic Books, 2015.
330. Steele, Shelby. The Content of Our Character: A New Vision of Race In America. St. Martin's Press, 1990.
331. Stephanie Shonekan, "The Role of White Allies in the Struggle for Racial Justice" (Civil Rights Journal, 2017).
332. Steven Hahn, "A Nation Under Our Feet: Black Political Struggles in the Rural South from Slavery to the Great Migration," (Cambridge: Harvard University Press, 2003).
333. Stevenson, Bryan. Just Mercy: A Story of Justice and Redemption. Spiegel & Grau, 2014.
334. Sven Beckert, Empire of Cotton: A Global History (New York: Knopf, 2014).
335. T.H. Breen and Stephen Innes, "Myne Owne Ground: Race and Freedom on Virginia's Eastern Shore, 1640-1676," (New York: Oxford University Press, 1980).

336. Ta-Nehisi Coates, "The Case for Reparations," The Atlantic, June 2014.
337. Tatum, Beverly Daniel. Why Are All the Black Kids Sitting Together in the Cafeteria? And Other Conversations About Race. Basic Books, 1997.
338. Tatum, Beverly Daniel. Why Are All the Black Kids Sitting Together in the Cafeteria? And Other Conversations About Race. Basic Books, 2017.
339. The Sentencing Project, "Report on Racial Disparities" (Washington, D.C., 2023).
340. The Sentencing Project, "Report: Black Disparities in Youth Incarceration." The Sentencing Project, 2020.
341. The Sentencing Project. "Report on Racial Disparities in the United States Criminal Justice System," 2018.
342. Thomas Shapiro, "Toxic Inequality: How America's Wealth Gap Destroys Mobility, Deepens the Racial Divide, & Threatens Our Future," (New York: Basic Books, 2017).
343. Thomas Sowell, "Black Rednecks and White Liberals," (San Francisco: Encounter Books, 2005).
344. Thomas Sowell, Discrimination and Disparities (New York: Basic Books, 2018).
345. Thompson, Mark. "In Defense of Cultural Exchange," Free Speech Review, vol. 8, no. 2, 2022, pp. 234-248.
346. Travis, Jeremy, Bruce Western, and Steve Redburn, eds. "The Growth of Incarceration in the United States: Exploring Causes and Consequences." National Academies Press, 2014.
347. Travis, John, and Western, Bruce. "The Growth of Incarceration in the United States: Exploring Causes and Consequences." National Research Council, 2014.
348. Travis, John. "Private Prisons in the United States: An Assessment of Current Practice." American Journal of Criminal Justice, vol. 20, no. 1, 1995.

349. Tuskegee Institute Lynching Statistics.
350. U.S. Bureau of Labor Statistics, "Labor Force Characteristics by Race and Ethnicity, 2019" (Washington, D.C.: U.S. Department of Labor, 2020).
351. U.S. Bureau of Labor Statistics, "Unemployment Rates by Race and Ethnicity" (Washington, D.C.: U.S. Department of Labor, 2023).
352. U.S. Census Bureau, "Poverty Rates by Race/Ethnicity" (Washington, D.C.: U.S. Department of Commerce, 2023).
353. U.S. Department of Justice, Bureau of Justice Statistics.
354. U.S. Immigration and Customs Enforcement, "Yearbook of Immigration Statistics," U.S. Department of Homeland Security, 2019.
355. U.S. Small Business Administration. "Access to Capital Among Young Firms, Minority-owned Firms, Women-owned Firms, and High-tech Firms." Office of Advocacy, 2013.
356. United States Census Bureau projections.
357. United States Department of Agriculture. "Community Gardens as Health and Wellness Initiatives." 2021.
358. United States Department of the Treasury. "Financial Literacy and Education Commission: National Strategy for Financial Literacy." 2020.
359. Useem, Bert and Piehl, Anne Morrison. "Prison State: The Challenge of Mass Incarceration." Cambridge University Press, 2008.
360. Vera Institute of Justice. "Race and Punishment: Racial Perceptions of Crime and Support for Punitive Policies," 2014.
361. Vincent Woodard, "Delectable Negro: Human Consumption and Homoeroticism within US Slave Culture," (New York: NYU Press, 2014).

362. Vitale, Alex S. The End of Policing. Verso Books, 2017.
363. W.E.B. Du Bois, "The Philadelphia Negro: A Social Study" (Philadelphia: University of Pennsylvania Press, 1899).
364. Wacquant, Loïc. Punishing the Poor: The Neoliberal Government of Social Insecurity. Duke University Press, 2009.
365. Wagner, Peter, and Sakala, Leah. "Mass Incarceration: The Whole Pie 2020." Prison Policy Initiative.
366. Washington, Booker. "Media Bias and Racial Perceptions of Crime," Journal of Sociological Studies, vol. 29, no. 3, 2016, pp. 456-471.
367. West, Cornel. Race Matters. Beacon Press, 1993.
368. Western, Bruce, and Becky Pettit. "Incarceration & social inequality." Daedalus 139, no. 3 (2010): 8-19.
369. Western, Bruce, and Pettit, Becky. "Incarceration & Social Inequality." Daedalus, the Journal of the American Academy of Arts & Sciences, 2010.
370. Western, Bruce. "Punishment and Inequality in America." Russell Sage Foundation, 2006.
371. Western, Bruce. "The impact of incarceration on wage mobility and inequality." American Sociological Review 67, no. 4 (2002): 526-546.
372. Wilkerson, Isabel. Caste: The Origins of Our Discontents. Random House, 2020.
373. Wilkins, Vicky M., and Marcia L. Whittaker. "The Impact of Incarceration on Wage Mobility and Inequality." American Sociological Review, vol. 76, no. 4, 2011, pp. 502-524.
374. Wilkinson, Richard, and Kate Pickett. The Spirit Level: Why More Equal Societies Almost Always Do Better. Allen Lane, 2009.
375. William Darity Jr. and A. Kirsten Mullen, From Here to Equality: Reparations for Black Americans in the

Twenty-First Century (Chapel Hill: University of North Carolina Press, 2020).

376. William Julius Wilson, When Work Disappears: The World of the New Urban Poor (New York: Vintage Books, 1996).
377. Williams, David R., and Pamela Braboy Jackson. "Social Sources of Racial Disparities in Health." Health Affairs, 2005.
378. Williams, Eric. Capitalism and Slavery. University of North Carolina Press, 1944.
379. Williams, Lisa. "Leveraging Privilege for Racial Justice," Equality and Equity Journal, vol. 9, no. 2, 2022, pp. 150-165.
380. Williamson, Vanessa, Theda Skocpol, and John Coggin. "The Tea Party and the Remaking of Republican Conservatism." Perspectives on Politics, vol. 9, no. 1, 2011, pp. 25-43.
381. Wilson, William Julius. The Truly Disadvantaged: The Inner City, the Underclass, and Public Policy. University of Chicago Press, 1987.
382. Winthrop D. Jordan, "White Over Black: American Attitudes toward the Negro, 1550-1812," (Chapel Hill: The University of North Carolina Press, 1968).
383. Wise, Tim. "White Allies in the Fight for Racial Justice." City Lights Books, 2015.
384. Wise, Tim. "White Like Me: Reflections on Race from a Privileged Son." Soft Skull Press, 2007.
385. World Health Organization, "Mental Health: Strengthening Our Response," WHO Fact sheet, March 2018.
386. Zehr, Howard. "The Little Book of Restorative Justice." Good Books, 2002.
387. Zucman, Gabriel, and Emmanuel Saez. "The Triumph of Injustice: How the Rich Dodge Taxes and How to

Make Them Pay." The New York Times, October 2019.

388. " The Economic State of Black America in 2020," U.S. Congress Joint Economic Committee, https://www.jec.senate.gov/public/_cache/files/23b0b4a9-4cda-463a-bbe9-ce4b63399c55/economic-state-of-black-america-in-2020---final-.pdf
389. " Wealth Gap Widens Between Whites and Families of Color." Pew Research Center, 2020.
390. "Racism without Racists: Color-Blind Racism and the Persistence of Racial Inequality in America," Eduardo Bonilla-Silva, Rowman & Littlefield, 2014.
391. "Retirement Savings for the Low-Income: The Untapped Potential of Government Policies," Brookings Institution, 2021.
392. Alec Ross, "The Industries of the Future" (Simon & Schuster, 2016).
393. Alexander, Michelle. The New Jim Crow: Mass Incarceration in the Age of Colorblindness. The New Press, 2012.
394. Anderson, Claud. "Black Labor, White Wealth: The Search for Power and Economic Justice." PowerNomics Corporation of America, 1994.
395. Anderson, Claud. "More Than Just Race: Being Black and Poor in the Inner City." PowerNomics Corporation of America, 2000.
396. Anderson, Claud. "Powernomics: The National Plan to Empower Black America." Powernomics Corporation of America, 2001.
397. Bates, Timothy. "Race, Self-Employment, and Upward Mobility." The Johns Hopkins University Press, 1997.
398. Berman, Ari. Give Us the Ballot: The Modern Struggle for Voting Rights in America. Farrar, Straus and Giroux, 2015.

399. Branch, John. "Colin Kaepernick and the Power of NFL Player Protests." The New York Times, September 2016.
400. Centers for Disease Control and Prevention, "Prevention for a Healthier America: Investments in Disease Prevention Yield Significant Savings, Stronger Communities," February 2009.
401. Cloud Atlas, directed by Lana Wachowski, Tom Tykwer, and Lilly Wachowski (2012; Los Angeles, CA: Warner Bros. Pictures), DVD.
402. Coates, Ta-Nehisi. "Between the World and Me." Spiegel & Grau, 2015.
403. Coates, Ta-Nehisi. "The Case for Reparations." The Atlantic, June 2014.
404. Community Resilience and Collective Efficacy: Emerging Concepts in the Sociology of Community", Journal of Community Psychology, 2016.
405. Crenshaw, Kimberlé. "Demarginalizing the Intersection of Race and Sex: A Black Feminist Critique of Antidiscrimination Doctrine, Feminist Theory, and Antiracist Politics," University of Chicago Legal Forum, vol. 1989, no. 1, 1989, Article 8.
406. Daley, David. Ratf**ked: Why Your Vote Doesn't Count. Liveright, 2016.
407. Darling-Hammond, Linda. "Unequal Opportunity: Race and Education." Brookings, March 1, 1998.
408. David R. Williams and Chiquita Collins, "Racial Residential Segregation: A Fundamental Cause of Racial Disparities in Health," Public Health Reports 116, no. 5 (2001): 404-416.
409. Department of Education. "Federal Student Loan Portfolio." 2021.
410. Derrick Bell, "Faces at the Bottom of the Well: The Permanence of Racism" (Basic Books, 1992).

411. Dolovich, Sharon. "State Punishment and Private Prisons." Duke Law Journal, vol. 55, no. 3, 2005.
412. Edmund S. Morgan, "American Slavery, American Freedom: The Ordeal of Colonial Virginia," (New York: W.W. Norton & Company, 1975).
413. Eduardo Bonilla-Silva, "Racism Without Racists: Color-Blind Racism and the Persistence of Racial Inequality in America" (Rowman & Littlefield Publishers, 2017).
414. Federal Reserve Bank of Atlanta. "2019 Small Business Credit Survey: Report on Minority-owned Firms." 2020.
415. Foner, Eric. "The Fiery Trial: Abraham Lincoln and American Slavery." W. W. Norton & Company, 2010.
416. Foner, Eric. Reconstruction: America's Unfinished Revolution, 1863-1877. Harper & Row, 1988.
417. Frazier, Garrison. Transcript of the Savannah Meeting, New York Daily Tribune, February 13, 1865.
418. Global Income Report, United Nations. "Disparities in Global Income and the Impact on Minority Communities." 2022.
419. Hughey, Matthew W., and Gregory S. Parks. "The Wrath of the Ancestors: Analyzing the Tea Party Movement." Sociology of Race and Ethnicity, vol. 1, no. 1, 2015, pp. 75-88.
420. Ibram X. Kendi, "How to Be an Antiracist" (One World, 2019).
421. International Renewable Energy Agency, "Renewable Energy and Jobs – Annual Review 2020," IRENA, 2020.
422. Jessica Gordon Nembhard, "Collective Courage: A History of African American Cooperative Economic Thought and Practice" (Penn State University Press, 2014).

423. Jill Litt et al., "The Influence of Social Involvement, Neighborhood Aesthetics, and Community Garden Participation on Fruit and Vegetable Consumption," American Journal of Public Health 101, no. 8 (2011): 1466-1473.
424. Johnson, Andrew. Presidential Veto Messages. Washington D.C.: Government Printing Office, 1866.
425. Joint Center for Housing Studies of Harvard University. "The State of the Nation's Housing 2020." Harvard University, 2020.
426. Kevin M. Levin, "Searching for Black Confederates: The Civil War's Most Persistent Myth," (Chapel Hill: University of North Carolina Press, 2019).
427. Kimberlé Crenshaw, "Mapping the Margins: Intersectionality, Identity Politics, and Violence against Women of Color" (Stanford Law Review, 1991).
428. Lincoln, Abraham. Presidential Endorsements of Reconstruction Policies. The Lincoln Archives, 1865.
429. Maggie Anderson, "Our Black Year: One Family's Quest to Buy Black in America's Racially Divided Economy" (PublicAffairs, 2012).
430. McKernan, Signe-Mary, et al. "Nine Charts about Wealth Inequality in America." Urban Institute, 2017.
431. Michael Marmot, "The Status Syndrome: How Social Standing Affects Our Health and Longevity" (Henry Holt and Co., 2004).
432. Michael Pollan, "In Defense of Food: An Eater's Manifesto" (Penguin Books, 2008).
433. Myers, Barton. Dismantling the Dream: The End of Reconstruction and the Betrayal of African American Land Rights. Oxford: Oxford University Press, 2015.
434. NAACP archives and legislative advocacy records.
435. Piketty, Thomas. "Capital in the Twenty-First Century." Harvard University Press, 2014.

436. Portes, Alejandro, and Robert L. Bach. "Latin Journey: Cuban and Mexican Immigrants in the United States." University of California Press, 1985.
437. Race and Punishment: Racial Perceptions of Crime and Support for Punitive Policies", Vera Institute of Justice, 2014.
438. Rachel Yehuda et al., "Holocaust Exposure Induced Intergenerational Effects on FKBP5 Methylation," Biological Psychiatry 80, no. 5 (2016): 372-380.
439. Robert Sapolsky, "Why Zebras Don't Get Ulcers" (New York: Holt Paperbacks, 2004).
440. Rothstein, Richard. The Color of Law: A Forgotten History of How Our Government Segregated America. Liveright Publishing Corporation, 2017.
441. Sara McLanahan, Laura Tach, and Daniel Schneider, "The Causal Effects of Father Absence," Annual Review of Sociology 39 (2013): 399-427.
442. Scott Ellsworth, "Death in a Promised Land: The Tulsa Race Riot of 1921" (Louisiana State University Press, 1982).
443. Sherman, William T. Special Field Order No. 15. January 16, 1865.
444. Stanton, Edwin. Records of the War Department: Dialogues on Freedom and Reconstruction, January 1865.
445. Steele, Shelby. The Content of Our Character: A New Vision of Race In America. St. Martin's Press, 1990.
446. Teju Cole, "The White Savior Industrial Complex" (The Atlantic, March 21, 2012).
447. The Effectiveness of Descriptive Representation: Black Legislators and Policy Preferences of Black Constituents", Political Research Quarterly, 2017
448. The Power of Buy Black: The Economic Impact of Black Consumers and Businesses", Nielsen Report, 2019

449. Thomas Shapiro, "Toxic Inequality: How America's Wealth Gap Destroys Mobility, Deepens the Racial Divide, & Threatens Our Future" (Basic Books, 2017).
450. U.S. Government Accountability Office. "K-12 Education: Better Use of Information Could Help Agencies Identify Disparities and Address Racial Discrimination." April 21, 2016.
451. West, Cornel. "Race Matters." Beacon Press, 1993.
452. Wilson, Valerie, and William M. Rodgers III. "Black-white wage gaps expand with rising wage inequality." Economic Policy Institute, 2016.

Printed in the USA
CPSIA information can be obtained
at www.ICGtesting.com
LVHW031317240524
781047LV00007B/151/J

9 798889 901990